HOLY COMPANY

HOLY

ELLIOTT WRIGHT

COMPANY
Christian Heroes and Heroines

Macmillan Publishing Co., Inc.
NEW YORK

Macmillan Publishing Co., Inc.
866 Third Avenue, New York, N.Y. 10022
Collier Macmillan Canada, Ltd.

Library of Congress Cataloging in Publication Data

Wright, H Elliott, 1937–
    Holy company.

    Bibliography: p.
    1. Christian biography. I. Title.
BR1700.2.W74   1980   280'.092'2   [B]   80–18924
ISBN 0-02-631590-4

10   9   8   7   6   5   4   3   2   1

Printed in the United States of America

For

a company of special people,

chiefly

JUANITA

and

BARBARA,

RICHARD, DAVID, JOHN PAUL, and JON,

and

especially for

PRISCILLA GANS

Contents

Foreword

WHAT IS HAPPINESS?

A friend and I fell to discussing that question one night a few winters ago; each had noticed the same advertisement for another of those books telling us how to become healthy, wealthy, and, if not wise, at least happy, by following the prescribed regimen.

We agreed, my friend and I, that the quest—indeed, the lust—for happiness today is matched only by the illusiveness of the goal. We wondered why.

For a while we talked about happiness in terms of "the good life," psychological adjustment, and self-affirmation; then the friend said, "We're after the wrong question."

"How so?" I asked.

"Because," he replied, "the important goal is not happiness but holiness: What is the holy life? At least, that's the important question for Christians, for religious people in general, and, I suspect, even for secularists, if they could admit it.

"Pascal said happiness is neither inside us nor outside, but in God, both beyond and within; happiness is a problem today because we've cut it loose from its moorings in religion, in God, in holy living."

What is holy living?

That is the subject of this book—specifically Christian holy living; not just the idea of holiness but the practice: the way of Christ mirrored in a company of great Christian lives, heroic in faith and love, ranging from the biblical age to our times.

More than seventy Christian heroes and heroines are set forth and discussed within a structure suggested by the Beatitudes of the Gospel of Matthew, printed on page xix. The Beatitudes do not exhaust the virtues and values of the way of holiness; they are a succinct, familiar statement of the bench marks of Christian living.

"Ecumenical" is the best word to describe the process of choosing the heroes and heroines. Ground rules were few. No living persons would be used; assessing the lives and virtues of the deceased is risk enough for one book. I wanted to avoid legendary characters or real persons about whom too little is authentically known to write a brief biography. Without setting quotas, I deliberately looked for individuals—lay and clerical, ancient, medieval, and modern—of many nationalities, ethnic backgrounds, and theologies within the main channels of Christianity: Roman Catholic, Protestant, and Eastern Orthodox.

Subjective inclinations unavoidably played a part in the selections; the heroes and heroines here are, finally, persons who appeal to me, though I have tried to hold broad affections, and in a few cases I did not choose so much as was chosen. I more than once laid aside Florence Nightingale, the nineteenth-century heroine of nursing. But Florence refused to stay laid aside. She came to me so often that I relented and am glad because she enriched the company and instructed me.

All of the lives in the book plus more for which there was no space have exerted individual and collective influence on me. They leaned into my mind and life, presenting models of spirituality that both complemented and, by challenging, refined my own sense of who I am as a Christian.

I knew none of the contemporary heroic Christians who lived into the post–World War II era, but I did meet two of them in passing, and a quality evident in them even in brief encounter bears mention because it illumines the entire Holy Company.

Martin Luther King, Jr. and Flannery O'Connor, the novelist and short story writer—although contemporaries, both born and reared in Georgia—were different in almost every way, especially formal theology and understanding of the church, he being a black Baptist and she a white Roman Catholic. Yet in their distinctness I sensed that each breathed of a common spirit: each knew what he or she believed as Christians and, more important, they knew they belonged to Christ; faith showed.

Faith showing—that quality, perhaps more than any other, is the mark of the way of holiness, the unity within the diverse Holy Company.

Acknowledgments

ONE OF THE PLEASING THINGS about books is the oppor-
tunity to acknowledge debts in print. In the writing of this book my
first debt, chronologically, is more than twenty years old. Dr. Evelyn
Wiley, retired professor of history at Birmingham-Southern College,
Birmingham, Alabama, gave me my first introduction to the excite-
ment of the past, and Dr. Bard Thompson, now at Drew University,
Madison, New Jersey, showed me church history in lectures at the
Vanderbilt University Divinity School, Nashville, Tennessee. If Dr.
Wiley and Dr. Thompson find their interpretations of events or
personalities in these pages, I ask them to take it as a compliment to
their scholarship, but I impute to them no responsibility for chal-
lengeable assertions I may have made.

In more recent days, friends, acquaintances, and strangers, (in the
person of librarians), have assisted me.

Special thanks to Patricia Brown, librarian of the Ecumenical Library of The Interchurch Center, New York, who allowed me unre-
stricted access to an invaluable collection.

The Reverend P. W. S. Schneirla of St. Mary's Antiochian Ortho-
dox Church, Brooklyn, directed me to relevant material on both
Eastern and Western Christianity; Dr. James Michael Lee of the
University of Alabama, Birmingham, advised me on the early

Church Fathers; and Cleveland E. Dodge set me on the trail of biographical data on his predecessor David Low Dodge.

My neighbor, the Reverend David C. Cockcroft of the Riverdale Presbyterian Church, the Bronx, not only lent me books at all hours, but helped me search the corpus of Dickens's works for the quotation I knew was there but could not find, and encouraged me and commiserated with me as only a friend can.

Other friends who aided me include Lillian Block, editor-in-chief emeritus of Religious News Service, New York, and my former colleagues at the news service, Laurence Mullin, Tammy Tanaka, and Darrell Turner; James Couchell, Martha Man, William Meyer, John Peter Paul, Betty Thompson, and Christopher Wuthman came to my rescue, often without knowing it, as did Charles and Janet Austin, Fred and Elizabeth Villegas, John and Diana Alicea, Nick and Jean Santoiemma, Carol May, Aida Notides, Elma Otto, Rose Grisetti, and Priscilla Gans. I thank them all.

Three persons were indispensable to me in accomplishing this book:

John Hochmann, friend and literary agent, originally proposed that I try my hand at a book on Christian heroes and heroines, and then advised me throughout the research and writing, read and criticized the first draft, offering able suggestions, and nobly represented me to a patient and superior editor: William Griffin of Macmillan.

The Reverend Richard John Neuhaus, theologian and senior editor of *Worldview* magazine, helped me in repeated conversations to focus the book, and always had time to listen and suggest when I called with questions large and small about sources or historical/theological points. He is the friend mentioned at the start of this foreword, but he shares in none of the potentially disputable conclusions I have reached.

Finally, my wife, the Reverend Juanita Bass Wright, who did not type the manuscript, did not keep the dogs quiet, or do any of those things spouses are usually thanked for in books, except that she corrected the spelling in a few chapters and numbered some pages. She was not home when most of this book was written, but was off appropriately engaged in her own ministries, and not incidentally, in making a living for us so I could read and try to comprehend Christianity, which she already understood. I thank her for the proofreading; much more, I thank her for loving me, and in that she always makes the greatest contribution to whatever I do and am. A debt of love is never repaid. Love can only be returned along with the Doxology.

ELLIOTT WRIGHT

Duff Cottage
Riverdale-on-Hudson
The Bronx, New York

February 1980

And Jesus taught the disciples, saying:

"Holy are the poor in spirit, for the kingdom of heaven is theirs.

"Holy are those who mourn, for they shall be comforted.

"Holy are the gentle, for they shall inherit the earth.

"Holy are those who hunger and thirst for righteousness, for they shall be satisfied.

"Holy are the merciful, for they shall receive mercy.

"Holy are the pure in heart, for they shall see God.

"Holy are the peacemakers, for they shall be called the children of God.

"Holy are those who are persecuted for the sake of righteousness, for the kingdom of heaven is theirs."

MATTHEW 5:2–10

Introduction: The Holy Company

In taking what James Agee called "each hobble toward the Promised Land,"[1] people watch others to see how the pilgrimage goes best. The ablest hobblers become the heroes and heroines.

But images of the promised land—the symbol of the goal of life —differ. The search for heroic models wanders through a maze, and at every corner guides advertise competing promised lands. A multitude of people think they glimpse the goal of life in sensual pleasure; their heroes/heroines flex and purr around the latest sex guide. Some claim the land of ego satisfaction and move with gurus selling mental plans; others lust and lurch toward kingdoms hot with gold—heroes stacking bullion—or find promise in power and copy Ghengis Khan. Promised lands of science, outer space, and boundless oil—these also beckon.

The Christian's promised land is God; the route to the goal is the way of holiness, a path not smooth—and Christians hobble, too. Halting, faltering, even saints trip, but Jesus Christ, who leads the way, who is the way, does not. Those following "The Way," as Christianity was first called, dare "to walk strongly"[2] through the rough.

The way of holiness can be pursued as a theological or ethical idea, but one means of grasping an idea is to see it exemplified, and the purpose of this book is to show Christian heroes and heroines from across the centuries walking strongly in the faith despite the hobbles no person can escape.

To exemplify the way of holiness in great Christian lives has immediate relevance to contemporary Christians and society. Jesus Christ is *the* Christian model. The Scripture, the traditions and teachings of the churches, and the sacraments are the channels of God's grace and truth, but lives show what it looks and feels like to be Christian, to believe, to be and act in faith.

This book heralds heroes and heroines who may serve as lessons in faith, holy leaven, in a world where society's heroic models are characterized primarily by quick passage through the revolving door of fame. The personalities sketched here could, if taken seriously, inspire modern Christians to be great hobblers for and in Christ, even if that should mean, as it often has, standing against cultural and religious trends in the name of Christ and truth, welcoming the chance to be maladjusted but joyful, stubborn but compassionate, and to suffer, if necessary, for the Gospel of the better way of Christlike love.

The heroes and heroines—saints, broadly defined, as will be discussed shortly—form a holy company grouped around the Beatitudes from the Gospel of Matthew. These Beatitudes, blessings and pronouncements of holy qualities spoken by Jesus to his disciples, are the biblical basis for many of the Christian virtues and values —righteousness and truth, mercy, humility, compassion, gentleness, peacefulness, and loyalty—essential to the way of holiness. Scholars disagree on whether Jesus gave these blessings at one time or whether they are Matthew's collection of sayings from different occasions, but that issue does not detract from the passage (Matthew 5:2–12) as a description of holy living on life's pilgrimage.

Matthew's Beatitudes (a shorter version appears in the Gospel of Luke) are united at their source, Jesus Christ, and the following chapters intend to preserve that unity even though the heroes and heroines are discussed under individual Beatitudes, each with a brief introduction.

G. K. Chesterton warned that the Christian virtues go "mad" in isolation from one another; wandering alone they cause all sorts of havoc, such as when scientists (or news reporters) pursue truth devoid of mercy for those affected, or when the roles of humility and love of truth get reversed so that persons assert themselves and are modest about asserting what is right. If the virtues must be unified, so must the Beatitudes. "A beatitude is the actuality of a perfect virtue; hence, all the beatitudes belong to the perfection of spiritual life," said Thomas Aquinas.

Naturally, some great Christians may embody a Beatitude or a virtue more clearly than others because of the time and place in which they lived, their personal abilities and interests, or the circumstances they faced. Not all Christians have been persecuted, and all martyrs certainly illustrate virtues besides the loyalty required to die for Christ. Keeping in mind the special situations and gifts of individuals, remembering that many heroes and heroines of faith exemplify all the Beatitudes, each chapter seeks to explore concretely a virtue or value through individual lives and through a group of diverse lives; the emphasis remains on one Holy Company gathered around all the Beatitudes.

The diversity appropriate to Christian discipleship is central to the "Holy Company" theme. Christianity, as the Apostle Paul said, has "one Lord, one faith, one baptism," but it has never had one language in which to praise its Lord, a single theological formula to express faith, or one mode of baptism. Christianity has always experienced diversity within a unity too often ignored—a unity in Christ that is fortunately being recognized today. The diversity within the company of heroes and heroines suggests the fullness of the way of holiness.

The great Christians surveyed here pursued the holy way in different cultures, against different historical backdrops, with different callings, and within different degrees of social acceptance or challenge to their faith. They also belonged to different branches of the one, historically divided Christian family, and expressed their praise and service to God through varying doctrinal traditions and liturgical forms. Their common denominators are the grace of God and the love of and for Christ—impressive common denominators; but on other scores they are neither set in competition nor are their differences erased. They do not merge into a single pattern of Christian discipleship. Karl Rahner has wisely summed up the danger of synthesizing: "You seek a 'synthesis' of everything and everyone and produce nothing but a characterless mishmash that claims to be for tomorrow merely because it has mixed up everything from yesterday."[3]

Heroes and heroines here retain their characters; indeed, their special features, even peculiarities, are needed to form the fullness of the way of holiness—a Holy Company diverse and exciting, constituting a continuity of faith relevant to particulars, united in Christ who gave the Beatitudes.

Albert van den Heuvel has offered a helpful analysis that both stresses the unity of the Beatitudes and indicates their significance for halting, sometimes strong-walking Christians. In a series of talks at a meeting in Louisville, Kentucky a few years ago, van den Heuvel, a Dutch theologian, explained the Beatitudes in terms of three interrelated portraits.

The Beatitudes are first, he said, a portrait of Jesus Christ; not, to be sure, the only portrait, but a summary of holy qualities seen in perfection only in the man from Nazareth, the epitome of all virtues and the supreme martyr. The Beatitudes hold together in Jesus Christ: none other has been so perfectly humble, gentle, merciful, pure, compassionate, and so loyal to God's cause of love and truth.

Next, the Beatitudes present a portrait of the Christian church as it would become through the grace of God, the wholly faithful body of Christ in the world, continuing the work of its Lord under the guidance of the Holy Spirit. The church, composed as it is of imperfect people, imperfectly embodies the way of holiness, but it prays for perfection and for strength to imitate Christ in its worship and service.

Third, Christians find in the Beatitudes a portrait of the ideal Christ-centered life. Perfect achievement of the model is impossible short of the kingdom of God, utterly unthinkable through one's own abilities and good works, and difficult with grace. The human inclination to sin is enormously strong; "vanity is as abundant as all the tones of the voice, all ways of walking, coughing, blowing the nose, sneezing," said Pascal. Still, there they are, the Beatitudes, the brushmarks of holiness in the life of Christ—impossible to ignore, virtues to imitate.

Partly because Christians wobble as well as hobble, the Beatitudes have at times been projected almost entirely into the future, seen as qualities or virtues more fitting to God's coming kingdom than to the here and now. The Beatitudes themselves, the Sermon on the Mount of which they are a part, and the New Testament as a whole do point ahead; they anticipate. In each Beatitude a second phrase in the future tense makes a promise—for example, the merciful "shall obtain mercy" and the pure in heart "shall see God."

The Beatitudes neither suggest a timetable for the realization of the promises nor say whether they will be fulfilled historically or spiritually, or both. But since the future-tense promises are stated as results, can it not be assumed that the virtues enumerated in each first phrase apply in the here and now? To project the Beatitudes wholly into the future is to render them irrelevant to Christian discipleship. Their significance to the way of holiness in this world is stressed in this book, and this conclusion is supported by the Beatitudes themselves.

The blessings in Matthew 5 are directed by Jesus specifically to his disciples, and the linguistic form is that of exclamation; the Beatitudes can be read as messages of congratulation,[4] joy-filled proclamations, as though Jesus were saying, "You are my disciples; you are special, and my disciples are poor in spirit, gentle, merciful, peacemaking, pure in heart; they mourn over the sins and trouble of the world, and are willing to suffer for my sake."

A great company of men and women, known and unknown, across the centuries have heard these exclamations addressed to them and, with Christ's help, have taken up the way of holiness that glorifies God, the difficulty of the task becoming "their pleasure and delight," to quote John Comenius, a seventeenth-century Moravian. The rough becomes smoother because their sole purpose in life is to love God and the neighbor God loves. Thomas More prayed:

Give me, good Lord, an humble, lowly, quiet, peaceable, patient, charitable, kind, tender, and pitiful mind, with all my works, and all my words, and all my thoughts. . . .

Give me, good Lord, a full faith, a firm hope, and a fervent charity, a love to the good Lord incomparable above the love to myself; and that I love nothing to thy displeasure, but everything in an order to thee.

To show that the Beatitudes are exclamations, the traditional translation from the Greek to English is the announcement, "Blessed are . . ." Several recent translations have changed *blessed* to other exclamatory words, primarily *happy*, and William Barclay in his popular Study Bible Series says the verb is so strong it should read, "O the Bliss of . . ."

In the phrases of the Beatitudes quoted at the top of each chapter and in the full text printed as the frontispiece, still another word is used as the repeated introduction: *holy*—for example, "holy are the poor in spirit." This choice involves an interpreter's stretch, but one that seems justified since these exclamations are spoken to those set on the way of holy discipleship.

Standing first in each Beatitude in the Greek manuscripts of Matthew's Gospel is the beautiful word *makarios*, translated in the traditional English versions with the meaning of the Hebrew for *blessed*. In Greek, the term is brighter, and the often neglected Beatitudes need linguistic brightening, their virtues judged quaint when compared with the world's delights. The newer translations attempt a restoration with a word such as "happy"—bright, but probably a poor choice since in English it is often a frivolous term. In the Greek of Greece, *makarios* meant more than everyday happy; it meant the highest happiness, the greatest joy, and was associated with the state of divinity; hence, the interpreter's stretch to a sense of holiness.

"Holy" is only of God; the way of holiness is living God's way, and, while disciples may stumble and trip, in having been called and blessed by Christ to pursue his work, they are endowed with the grace of faith, hope, and love; their obedience is holy obedience to the holy, and they receive a holy welcome to the way of holiness.

Earlier, the heroes and heroines of the way of holiness were called saints, broadly defined. That passing comment must be expanded, because holy living and sanctity (the condition of sainthood) are closely related.

Saint in Christianity is both a general and a specific term, and the theological and historical relationship between the two usages can be sketched briefly. The Latin from which the English comes means "holy" or "consecrated," that is, those who are sanctified.

The language of saints and sanctity is not characteristic of the four Gospels and appears infrequently in the Old Testament; it is found in the writings of the Apostle Paul whose letters are the oldest material in the New Testament. Paul addressed himself to the saints of the various churches to which he wrote, and also conveyed greetings from saints in one church to another. In at least most of the Pauline references, *saint* is a synonym for *Christian*, those who belong to Christ—the living and the dead in Christ.

Paul's use of the term became widespread in the early Christian church and is reflected in the phrase "communion of the saints" included in the first (Nicene) creed, adopted by a church council in 325. "Communion of the saints" is also found in the Apostles' Creed, which does not date from the original Apostles but is ancient, probably from the third-century church in the city of Rome. The communion or fellowship of the saints in both of these creeds refers to the whole company of Christians in the church militant (on earth) and the church triumphant (in heaven).

Another, more specific use of the word *saint* also developed in early Christianity. This was as a designation for Christians reaching the church triumphant through martyrdom. Martyrs were honored and the dates of their deaths marked by specific observances at least by the mid-second century. Recognition of the special status of martyrs was the first step toward the official canons (lists) of Roman Catholic and Eastern Orthodox saints.

The concept of canonizing saints by church action unfolded slowly, more slowly than the practice of veneration, or reverence for (not worship of) departed saints, including the making of prayers to God through sanctified heavenly souls. Of course, there was protracted discussion of whether saints could, or should, act as mediators between the living and God, but the idea that the departed are of spiritual benefit to believers on earth is very old in Christianity. Origen, a theologian of late second-century Egypt, wrote that the saints who were fallen asleep exercise love toward "those who are struggling in this life much more than those who are compassed about with human weakness and are struggling in the company with feebler folk."

Procedures for canonizing Roman Catholic saints were not commenced until the tenth century, and the regulations were refined over several hundred years, coming to include the requirement of miracles performed by the nominee after death. Canonization in Eastern Orthodoxy is less complex.

The Protestant reformers of the sixteenth century wished to return to the concept of saints found in the Apostles' and Nicene Creeds, that is, the communion of Christians living and dead. For example, John Calvin, the Swiss reformer, spoke often of the glory of the saints in heaven, but he did not approve prayers offered to God through them. He and the other early Protestant leaders generally agreed that saintly mediators with God were unnecessary, even ill-advised, since everyone can pray to God directly.

In Puritan New England the godly on earth were regularly called saints, and the term is still heard in Protestantism as a name for church members. This general use is also known in Roman Catholicism and Eastern Orthodoxy.

Anglicans (Episcopalians) and Lutherans have calendars of saints whose special days may be observed. Among these groups, the departed are usually not venerated as mediators, though some Anglicans and Lutherans elect a more Roman Catholic practice.

While most Protestants have no canonical saints, they have heroes and heroines who are held up as moral and spiritual models. Until fairly recently, books recounting the lives of great Christians were almost as popular among American Protestants as were lives of the saints among Catholics in an earlier day. Everyday Protestant reading matter into the 1950s included the adventures in faith of evangelists, missionaries, businessmen, mothers, and heroic pastors. Such accounts show signs of making a comeback.

Protestants generally are a people of immediacy, so that their heroes and heroines tend to be persons living or recently dead, or perhaps an early denominational founder understood to have direct and immediate influence on the life of the community.

Since the emphasis here is on the earthly lives of the heroes and heroines discussed, *saint* is used in the more general sense, except when it is said that an individual was canonized by a church. *Hero*, *heroine*, and *saint* are almost interchangeable terms in the following chapters, but no suggestion is intended that persons outside the official canons of any church are, or should be, canonical.

The heroic Christian company here comes from a broad spectrum of history. This holy company includes Roman Catholic, canonical and noncanonical, Protestant, and Eastern Orthodox Christians, and there are even some persons considered heretics in more than one church. Some were famous in their lifetimes; others were public nobodies, but when it came to their faith even the best known were able, to borrow a phrase, to keep from being "asphyxiated in fame."[5] Some had a sense of comedy and irony; others were Sunday sober, which is not joyless. Some left written records of their pilgrimages; others did not.

Some hobbled in long, agonizing struggles with doubt; others had unbroken constancy in faith. All were human beings, imperfect in many respects compared with their Lord, and their warts are as interesting as their halos because they were warts dedicated to God. The motif of the way of holiness is not repeated needlessly in the narratives. The brief biographies and the chapters speak for themselves, telling their own stories within the frame of the Holy Company.

The number of great Christians of the past who rightfully belong in the Holy Company is uncountable, and a mere seventy-seven are included here: examples, only fleeting examples of the host that has walked the way of holiness.

Only two other generalizations about this small but diverse company may be helpful.

First, the saints are not on trial. Modern people have an understandable tendency to read history through the eyes of the "reasonable" culture of science and moderation developed, at least in Europe and North America, since the late eighteenth century. Consequently, persons and events in earlier ages are often unfairly judged on the basis of standards and ideas alien to their worlds. As a simple example, people today sometimes have difficulty understanding why early Christians allowed themselves to be killed for their faith. Moderns are apt to ask, "Why didn't they fight? Or do whatever simple religious act the Romans asked as a sign of loyalty to the state? They could have lived and kept Christianity despite a show of Roman patriotism." There were not enough of them to fight, and besides, most early Christians rejected violence. And a little act of patriotism meant putting Caesar over Christ—a lie of faith, and truth mattered. A virtue for modernity would be to check its arrogance toward the past.

Second, great Christians—living or dead, known or unknown to the public—can be intense people; they take faith and the way of holiness with the utmost seriousness, and may seem a bit unusual, even abnormal, judged by the common standards of somewhat lax adherence to religious practice and of a socially weak commitment to God's truth. Christians great in faith do not mind standing apart from the crowd; cutting loose from everyday expectations is a saintly quality.

Christian saints and heroes are great in faith for faith, but they seldom claim greatness; they are more apt to praise God's greatness. God grants favors, Teresa of Avila said, "not because those who receive them are holier than those who do not, but in order that His greatness may be made known, as we see in the case of Saint Paul and the Magdalen, and in order that we may praise Him in His creatures."

. . . and as is seen in the case of Teresa of Avila, John Vianney, Mary Slessor, Martin Luther King, Jr., John Wesley, Vincent de Paul, Catherine of Siena, Dietrich Bonhoeffer . . . and the whole Holy Company.

CHAPTER I

Rescued from Pride

"Holy are the poor in spirit . . ."

"ARE YOU CONTENT NOW?" the caterpillar asked Alice in wonderland.

"Well, I should like to be a *little* larger," she said. "Three inches is such a wretched height to be . . . I'm not used to it!"

Pride, the human boast, is not content either: "a little larger," it insists. "Still more!" And larger, larger, larger, until, like Alice in another phase, it fills the whole space. Small is a wretched size for pride; it is not used to it. Pride likes bigness because, to quote Dorothy Sayers, it intends to "creep under the ribs of God,"[1] to assert human divinity and push God out of the universe.

Pride, understandably, is the first deadly sin; the First Beatitude is appropriately anti-pride. The Christians poor in spirit refuse to take part in the deification of humanity. They resist, are able to resist on the strength of what Dietrich Bonhoeffer called the "call and promise of Jesus," the grounds on which pride can be dedicated to God along with possessions, pleasures, pains, hopes, and sciences. Their boast is of Christ; the condition, in Bonhoeffer's words, is "the utter poverty of the cross."

"Spirit" in the First Beatitude (Matthew 5:3) means the internal, animating life force, the consciousness of self and of the world. To be "poor in spirit" is not so much to adopt a particular pattern of behavior as to live *in* Christ, for the whole self to be so attached to the call and promise of Jesus that life is detached from worldly things and freed from all claims to human self-sufficiency. The poor in spirit sing with the Psalmist:

> I will bless the Lord at all times;
>   his praise shall continually be in my mouth.
> My soul makes its boast in the Lord . . .
>
> (Psalm 34:1–2b, RSV)

But what of the economic overtones of Matthew 5:3? How is Matthew's First Beatitude to be understood when compared with a companion passage in the Gospel of Luke which reads not "poor in spirit" but simply "you poor" (Luke 6:20)?

Some interpreters across the years have said Luke's version is the more authentic and that Matthew "spiritualized" Jesus' original stark declaration that God's kingdom belongs to the economically poor. Luke was important in shaping medieval monasticism's idea of the virtue of poverty; the special recognition of "you poor" in Luke 6:20 is used today both by those who say the church must champion the cause of the poor and also by those opposed to Christian social action; after all, it can be argued, though not sensibly, that to lift persons from poverty is to end their favored status with God.

There is no doubt that Jesus directed his "good news" in large part toward the often impoverished "people of the land" who had no social and little religious standing in first-century Palestine. He went with healing and acceptance to the lowly and outcast; he criticized the prideful rich to whom he promised the last seats at God's banquet, and in this reversed a common ancient belief that riches showed God's favor and poverty was a divine curse.

But to interpret the message of Jesus as solely or primarily economic is a mistake. Contrary to both capitalism and Marxism, life is more than bread. The Christian Gospel cannot be reduced to economic categories. Bonhoeffer is right in *The Cost of Discipleship*, a meditation on the Sermon on the Mount, to insist that Matthew and Luke not be set in opposition, one (Matthew) interpreted as sanctifying spiritual renunciation, and the other, material privation. "On the contrary," Bonhoeffer wrote, "both gospels recognize that neither privation nor renunciation, spiritual or political, is justified, except by the call and promise of Jesus, who alone makes blessed those whom he calls, and who is in his person the sole ground of their beatitude."[2]

The holiness of the poor in spirit is their awareness that in and of themselves they have no holiness, no worth except as it comes from God. Christians following the poverty of the cross are, like Jesus, ready if need be to suffer any privation or pain for God; to renounce everything—everything, including the expectation of merit for making sacrifices. What difference is there between thinking of riches as a sign of divine favor and expecting reward for poverty? Pride, the human boast of rich or poor, is Christian anathema.

William of Sens, the master builder of cathedrals in Dorothy Sayers' *The Zeal of Thy House*, is much the modern in his initial inability to fathom why he cannot have salvation and self-designed human glory at the same time. Informed by the Archangel Michael that his confession of sin is superficial, dealing only with matters of flesh, the architect is perplexed. What more can he confess? he asks.

"Where one's treasure is, the heart is also," Michael replies. "Sin is of the heart."

"But all my heart was in my work," William says, and then the light begins to dawn. His sin was in his work, his marvelous talent so great in his own eyes it rivaled God, who could not build a church, he says, without an architect. And William, at first, will admit no wrong in his attitude: "My work is mine; He shall not take it from me"—not with torture or death.

Michael responds that no suffering and pain can befall the architect that humanity has not inflicted on God; Christ had to leave his work to others—"He made no reservation of Himself."

William of Sens can finally say, "O, I have sinned. The eldest sin of all, Pride . . ."[3]

No single style of discipleship characterizes the "utter poverty of the cross" that rescues believers from pride. Monastics withdrawn from the world and lay Christians engaged in the world are in the company of the poor in spirit. The important quality is the cry, "I believe, Lord, help thou my unbelief" (Mark 9:24).

Partly because of their emphasis on interior love as replacement for pride, Christian mystics come to mind as examples of the poor in spirit. Mystics can illustrate the dimension of discipleship highlighted in the First Beatitude, though they hold no monopoly on poverty of spirit, which Thomas Aquinas said is the starting point of holiness. However, since a number of mystics are included in this chapter (and subsequent chapters), brief comment on Christian mysticism is in order.

Walter Rauschenbusch (see page 161), the great exponent of the social gospel, considered mysticism a temptation to be resisted in the imitation of the "religious personality" of Jesus. In his opinion, mystics with their "inner way" forget the concrete realities of life and turn in disdain from the world where, in his view, Christ should be served by serving others.[4] In other words, Rauschenbusch saw mystics as self-centered, and he wondered what good they are.

Disdain for mystics, ancient or modern, is not uncommon among today's Christians, for whom spiritual rigor is neither encouraged nor expected in a culture glorifying physical gratification. If they are considered at all, mystics are thought of as strange, otherworldly people.

Rauschenbusch's criticism, which has had its influence, is as unfair as it is misinformed. First, not all mystics shut themselves off from the world. Francis of Assisi, Catherine of Siena, and Evelyn Underhill, to name only three of the dozen or so mystics in this book, were persons very much in the world, often dealing with totally concrete social realities. But even reclusive mystics can hardly be accused of forgetting the world.

Mysticism is by definition—at least one garden-variety definition —a form of religious faith seeking interior communion, or union, with the Divine by means of love, contemplation, or some form of spiritual exercise; it makes little appeal to reason. Evelyn Underhill put it more simply: "Mysticism is the art of union with Reality."[5]

Mysticism occurs in all religions, and sometimes outside formal religion. Christian mysticism emerged in the Eastern, Greek-speaking branch of the Church at an early date and, in general, is usually less concerned with systems of theology than with the experience of Christ. But true Christian mysticism is not merely subjective; it arose in large part around the objective reality of Christ's presence in the sacrament of Holy Communion, the "discovery of the inward in the outward," as Underhill has said.[6]

While a great many monastics across the Christian centuries have been mystics, monasticism and mysticism are not synonymous, and the mystic's aim of spiritual union with God is motivated not by a loathing of the world but by a love of the world. A favorite biblical text of mysticism is John 3:16: "For God so loved the world. . . ." Mysticism at its best accounts for evil by facing it with the joy of love radiating into the world, glorifying God and God's creation.

Many mystics, says one historian, burn with "an uncontainable love," a boundless sympathy toward every creature in God's world.[7] These love-filled, often ecstatic souls are important to the Church because they take with utter seriousness the Incarnation of God's love—a love shown on the cross of Christ—in the world.

To repeat, mystics have no monopoly on poverty of spirit. Christians concerned with the more intellectual, the rational, dimensions of faith can also exemplify the First Beatitude—when intellect is dedicated wholly to God, emptied of pride, and pinioned to the call and promise of Jesus.

Mystic or nonmystic, the poor in spirit affirm with Patrick of Ireland:

> Christ with me, Christ before me, Christ behind me,
> Christ in me, Christ beneath me, Christ above me,
> Christ on my right, Christ on my left,
> Christ when I lie down, Christ when I sit down,
> Christ when I arise . . .

Of such is rescue from pride.

Cyprian (200?–258)

The garden was cheerful; glancing at the bright Mediterranean sky through a shade of vines, he felt serene—for a moment.

Beyond the enclosure, on the city streets, from the top of the mountains to the West, the world looked different, he knew. The middle-aged lawyer plied his trade in Caesar's Carthage, Rome in Africa, proud in commerce beside the Gulf of Tunis.

Out there: robbers on the highway, pirates on the sea, bloody gladiators regaling crowds; misery at the hearth, and selfishness.

"A bad world . . . an incredibly bad world," he continued writing in the letter on his lap. "Yet in the midst of it I have found a quiet and holy people. They have discovered a joy a thousand times better than the pleasures of this sinful life. They are despised and persecuted but they care not. They have overcome the world. These people . . . are the Christians—*and I am one of them.*"

Cyprian—glib-tongued Cyprian, his voice for hire by day, his nights for "liberal banquets," his mind playing hopscotch for truth —a Christian! He and his friends at court were surprised; Cyprian had abandoned "the good life" to join the ranks of the "sacrilegious."

Religion in third-century Carthage and across the Roman Empire, meant the state cult—Jupiter, Venus, and their kindred, relaxing in their myths while divine emperors reigned; religion, a pinch of incense to Caesar's genius. Christians were *de facto* illegal for refusing religion; yet they could not be silenced about "The Way."

Cyprian knew the sect and had been confused by its preachers urging "conversion." He listened—"irrational," he thought, "that a man should be capable of being born again." But he kept listening, especially to an old priest named Caecilian, and there he was in 246 sitting in a garden, born again, baptized, and beginning a new life.

"By the help of the water of new birth, the stain of former years had been washed away," he said. ". . . doubtful things at once began to assure themselves to me . . . dark things to be enlightened."

The church at Carthage not only had a new member, but also its leader, its bishop for the next difficult decade—a leader of no riches but the cross of Christ and faith in a living Christ: "Let us walk by the example of Christ, as the Apostle John instructs us, 'He who says he abides in Christ, ought to walk even as He walked'."

Cyprian walked all the way with his new Lord. Ten years after he was elected bishop of Carthage, he was executed with a Roman sword. His crime was refusal to worship Caesar. He willingly died for his faith, but he did not always find it easy in the episcopal office to walk as Christ walked.

Christianity came early to Carthage and prospered. The local church in Cyprian's day was renowned for valor in the face of sporadic Roman persecution, and another wave was at hand when Cyprian, who felt ill-prepared to be a bishop, reluctantly took the mitre in 248. As will be discussed in Chapter Eight, neither the reasons for the Roman hostility to Christianity nor the full extent of the persecution are clear. Most likely for combinations of reasons, rulers of the empire from time to time decided that Christians were a menace and must, on pain of death, formally recognize the state religion.

In 250 Emperor Decius ordered all provincial officials to require all persons to sacrifice to the Roman gods and to the genius of Caesar. Christians resisted; arrests followed, and Bishop Cyprian sought a safe haven—an acceptable and expected course for bishops under persecution in some parts of the church, but not in Carthage. In North African theology martyrdom was considered the surest way to salvation, the most glorious act of obedience to Christ. But theology is not always put into practice, and having no bishop to set the martyr's example, many Christians sacrificed to the pagan gods or bought certificates saying they had.

When persecution subsided, Cyprian came home to criticism, compounded by the practical question of the "lapsed"—Christians who had bowed to the Roman pressure. Cyprian took a moderate position between extremes, one saying that all the "lapsed" should be pardoned forthwith, and the other saying they should never be readmitted to the church. The Bishop of Carthage advised patience in dealing with the controversy.

Cyprian said that anger, discord, and strife in the church grieved the Holy Spirit. Issues of disagreement, he taught, should be settled within the unity of the church by councils. The church was all-important in his thinking; he called it the mother that bears and feeds Christians whose faith dies away from its bosom. By "church" Cyprian meant the channel of grace in sacraments, the preached word, and true teachings protected by true bishops, each equal to the other.

If Cyprian worried some of the priests by avoiding martyrdom in 250, he won the admiration of the whole city two years later. Carthage was struck by plague. The bishop rallied Christians one to another and to the care of non-Christians. Walking in the way of Christ, he said, meant a servant ministry to strangers and even persecutors. "Love your enemies; care for those who despitefully use you," he admonished. Cyprian's ten-year ministry was marked by keen consciousness of Christian responsibility to relieve poverty, no matter how poor Christians themselves were. Believers who could not contribute money, he said, could donate labor and love to those equally poor or poorer. And to the affluent, he said, "Do not let that sleep in your coffers which may be profitable to the poor."

Persecution resumed in 257. Emperor Valerian first ordered Christian worship to cease and then, according to Cyprian, decreed that all Christian clergy and men of rank "should be degraded and lose their property, and if, having been deprived of their possession, they should remain Christian, then they should also lose their heads; that matrons should be deprived of property and banished."

Summarily arrested, Cyprian was exiled to a residence fifty miles from Carthage; in 258 he was recalled for trial. The preserved testimony on the basic charge is short:

Roman Official: The most sacred emperor orders you to sacrifice.
Cyprian: I will not.
Official: Think about it.
Cyprian: Do what you must; there is no reason to reflect on so clear a matter.

The sentence took little time to consider. Said the judge:

You have lived long in sacrilege; you have gathered round you many accomplices in unlawful association; you have made yourself an enemy of the Roman gods and their religion: and our most pious and sacred princes and . . . the most noble Caesar, have not been able to recall you to the practice of their rites. Therefore, since you are found to be the author and leader of shameful crimes, you yourself shall be an example to those whom you have led in your wickedness: your blood shall confirm the laws. Cyprian shall be put to death by the sword.

Cyprian was beheaded in a public garden outside the city as a throng of spectators, including Christians, looked on. The body is said to have been laid by the path so the curious could see it. That night the faithful took their bishop for Christian burial, and they undoubtedly remembered his words: "We must endure and persevere, beloved, in order that, being admitted to the hope of truth and liberty, we may attain to truth and liberty itself."

Macrina (327–379)
Basil of Caesarea (329–379)
Gregory of Nyssa (335–395)

The Roman Emperor Valens cautiously approached the city of Caesarea, capital of the province of Cappadocia. Valens, a Christian with a theology condemned by the church, was traveling around what is today central Turkey replacing bishops and generally harassing Christians who disagreed with his imperial beliefs.

Caesarea in 371 merited special care, for there lived a newly elected bishop, a member of a formidable Christian family, hard even for an emperor to intimidate, and Basil, the new bishop, declared Valens a menace to Christianity.

Valens sent an emissary to ask Bishop Basil to be more reasonable. Must the bishop call the emperor a heretic? Could they not strike a compromise on their theological differences? "Nothing short of violence can avail against such a man," the emissary reported to Caesar.

Caesar Valens passed through the city without attempting violence; he caused Basil to lose half of his diocese and ousted Basil's brother Gregory as bishop of the small town of Nyssa, but these measures accomplished little. When Valens died in 378 at the hands of German tribesmen, the heresy he represented was well on its way toward defeat, the resistance led by members of a remarkable family equipped only with spiritual poverty and a love of Christian truth.

Basil, Gregory, and their older sister Macrina were born to wealth, which they gave away or used up in the service of others. The fewer material goods they had, the fewer they wanted. Basil could have been speaking for the whole family when he prayed for "growth in virtue and perfection, to Thy commands' fulfillment."

Macrina was probably the eldest of the ten children born to Basil the Elder, a lawyer, and his wife Emmelia, a prosperous, landed couple of Cappadocia. The family had been Christian for at least two generations. As the eldest daughter, Macrina naturally helped tend the younger children and seems to have been more mother than sister to Gregory and another brother, Peter, who also became a bishop. She may have taught her brothers their first school lessons; Macrina in maturity was unusually well-educated for a fourth-century woman, but part of her instruction, especially in theology, was arranged by Basil, who recognized the natural talents of the one he and Gregory called "the great sister." Macrina was keenly sensitive to signs of pride in her brothers, young men of advantage and professional promise. Conceit she considered an affront to God, and she is said to have reeducated Basil in humility when his studies in Athens filled him with intellectual arrogance.

While both Basil and Gregory were schooled in theology, neither set out to be priests. They mastered non-Christian philosophy, and each began his career as a teacher of rhetoric in Caesarea. Gregory may have married; if so, and a woman did figure in his young adulthood, the experience was unpleasant, because he later could not say enough to praise celibacy—"glorious virginity," which he lacked.

Eastern Christianity was strongly attracted in the fourth century to asceticism, the renunciation of worldly goods and pleasures in favor of restricted lives of celibacy, self-discipline, and prayer. The original ascetic model was the lone hermit (see Anthony of Egypt, page 55), but by the middle of the fourth century the number of monastic communities was increasing.

Macrina and a small company of women retired around 355 to a semi-cloistered life on a family estate in the region of Pontus. Meanwhile, Basil, tired of rhetoric, undertook a long study tour of monastic centers in the Middle East. He was most impressed by linked communities for men and women in Egypt, and he proposed that he and Macrina establish similar houses. They chose a spot on the Iris River in Pontus.

Basil intended to spend his life as a monk, but it would not be so. The church had need of him and of Gregory who, married or not, had followed his brother and Macrina into the monastic way. A doctrinal dispute was causing havoc in the church; the issue was the interrelationship of the persons of the Holy Trinity—Father, Son, and Holy Spirit. This was an old controversy which the first Christian council, held at Nicaea in 325, had presumably resolved. Arius, a priest of Alexandria, had in effect, denied the divinity of the Son on the grounds that Jesus, as a human being, could not share the essential nature of God.

Although rejected by the Council of Nicaea, Arianism spread across the church, threatening at times and places to replace the confession of Christ as divine and human. The threat was particularly great during the reign of Valens, an avowed Arian. One problem faced by the defenders of orthodoxy was that of language: how best to say that God is three in one, keeping the unity, but recognizing distinctions in what theology calls the Godhead.

Basil and Gregory held the orthodox theology and, along with a friend, another Gregory, played major roles in building the defense against Arianism and the Emperor Valens. Their contributions were both ecclesiastical and theological.

Partly to counteract Arian tendencies in Cappadocia, Basil agreed to ordination, but he got along badly with his bishop and again withdrew to the monastic life. In 365 he was recalled to assist a different bishop in Caesarea and five years later became bishop himself and, as such, head of the Cappadocian church.

To strengthen the orthodox position, Basil named friends and relatives bishops of outlying towns. Gregory was sent to the village of Nyssa, where he initially proved a fumbling bishop. Basil spoke of his brother's "simplicity" and "inexperience" in church affairs, although Gregory was never a simplistic theologian. Valens used Gregory's lack of experience as an excuse for exiling him from Nyssa in 375, but Gregory returned on Valens' death in 378 and thereafter acquitted himself well as a bishop.

Basil and the two Gregorys set out to refute the Arians in a flow of writings. Their major contribution was a linguistic formula expressing the unity of the Holy Trinity while preserving the distinctions among Father, Son, and Spirit. God, they said, is "three Persons in one substance." In working out the language, they made use of Greek philosophical concepts, notably Plato's idea of the one and the many. "The Father is God and the Son is God; and yet by the same affirmation God is one, because no distinction of nature or of operation is to be observed in the Godhead," said Gregory of Nyssa.

While her brothers wrote against the Arians, Macrina developed her convent and ran a hospital attached to it. She assumed a large part of the family wealth, but at her death, according to Gregory, she owned no garment suitable for burial. Basil shared his "great sister's" philanthropic urges, organizing in Caesarea one of the first systems of Christian social institutions—hospitals, orphanages, and homes for the elderly.

Basil outlived Valens by only a few months. He died January 1, 379, and is still commemorated as a major saint in Eastern Orthodoxy, whose liturgy he helped to shape. His eucharistic (communion) prayers are among the most beautiful ever written, for example:

> Let Your precious Gifts to health restore me,
> to cleanse, enlighten, and protect me,
> to sanctify body and soul and save me.
> All phantasies and evil doing to avert:
> the devil's urges in the mind conceived
> and by the body effected.[8]

Macrina died a few months after Basil. Gregory, stopping at her convent for the first time in years, found her on her deathbed. He stayed with her until she breathed no more, and saw her buried. Macrina told her younger brother that God and the Church were calling him to important work that he must accept as a blessing.

Gregory of Nyssa lived almost twenty more years, finishing the work of refuting the Arians, a task made easier by the orthodox Emperor Gratian who succeeded Valens. He traveled throughout the Middle East defending the Nicene Creed adopted in 325, and was present as the leading theologian at the Council of Constantinople (381), which affirmed the teaching on the Holy Trinity as he understood it.

The other Gregory mentioned as taking part in the Cappadocian defense of orthodoxy was named Gregory of Nazianzen, a friend of Basil's from student days. What he said of himself and Basil also applied to Macrina and Gregory of Nyssa: "Our great pursuit, the name we wanted, was 'Christian,' to be called Christians."

Francis of Assisi (1181–1226)
Clare of Assisi (1193?–1253)

Biographers seldom agree on either the details or the meaning of his life. Here is Francis the nature lover—"ecologist" before his time; there, Francis the missionary, preaching to birds and Saracens. Some liken Francis the knight to his lady, Poverty; or Francis the troubadour of God singing songs of joy as the dark ages ended with a Franciscan sunrise; some the institutional Francis, "mother" (the monks called him that) of the religious orders bearing his name.

Francis of the word-portraits can be tormented mystic, clown of God, inspired church reformer, or incipient heretic. The "simple and unlettered man, delightful to God and man," as a contemporary said, can be molded to the prejudices and pleasures of any generation, romanticized, or made a target of skeptics.

He escapes the words no matter how narrow or broad, and, without ceasing to be a man of his times, emerges from romantic or skeptical biographies as the most attractive Christian between Jesus and yesterday—the epitome of the poor in spirit, demanding nothing, least of all sainthood.

Francis had asked to be buried in a cemetery for criminals; the people of Assisi and the Franciscan leaders could not permit that. They wanted a saint—good for the reputation—and had posted guards near his deathbed at tiny Saint Mary of Angels Church, outside the town, to prevent the theft of his body—their relic. They conducted their relic to Assisi's largest church for temporary burial while awaiting a new mausoleum, but on the way they made a stop that did honor the unpretentious holy man who had owned nothing.

The procession paused at a convent next to Saint Damian's, a church that Francis had in his youth repaired with his own hands. Through the convent grille a nun, not old but no longer able to stand, looked out upon the withered corpse. Francis was paying his last visit to Clare Sciffo, a closer friend than "Brother Sun," founder with him of the Ladies of Poverty, today the Franciscan Sisters of Poor Clare.

Clare and Francis lived different kinds of lives—she in the cloister, he as a wandering preacher, but their stories belong together; she, the first woman to join his movement, understood and shared as few others the newness of spirit he brought to late medieval Christianity, and theirs is a story not only of tame wolves and friendly stars, but also—and mostly—of people and the love of Christ.

Both Francis and Clare grew up in Assisi, picturesque in the mountains of central Italy. Theirs was a feudal world of knights, castles, peasants, warring popes and princes, and a new middle class. Her father was a landed lord; his, a seller of cloth, Pietro di Bernardone, prosperous, not aristocratic, one of the new middle-echelon capitalists.

Pietro apparently liked France and was there on business when his son was born and baptized Giovanni (John). Back home he either formally changed the name or used Francis as a nickname. Young Francis learned a bit of Latin and French but was indifferent to school; as a pampered son of the new merchant class, education meant less to him than spending money on happy times with lively young friends. Knighthood and military valor intrigued him. At the age of about twenty he joined an Assisian campaign against neighboring Perugia, was captured, and spent almost two years as a prisoner of war.

Probably ransomed by his family, Francis returned to his old life but soon fell ill. He had recovered enough by 1205 to set off on another military venture, but he never reached his destination. A dream or a heavenly voice told him to go home "to serve the Master rather than the man." Assisi was no longer the same to him; nor he to it. The young man-about-town became moody, neglected his friends, and wandered about old churches. Told he needed a wife, he is said to have replied, "I am going to take a wife more beautiful and worthy than any you know."

Townsfolk in Assisi knew something was the matter when Francesco di Pietro di Bernardone started helping in a leper hospital. This experience deeply impressed him. In a "Testament" dictated later in life he said, "When I was yet in my sins it did seem to me too bitter to look upon the lepers, but the Lord Himself did lead me among them, and I had compassion upon them. When I left them, that which had seemed to me bitter had become sweet and easy."

Reports vary as to where Francis was when his "conversion" took place—some put him in Rome on pilgrimage, and others in Asissi; but they all mention Saint Damian's Church, a crumbling structure near the town. Perhaps in Rome, perhaps at Saint Damian's, Francis heard a voice saying, "Go, repair my house which is falling down." Francis would later interpret this as a mandate to shore up the walls of Christianity itself, but immediately it meant repairing Saint Damian's. He had already given away what he owned, so he generously helped himself to Pietro's fine cloth and sold it, taking the money to the priest at Saint Damian's, although the latter was reluctant to accept it.

Pietro then accused his twenty-five year old son of theft. The hearing, at Francis' insistence, was before the local bishop, who directed him to return the money. He obeyed and, as the famous account goes, took off his own clothes, down to a hairshirt, returning them to Pietro and declaring, "I have called you father on earth, but now I say, 'Our Father, who art in Heaven'."

For two years Francis lived a hermit's life near Saint Damian's, begging for his food and for the materials he used in repairing the old church. In 1209 he chanced to hear a sermon on Matthew 10:5–15, a passage in which Jesus sends his disciples out to heal and preach, telling them to take no money or extra clothes. Francis had found his calling. He also took a wife, his lady Poverty.

As he preached and practiced poverty in Assisi, Francis attracted followers, some of them, like himself, the sons of the new middle-class capitalists. A cow shed served as the first Franciscan "house," but Francis did not intend that there should be any permanent establishments; members and the order were to be totally without possessions. In imitation of Christ, Franciscan friars were to wander, preaching and helping people, neither taking money for their work nor paying for their keep.

The appeal of Francis must be seen in the light of the religious situation of the early thirteenth century. Both church and established religious orders were politically powerful, rich, and somewhat removed from the daily cares of the people, the vast majority of whom were peasants. Neglect of spiritual and physical needs was rampant, thought not universal, and ethical guidance for the laity was at best spotty. In some areas, reform movements of questionable orthodoxy were making great headway by introducing emotional religion tempered by strict moral standards. *Living* the faith as well as *confessing* it was becoming important. The appearance of wandering, mendicant (begging) preachers concerned about everyday people fired imaginations.

Francis and the early Franciscans brought a message of joy based on an awareness of the love of Christ. God's love demonstrated in the cross was the heart of Francis' preaching, and his stress on poverty and humility emerged from a theology of love. He did not say that money and other material goods are evil; he said that they divert attention from God, and he felt the same way about education. Humility, self-emptying to God, was for him the way to witness to the love of Christ in the world.

The love of Christ is the context for considering the accounts of the stigmata (signs of Christ's suffering on the cross) said to have appeared on Francis' body in 1224. With or without stigmata, Francis was willing to participate in the suffering of his Lord.

By 1210 the group around Francis had grown to a dozen. Francis went to Rome to ask permission to found an order, but Pope Innocent III was reluctant to approve new orders, especially one preaching poverty and personal purity—the papacy was having enough trouble with a puritan group called Cathari in southern France. Convinced that Francis respected church authority, the Pope gave his verbal blessing (formal charter came in 1216), but Rome worried about Francis' insistence on the order's absolute poverty, and helped to modify that point when a permanent Franciscan rule was written in the early 1220s.

Francis called his order the Humbler Brethren, or Friars Minor, and as the brothers moved north and south and beyond Italy in their brown robes, new recruits came from all directions. By 1219 the Franciscans numbered 5,000. No organization for women was originally planned, and Francis questioned the wisdom of starting one, since the sisters would need a cloister, it being impossible for them to be wandering preachers.

The question of a second order for women was both raised and solved by the arrival of Clare Sciffo, who had first heard Francis preach when she was sixteen years old. Spiritually and perhaps otherwise attracted to the preacher, she sought his counsel and soon vowed to become a nun under his care. Clare's prominent family vigorously protested; she was unmoved, and on the night of Palm Sunday, 1211, slipped away to the Franciscans at Saint Mary of Angels.

Francis really did not know what to do with the young woman, then eighteen. He first lodged her with a community of Benedictine nuns, then arranged a house for her and her sister next to Saint Damian's. Tradition has it that she never left Saint Damian's again and that her personal austerity caused her to lose the use of her legs. Other women attracted to the Franciscan movement found their way to Clare, and together with Francis she shaped the Order of Poor Clare. She expanded the order into all parts of Europe by dispatching groups of sisters to open new houses to care for the sick and the poor.

Clare was a large blossom among "the little flowers of Saint Francis."

Francis himself could never have lived cloistered. He had too much energy, too much missionary vision, and he wanted personally to preach to the Muslims. An attempt to reach Palestine in 1212 ended in shipwreck, and a later journey toward Muslim Spain was stopped by sickness. His one opportunity to proclaim the love of Christ to Muslims came in 1219, when he and twelve brothers went to Egypt to minister among crusaders laying seige to Damietta, a town considered important to the protection of the Latin Kingdom of Jerusalem.

Distressed by the moral turpitude of the Christian soldiers, and perhaps bewildered by the military strategists, he decided to end the war by converting the sultan of the Saracens to Christianity. Taking one brother with him, Francis marched toward the camp of Al-Kamil. The pair was arrested and chained, but managed to see the sultan, who liked Francis enormously and listened to his preaching for several days and, though he did not convert, sent the monks back to the Christians with a request, "Pray for me, that God will be pleased to give me the laws and faith which so greatly delight you." And, legend says, Al-Kamil gave Francis a horn which the preacher later used to convene congregations.

From Egypt Francis went to the Holy Land, where he received a message urging him to return swiftly to Italy in the interest of the order. His brief absence had given those he left in charge enough time to begin transforming the Franciscans into a traditional monastic order of established houses and educational centers. He was horrified, but a process had begun that he could not stop. Back in Italy, Francis was told the order needed a new, fully developed rule. He wrote, and the administrators he had named and high church officials revised his words. The Franciscan order would not henceforth cling to absolute poverty—property would be acquired and held in the name of the Roman Catholic Church.

When the new rule was approved in 1223 Francis withdrew, in effect, from Franciscan affairs. He preached when he could, his health rapidly failing as a result of multiple diseases, including an eye ailment contracted in the Middle East. Christmas of 1223 he spent at Grecchio, where to his great delight the celebration included a crèche, not the first ever seen, but the one which popularized the portrayal of the Holy Family in the Bethlehem stable.

To the period between his withdrawal from the everyday affairs of the order and his death belong the stigmata and his most famous literary composition, "Song of the Creatures," also known as the "Canticle of Brother Sun." Francis wrote relatively little, and some of that attributed to him is no longer considered genuine, but there is no doubt about his hand in the "Song of the Creatures." Francis believed that people and nature, other creatures and the elements, form a family beloved of God. He praised God through and for the other members of the family—Brother Sun, Sister Moon, the air, water, and fire:

> Be praised, my Lord, for our sister mother earth:
> she supports, nourishes, and gives forth vegetations—
> colorful flowers and grass.

According to scholars, the poem originally ended with the praise for mother earth. Two other sections, on forgiveness and "Sister Death" were added by Francis to commemorate specific occasions, the last when he was told medicine could do no more for him:

> Be praised, my Lord for our sister bodily Death,
> from whom no man can escape.
> How sad those who die without you!
> Happy are those who follow your holy will—
> the second death shall be powerless to
> harm them.

Francis died in his forty-fifth year, blind and in great pain, asking the monks to sing the "Song of the Creatures." The saintmakers around him thought music unfitting for his final hours, but he got his song, they got their saint, and the world got a Christian life it cannot forget:

> Praise, blessings, thanksgiving to my Lord—
> Let us serve Him with great love.

Teresa of Avila (1515–1582)

"O, Lord, how little do we Christians know Thee," she said.

Teresa of Avila spent her sixty-seven years trying to know God, and to know herself in relation to God. All self-knowledge, she taught, depends on recognition of the dignity and beauty of the soul created in God's image. "It is no small pity, and should cause us no little shame that . . . we do not understand ourselves, or know who we are," wrote Teresa.

For her the response of the self, the soul, to Christ was an arduous, mystical pilgrimage toward a poverty of spirit, a spiritual perfection, never fully achieved by human effort; to claim perfection, she knew, was to admit imperfection. Be patient, she advised the nuns in her care; let grace be the guide through the rooms of the soul's "interior castle." But she was not a spiritual quietist awaiting the dawn of holy light. The spirit, the mind, and the bended knee could act: "Be brave and dare with a holy boldness."

She was brave, bold, and, some thought, overbearing in her two-fold calling as spiritual guide (through her writings on the mystical experience) and as a reformer of her Carmelite religious order. Historically, Teresa belongs to the Counter-Reformation, that movement within Catholicism stimulated by the Protestant Reformation. Without tending toward Protestant theology, the Counter-Reformers saw reason to spiritually purify the church and its monastic orders. Teresa's Carmelite reforms reflected an urge to reassert apostolic simplicity among cloistered and mendicant religious orders.

Her mysticism with its emphasis on the soul's union with God also complemented a Counter-Reformation theme. One complaint against the Renaissance Catholic Church was its cold formalism, and Protestantism came preaching a personal faith that appealed to many sixteenth-century Christians. Through efforts that both recognized the validity of the complaint and tried to stem the Protestant appeal, the Counter-Reformation emphasized personal faith within the Roman Catholic context.

The Spanish Counter-Reformation drew heavily on mysticism in bringing believers closer to the spirit of the Gospel, as well as in confirming them in the forms and sacraments of Catholicism. Teresa and her friend John of the Cross were the fountainheads of a school of mysticism that strongly influenced the Counter-Reformation in France and elsewhere (see Vincent de Paul, page 149). Their main emphases were on personal communion with God through prayer and the inexpressible joy of direct encounter with Christ.

Teresa was one of two daughters (and seven sons) born to Alonso Sanchez de Cepeda and his second wife Beatrice y Ahumada. Her father was a gentleman of Avila, the marvelous fairytale fortress town in central Spain; her mother died when Teresa was twelve years old. It being the kind of world it was, she and a brother, Rodrigo, played at saints and martyrs, and once, according to the story, headed south toward Muslim Africa where they expected to make the supreme sacrifice for their immature faith. (An uncle is said to have met them on the road and taken them home.)

Her late teen years were divided about equally between lying sick at home and living in a convent, first as a student, then as a novice, and there seemed to be a cause-effect relationship between convent and sickness until, during a three-year bout with bad health, she discovered "mental prayer"—mental, as opposed to formal prayer. Mental prayer is similar to what Brother Lawrence (see page 85) called "the practice of the presence of God"; Teresa said, "Mental prayer is . . . friendly conversation, frequently conversing alone, with One Who we know loves us."

The necessity of mental prayer, which can be vocal or silent, Teresa developed in her book *The Way of Perfection*, but she herself apparently abandoned it for more than a decade after she recovered and returned to Avila's Carmelite Convent of the Incarnation in about 1538, when she was twenty-three years old. For those years Teresa was not an especially distinguished nun; she later saw herself as divided between worldly and spiritual interests.

Teresa's major work did not begin until she was past forty. After a religious experience in which an image of the wounded Christ pierced her heart, she was ready to do whatever Christ commanded:

> Thine am I, I was born for Thee,
> What wouldst Thou, Master, make of me? . . .
>
> 'Tis Thou alone dost live in me.
> What wilt Thou I should do for Thee?

Her objective service to Christ and the church would be to return the Carmelite order in Spain to its original simplicity and austerity.

The Carmelites formed one of the great new religious movements of the Middle Ages. An order of hermits began in the late twelfth century on Mount Carmel in Palestine. As it moved west it took on the mendicant style of the Franciscans and Dominicans. The formal order of Carmelite nuns was chartered in 1452. Like the Franciscans and Dominicans, the Carmelites lost much of their original vigor and also acquired properties as the order aged. Teresa came to consider her own convent much too lax and too dependent on revenues from endowments; like Francis, she believed that nuns and monks should live from alms and go barefoot (in sandals).

A resident of the Convent of the Incarnation for twenty-five years, Teresa pulled up stakes in 1562 by opening her own convent (Saint

Joseph's) for barefoot (discalced, as opposed to calced, or shod) Carmelite nuns. Her nuns wore coarse brown habits and veils with no
pleats, slept on straw, ate no meat, and rarely if ever left the cloister.
The town of Avila was distressed; no revenues could be realized from
a convent of such austerity—and what if the reform movement grew?

For five years Teresa was the constant mother superior of Saint
Joseph's, schooling the nuns in the way of prayer and meditation; a
ministry of "reparations" for human sinfulness, she said. She was
unsure until 1567 that the Carmelite officials in Rome would approve
her reform. In that year the prior general visited Avila and blessed
Saint Joseph's and other new reform convents he hoped Teresa would
establish.

She needed no more than an invitation to move across Spain,
founding barefoot communities, usually of only thirteen women
each. On her travels in 1567 she encountered Juan de Yepes, a young
Carmelite priest, whom she recruited to begin a barefoot reform
among the men of the order. De Yepes, better known as John of the
Cross, became Teresa's chief collaborator in reform and in the spread
of Spanish mysticism. A brilliant man, highly educated, John of the
Cross wrote numerous spiritual classics, including *Ascent of Mount
Carmel*, which not only traces the mystic's path to God but also warns
against the "vainglory" that can spoil the pilgrimage.

Both Teresa and John were accused of vainglory by opponents of
their Carmelite reform. Misrepresented to the order's general in 1577,
she was directed to cease founding new convents, and he was imprisoned in Toledo for a time. Teresa was what the modern world would
call a "tough" woman; she considered many women slow-witted. She
had a temper, which she used, and though she exaggerated her own
ignorance and impatience, vainglory was not among her faults.
Forced into retirement, she must have often pondered the poem
found in her Breviary after her death:

> Be not perplexed,
> Be not afraid,
> Everything passes,
> God does not change.
> Patience wins all things.
> He who has God lacks nothing;
> God alone suffices.

The crisis in the reform passed. King Philip II of Spain intervened
for Teresa and John, and a division was effected between the barefoot

and shod Carmelites—each would operate independently. Teresa, her health failing, resumed her organizing, traveling by carriage over rough roads to administer the seventeen convents she had founded, and to lay plans for others. A patched habit was the symbol of her authority.

Of her five books, the most widely read is *Interior Castle*, her analogy of the soul's progress from self-knowledge into the presence of God. She wrote it for her nuns, ending it with a prayer that she might, through Christ's merits, accomplish the ascent of the soul she had described.

She fell ill for the last time at Alba de Tomes. Asked by a priest if she wanted to be buried in Avila, she replied, "Will they not give me a little earth here?" They did.

Teresa was declared a Catholic saint in 1622, and in 1970 Pope Paul VI made her the first woman "doctor" (primary teacher) of Catholicism.

Jonathan Edwards (1703–1758)
Sarah Pierrepont Edwards (1710–1758)

Stockbridge, Massachusetts, in 1751 was the American frontier—remote, rustic, primarily an Indian town with a small settlement of white pioneers; not a likely home for New England's foremost Puritan divine, a preacher whose sermons raised debate in Boston and London.

Yet there he was, Jonathan Edwards, newly arrived pastor to the pioneers; missionary to the Indians, and also their defender against white exploitation. Edwards, his wife Sarah, and their seven dependent children (they had eleven) had come from Northampton, farther east. They were, in a sense, exiles; his twenty-three year ministry in Northampton had ended when the congregation fired him for challenging set ways of thinking.

Edwards was America's first major theologian-philosopher, and remains major although he is not well known today, except among scholars and seminarians. His relative obscurity results in part because popular history has unfairly chosen to remember him as a "fire and brimstone" preacher and, more important, because the theology he represents was swept aside in the American religious currents.

Mighty among the poor in spirit, Edwards breathed, ate, raised his children, preached, wrote, and engaged in theological controversies to one end—to glorify the sovereign God Almighty, maker of heaven and earth, and source through Christ of beauty, virtue, love. He was not sour in the stereotype of the Puritan, though a Puritan he was, stern on the moral front but also a man of abounding joy, a lover of nature—God's creation—and lyric in thanksgiving for having been surprised as a young man by God's saving grace. "God's excellency, his wisdom, his purity and love seemed to appear in everything," he wrote after a religious experience during his student years at then new Yale College in New Haven, Connecticut.

The proper evidence of a fig tree, Edwards said, "is that it actually bears figs"; likewise, to him, the evidence of a life regenerated by God is Christian practice—holiness public in fruit and effect.⁹ He found a prime example of Christian practice in his own home—Sarah Pierrepont Edwards. Before they married, he wrote in his notebook, "She is of a wonderful sweetness, calmness and universal benevolence of mind, especially after . . . God has manifested himself to her mind. She will sometimes go about from place to place, singing sweetly; and seems always full of joy and pleasure; and no one knows for what." Almost twenty years into their marriage, Edwards used his wife without naming her, as a case study of a visible saint. He found continuing delight in her God-centered affections and her charity. Not that Sarah Edwards did anything such as found a hospital or run a school—her charity was more everyday, in the home, as a neighbor, and in coping with a husband who sometimes spent thirteen hours a day in his study.

Sarah and Jonathan Edwards were both children of parsonages, she born in New Haven and he in East Windsor, Connecticut. He entered Yale College at age thirteen and stayed on for two years after graduation in 1720 for advanced study. For a few months he pastored a Presbyterian church in New York, then returned to Yale as a tutor. Edwards went to Northampton in 1727 as associate to his maternal grandfather, Solomon Stoddard, pastor in the Massachusetts town for sixty years. He and Sarah Pierrepont married that same year, and in 1729 Grandfather Stoddard died, leaving Edwards sole minister.

The New England into which Edwards was born was a unique place, part of the British colonial realm in America, but different from the colonies to the south. Massachusetts, for example, was really a holy commonwealth—God's own commonwealth governed by the saints—in the eyes of the Puritans, who drew little distinction be-

tween church and society. A town meeting and a church meeting
were one and the same in Northampton in the days of Solomon
Stoddard.

By the 1740s the holy commonwealth was entering its last phase;
this Edwards saw long before the other Puritan divines. The Calvin-
ism (Reformed theology coming from Switzerland via Scotland and
the English Dissenters) underlying the commonwealth was being
challenged; moral behavior was deteriorating. "Licentiousness," Edwards said, prevailed among the youth of Northampton in 1730;
"they were many of them very much addicted to night walking, and
frequenting the tavern, and lewd practices."

As much as he opposed lewd practices, Edwards did not believe
Christian practice could be assured by stretching a Christian canopy
over a community. A Christian commonwealth could not guarantee
Christian behavior or faith; religion to him was chiefly a matter of the
converted, purified, and holy heart. And, unlike many of his fellow
Puritan preachers, Edwards did not object to emotion in religion, so
long as the experience was not mistaken for the reality of faith.

Primarily through his preaching, a religious "awakening" swept
Northampton in the late 1730s. It began with the young people who
gave up "night walking" for serious concerns; the fervor spread to the
adults, and soon the whole town was talking of the "great things of
religion." Other towns were affected, and the New England revival
combined with similar outbreaks in other colonies to form the "Great
Awakening," or the "First Great Awakening."

To this period belongs the sermon for which Edwards is unfortunately best remembered. He preached "Sinners in the Hands of An
Angry God" in Enfield, Connecticut in 1741. True, the sermon did
dangle sinners over the fiery pit of hell on a slender thread, but it was
atypical of Edwards's preaching, and if the whole text is read, its
intent is to acknowledge the majesty of God rather than to frighten
people into grasping onto God to stay out of hell. Edwards did not try
to compel conversion by fear—that was against his basic theology; he
proclaimed the possibility of people being grasped by God.[10]

The "Great Awakening" yawned and fell asleep in New England in
the mid-1740s. Some of the new saints were steadfast, while others
went astray, leaving Edwards with a theological and psychological
question: Why were some conversions genuine and others not? One of
the first exponents of the psychology of religion, he tackled the question in terms of "religious affections," and by observing people and

studying the Bible, he developed a practical understanding of the operation of saving grace. The first eleven of the twelve grounds of "gracious affections" he enumerated are internal—indications by which a person knows the Spirit is at work. Among these is a sense of humility that continues after the guilt of wrongdoing is removed in conversion. The final indication is objective, visible; namely, that one makes the "practice of religion eminently his work and business."

It was specifically in putting his conclusions on religious affections into practice that Edwards angered his Northampton congregation. He decided it was hypocritical to admit to Holy Communion, as was customary, any and all who presented themselves. When it came to new members, only fig bearers would be called fig trees; only visible saints could approach the Lord's Table: No fruit in practice meant no conversion, and no conversion meant no access to the sustaining means of grace.

Edwards' theology on the point is debatable. His grandfather Stoddard had considerable Christian tradition in his favor when he opened the table on the grounds that the sacrament contributes to Christian regeneration. Edwards, however, did not act out of spiritual arrogance. His major concern was that the church assume its responsibility to define the nature of the Christian life; to let social custom determine the qualifications for admission to Communion was to him hypocritical because it allowed the unconverted to make liars out of themselves.

Without work and controversial, Edwards remained in Northampton a year before accepting the offer of a missionary society to relocate in Stockbridge. His seven years on the frontier were among his most productive as a theologian. There he wrote significant books on free will (he rejected it), original sin (he accepted it), and a philosophical defense of his belief that God's glory, not human happiness, is the goal of life and all creation.

The philosophical treatise, called *The Nature of True Virtue*, allowed humanity a limited "natural" goodness. True virtue Edwards identified with the love of God for God's sake; that too is true sainthood and true beauty, he said. As one historian has well stated, for Edwards "true religion is not to achieve moral goodness but to receive holy beauty."[11]

Reluctantly, Edwards agreed in 1757 to leave Stockbridge to become president of the young College of New Jersey (later Princeton University), replacing a son-in-law who had died. Before he was inaugurated, Edwards died from a smallpox inoculation in March, 1758. Sarah joined him a few months later.

Sarah and Jonathan Edwards enjoyed a lifelong love affair with each other; they loved God more because physical and domestic love were to them only "private affections." Edwards spoke for both of them in writing in *The Nature of True Virtue:*

The reason why men are so ready to take these private affections for true virtue, is the narrowness of their views; and above all, that they are so ready to leave the divine Being out of their view, and to neglect him in their consideration, or to regard him in their thoughts as though he did not properly belong to the system of real existence, but was a kind of shadowy, imaginary being.

God was very real to the Edwardses, real and to be glorified.

Søren Kierkegaard (1813–1855)

He inherited from his father a belief that the family was cursed and he, like five of six brothers and sisters, would die young—before his thirty-fourth birthday. Therefore, Søren Kierkegaard pursued with a sense of urgency the God-given task that came upon him in his twenty-sixth year.

His task was that of becoming a Christian, and of inciting others toward becoming Christian, in a culture, nineteenth-century Denmark, that claimed to be Christian but, to him, was not, or at best merely spread an umbrella under which people sat as "Christians of a sort." Kierkegaard was uninterested in Christianity "of a sort," except to attack it; he considered Christianity the truth worth living and dying for—a faith, not a philosophy or ethical system; a personal faith requiring self-denial and risk.

The key word in his task is *becoming*. Kierkegaard could not imagine Christianity as a static condition achieved today for tomorrow, but when he said "becoming a Christian" he was not using evolutionary language. His language was that of the clash of opposites—doubt and belief, for example—dispelling illusions, letting one clearly see the good sense of a faith-filled "leap" in the dark.

His own becoming was a series of epiphanies and pains, enlightenment, lapses, and deep psychological suffering. At times he was shrouded in dread and guilt, knowing sin as despair before God, and not until relatively late in his forty-two years experiencing a decisive sense of forgiveness.

"Here I stand, a great question mark," he once said, and as a question mark he set forth in "fear and trembling," knowing the "sickness unto death" (despair), hoping in faith to receive "purity of heart" and be equipped to the "acts of love."[12] Søren Kierkegaard inherited a fortune; he lived the poverty of the spirit.

Evidence of his inward "God-relationship" erupted in a virtual mountain of books written and published between 1842 and 1846. The latter year he thought would be his last; he would soon be thirty-four, and in the title of a large volume called a "postcript" he included the word "concluding." But he did not die, and in 1847 resumed his task of becoming a Christian. His writings during the last eight years of his life, his years of grace, as it were, had a new boldness, a more direct affirmation of his faith, a stronger resolve to "have one thought, to will one thing"—to learn and live Christian love.

Kierkegaard's amazing literary output did not go unnoticed in his lifetime as is sometimes alleged. He was both famous and infamous in Denmark, especially after launching the project, the campaign that consumed the last two years of his life. He set about to introduce the Church of Denmark (Lutheran) to Christianity. The state church, he said, had reduced the clergy to the status of civil servants, and in that and other ways had so departed from New Testament faith that he believed "Christianity no longer exists."

Partly because Danish is a little-known language outside Denmark, his works lay dormant for almost half a century after his death. They found a popular audience first in Germany, and between the two world wars, throughout the world. Thirty years ago it was fashionable to say "Kierkegaard's time has come"; today, his time may have passed in the way in which he was first used in Europe and America. He was used in building modern existentialism, a philosophy asserting human freedom and responsibility against rigid systems of thought and social organization. Since it has a hard time accounting for the reality of sin and evil and can project little hope, existentialism has fallen on hard times in the late twentieth century.

Kierkegaard lives on as his reintroducers fade because his work is more basic than theirs. He was neither philosopher nor theologian in a formal sense, and not always an existentialist in the sense that French writers Albert Camus and Jean-Paul Sartre were. He was a religious writer, a spiritual writer, who experienced the anxiety and dread the modern existentialists write about, but without stopping with dread. He insisted that he be viewed as a Christian writer: "My whole work as an author is related to Christianity, to the problem 'of being a Christian,' " he said.

He was born and lived all his life in Copenhagen, except for four trips to Berlin and limited travel in Denmark. His father, Michael Kierkegaard, began life as a poor farm boy in Jutland and moved to the capital, where he made a fortune in business. Young Søren adored his father; his mother, also from Jutland, seems to have made little impression on the youngest child of seven. The Kierkegaard home was marked by strict Lutheran orthodoxy, super-strict morality, and frail children. As a youngster Søren had a fall resulting in a spinal curvature, but none of the children was physically strong, and many of them, including Søren, inherited a melancholy that today would probably be diagnosed as depression. Of the seven children all but one, who expired at age twelve, reached maturity, then started a parade to the grave. Three children and their mother died in a three-year period (1833–34), causing the father to predict the deaths of Søren and his older brother, Peter, before they were thirty-four, the most advanced age of any of their brothers and sisters. Peter survived Søren and became a Lutheran bishop who vigorously disliked his brother; he tended toward emotional instability in his declining years.

Søren entered the university at age seventeen; theology was to be his subject, but he found philosophy more interesting and actually had no professional direction, a situation that worsened after his twenty-second birthday. About that time a "great earthquake" shook him. He never disclosed exactly what this was. Scholars can only speculate, but it had something to do with discoveries about his beloved father—possibly evidence that the parent who had raised his children in strictest morality had been sexually promiscuous as a youth, and perhaps also the knowledge that his father believed the family to be cursed because he, as a lad, had cursed God for his poverty.

Whatever the "earthquake," it caused a breach between father and son and sent Søren into great despair, accompanied by a rejection of religion, episodes of drunkenness, and at times the contemplation of suicide. While he looked back on that period as one of moral debauchery, the evidence suggests the possibility of one sexual encounter.

Father and son were reconciled on Søren's twenty-fifth birthday, only a few months before Michael Kierkegaard died. The reconciliation brought the young man back to religion. During Lent, 1838, he recorded in his *Journal* an experience as of a conversion:

There is such a thing as an *indescribable joy* which glows through us as unaccountably as the Apostle's outburst is unexpected: "Rejoice, and again I say, Rejoice!"—Not a joy over this or that, but full jubilation, 'with hearts, and souls, and voices': 'I rejoice over my joy, of, in, by, at, on, through, with my joy'—a heavenly refrain, which cuts short, as it were, our ordinary song . . .

He resolved to return to the study of theology, and in mid-1840 graduated from the University of Copenhagen, though he did not seek ordination. His inheritance meant he could pursue an interest in writing. Also, he was involved in his first and only love affair.

Regine Olsen was ten years his junior, but Kierkegaard wooed and won her. They became engaged in the fall of 1840 and, in his paradoxical manner, he almost instantly regretted the proposal. He could not marry, he decided, because of the family curse and because he believed marriage required total truthfulness—and he had the secret of the "great earthquake," which he could not, would not, divulge. He broke the engagement, forcing Regine to accept this by acting roguish (all he did was say he had not yet sown all the "wild oats" he planned, and that was roguish in Copenhagen in 1841).

Kierkegaard never stopped loving Regine, never gave her up in his heart, even though she married another. His writings would repeat over and over the sad story of the ill-fated romance.

In his pain, he fled to Berlin where he wrote much of his first major book, *Either/Or*, the introductory volume of a number dealing with aesthetic and ethical concerns. These books are usually termed "philosophical" as opposed to his later "religious" writings, but according to Kierkegaard himself the purpose of these books was to show that aesthetics—matters of the senses—and even ethics are dead-ended as substitutes for religious faith.

He used pseudonyms for many of the early books, not necessarily to hide his authorship but because they were in large measure dialogues with himself as he was becoming a Christian. Irony and wit, often in the forms of stories, even novellas, punctuate the works. His last book in this period was *Concluding Unscientific Postscript*, an attack on the philosophy of Hegel. Kierkegaard found Hegelianism, then the rage in Europe, comical in its attempt to organize the whole of life into objective categories. He said that truth was more subjective.

Approaching death, he thought, in 1846, Kierkegaard, who has his own comedy, decided to continue his direct appraisal of things and ideas he did not like. One thing he disliked was a newspaper called the *Consair*. While the paper had praised his works, the politically conservative Kierkegaard disapproved of its muckraking attitude. He insulted the editor, who then proceeded to vilify the writer in every issue, portraying him as such an ill-dispositioned, unkempt, and physically deformed character that for years Danish mothers were reluctant to name their sons Søren. The abuse hurt, but out of it Kierkegaard gained new resolve to say what he must say, and that was strictly religious. Public ridicule, in his words, "put a new string in his instrument," and he intended to play it.

His playing took the form of his greatest books, including *Training in Christianity*. These works indicated awareness of the need to imitate Christ in love and suffering. He prayed: "Lord Jesus Christ! A whole life long didst thou suffer that I too might be saved: and yet thy suffering is not yet at an end; but this too wilt thou endure, saving and redeeming me, this patient suffering of having to do with me."

In these last years, Kierkegaard felt God was entrusting him with a definite message, and that message was directed against the religious establishment. His target was not administrative corruption in the Church of Denmark, but spiritual indifference, derived, he believed, from a rationalistic approach to faith, supported by the "official" system. Denmark, like Scandinavia in general, had and has official state churches, Lutheran by tradition and based in some degree on the idea of Christendom—church and state linked in forming a single Christian society.

To Kierkegaard, Christendom was a myth, a deceit, a figment of the establishment's imagination, giving people the false notion they had no personal responsibility in obedience to Christ. His attack on "Christendom," which he said had destroyed Christianity, came in articles and a series of pamphlets that pitted him against the Danish hierarchy, and also won for him the largest public following of his career. The possibility of fame troubled him, but he was relentless in the assault, going so far as to encourage Danes who wanted to become Christian to boycott the established churches and "shun the parson."

Kierkegaard made many of his points in stories and parables, and the passion behind his anger at the religious establishment can be

sampled in his account of "The Wild Goose." In the story a wild
goose decides to tarry with some tame geese he likes and hopes to
persuade them to accompany him on the migration south; the tame
geese are uninterested in learning to fly, and acquire power over the
wild goose so that he remains with them when the wild flock leaves.
"The thing Christianity teaches," he said in drawing the moral, "is
what a man can *become* in life. Here then is the hope that a tame goose
may become a wild goose." Christians, he continued, should stay
with people as long as possible in an attempt to win them to love, but
"as soon as thou dost observe that the tame geese are beginning to
acquire power over thee, then off, off and away with the flock, lest it
end with thee becoming a tame goose blissfully content with a pitia-
ble condition."

Soon after the writing of "The Wild Goose," Kierkegaard was off
and away to another flock. He had not finished his attack on Christendom, but his point had been made when he collapsed on the street in
early October, 1855. Though he rallied in the hospital and lingered
forty days, his legs were paralyzed. Told by a friend he looked well
enough to go home, Kierkegaard replied:

Yes, the only trouble is, I can't walk. But indeed there are other means of
transportation, I can be lifted up; I have had a feeling of becoming an angel
and acquiring wings; and that indeed is what is to come to pass: to sit astride
the cloud and sing,

Hallelujah!"

Amanda Smith (1837–1915)

Tennessee, she knew, was far below the Mason-Dixon line, and in
the 1870s she was reluctant to go there, but the black scrub woman,
living in New York, felt a calling to a meeting in Knoxville and put the
matter to God: "Lord, if being a martyr for Thee would glorify Thee,
all right; just to go down there and be butchered by wicked men for
their own gratification, without any reference to Thy glory, I'm not
willing."

The Lord told Amanda Smith to go, and she did, to Knoxville, and
on to Texas and towns between, not always finding places to eat or
sleep, but always believing the voice that said, "My grace is sufficient
for thee."

She was an unusual sight in post–Civil War America—a black

woman evangelist, an ex-slave, traversing North and South preaching to all races and then spending fourteen years—only God knows how she did it financially—evangelizing in England, India, and Africa.

Amanda Smith felt rich scrubbing floors and washing clothes; she belonged to Jesus and wanted to share that treasure with others. She was not ordained, not a missionary commissioned by her denomination, the Methodist Episcopal Church; no organization ever paid her a salary. She wanted social improvements for her race, but was convinced that no benefit outranked the presence of Jesus alive in the heart.

She called her autobiography *The Lord's Dealing with Mrs. Amanda Smith*. The direct dealings began around 1850 in a Methodist revival near York, Pennsylvania. A thirteen-year-old freed slave, working for a white widow, slipped into a back pew during an evening service. A friendly woman noticed her, entreated her to give her life to Christ, and Amanda did, though it would be years and many heartaches later before God summoned her to preach.

Amanda Smith's dealings with life began in 1837 on the plantation of Dr. Shadrach Green near Long Green, Maryland. Her mother was Green property, and her father belonged to a neighboring squire. Her father, Samuel Berry, worked round the clock to buy the freedom of himself, his wife, and five children. He succeeded in his Herculean task, according to one account, but another says Amanda was freed in order to comply with the deathbed wish of her owner's young daughter. Bought free or set free, Amanda was free and working in Pennsylvania when she was thirteen years old. Somewhere along the way she got about three and a half months of schooling.

An early first marriage ended with her husband's marching south with Federal troops and never returning. A daughter was born. The second marriage, to a man she thought was a preacher, was longer but little happier. Mr. Smith had decided to leave the ministry without informing his fiancée; this grieved her because she had been attracted to him partly because he was a preacher.

After a few years in Philadelphia she moved to New York City, where the turning point of her life occurred in 1855 at another Methodist revival. Converted in Pennsylvania, she was "sanctified" in Methodist fashion at the Green Street Methodist Episcopal Church. "O what a mighty peace and power took possession of me," she later recalled.

Mrs. Smith began to worry for the unsaved. She had to urge them toward Christ by witnessing to the peace and security she felt, and she did feel secure, although she earned only a few dollars per week as a cleaning and washer woman. Her tubs and buckets were her altar; she prayed as she worked, and finally found the courage to begin testifying in church. Eloquent and passionate, she received invitations to speak in other congregations. Her lack of education or ordination was no barrier in the 1870s. The United States was caught up in a lay-led Protestant revival. Women as well as men preached.

Popular audiences in the late nineteenth century adored the women preachers, one of whom, the Widow (Margaret) Van Cott, was on the sawdust trail for thirty years, her hair "nicely fixed and frizzed" and her face glowing with "conscious splendor." Amanda Smith's preaching career in the United States was much shorter, though for a time she commanded a popular following and preached in many notable churches, including Brooklyn's Bethany Church, the pulpit of Henry Ward Beecher, a clergyman so popular that his endorsement was sought by soap makers.

Mrs. Smith, of course, was not accepted by all audiences north or south because she was black. Experiences of discrimination no doubt encouraged her to consider Eng;and, but the thought was amusing to her when God put it in her mind. "Go to England!" she said to herself, "Amanda Smith, the colored washwoman, go to England! No, I am not going to pray a bit; I have to ask the Lord for so many things that I really need that I am not going to ask Him for what I don't need—to go to England."

Was she afraid? The realization dawned that God wanted her to go. "Oh, such a sense of shame filled me. I prostrated myself on the floor . . . and I cried out, 'Lord, forgive me, for Jesus's sake, and give me another chance, and I will go to England.' "

Friends arranged ship's passage, and with her bonnet and Quaker cloak, she sailed east in 1876, finding a warm welcome among the evangelical Protestants in England and Scotland. She preached in the British Isles for almost nine months. India beckoned; she was there eighteen months, then back in London for a world Methodist meeting, then off to Liberia.

Amanda Smith spent most of the next dozen years in West Africa, evangelizing, organizing women's groups, advocating temperance, and promoting the religious education of children. Money for her work came in dribbles from America and England. Once despairing of a letter with a check, she realized she was putting her faith in

America, not in God. "Lord forgive me," she prayed, "and help me to give up every hope in America and trust in Thee, the living God."

She left the United States penniless, and returned penniless in 1890. Back home Amanda Smith settled in Harvey, Illinois, a Chicago suburb, and opened an orphanage for black children. She supported the home with the income from her autobiography and by contributions. She also preached, but on a less extensive scale than before her missionary journey. Mrs. Smith maintained the orphanage until shortly before her death in 1915.

In India one of the persons she met and impressed was an American Methodist missionary, later a bishop, James Thoburn. He wrote of Amanda Smith:

The penetrating power of discernment which she possessed in so large a degree impressed me more and more the longer I knew her, indeed, through my association with her I learned many valuable lessons, more that has been of actual value to me as a preacher of Christian truth, than from any other person I ever met.

Pandita Ramabai (1858–1922)

The future looked bleak to the young Hindu woman arriving in Calcutta with her brother in 1878. She was twenty years old, past the usual marriage age for Brahman (high-caste) girls, and jobs for women were almost nonexistent. The brother was ill; they had no family and, despite their caste, for two years had done what the homeless poor of India often did. They had wandered.

Destitute, determined, and soon alone—the brother died—she turned to her only resource, her mind. Though poor and hungry, she had something few Indian women of her day possessed—an education; not a well-rounded education, but a very specialized one. She knew Sanskrit, the sacred language of her religion, and could recite thousands of verses conveying the wisdom of India.

She would recite on the streets, near temples, wherever, for her keep. Such a novelty—Sanskrit from a woman's lips; tradition discouraged it, but she was so proficient she came to the attention of the British colonial government and the Hindu teachers. She so impressed a group of learned men that they hailed her as "pandita," mistress of wisdom.

Pandita Ramabai used her public recognition to popularize two social abuses close to her heart: the bias against education for women, and the practice of marrying small girls—mere babies—to older men, so that India was full of child-widows nobody cared for.

She laid out her causes in Calcutta, and there she also encountered Christianity for the first time. Ramabai thought it a strange religion —people gathered in rooms without idols, reading and singing, down on their knees praying to something unseen or, she wondered, "were they paying homage to the chairs before which they knelt?"

Despite the strangeness of its practice, one feature of Christianity as she saw it in Calcutta immediately appealed to her. That was the attitude of its women. The Christian women she met did not consider themselves the property of husbands or fathers—they had a part in worship, and their souls mattered. She eventually went to Christianity because of its attitude toward women; she stayed because Christ claimed her. Pandita Ramabai could have been a university professor, if not in India then in Europe or America; she had offers, but she chose to serve Christ by serving women and the poor of India.

Her interdenominational mission at Kedgaon, near Poona, became a center of education, agricultural experimentation, and refuge for widows and starving people. Pandita Ramabai knew a great deal about both widowhood and starvation.

Ananta Shatri Dongre, her father, was a Brahman priest and scholar of Mangalore who married her mother when the bride was nine years old and he forty-three. He decided to instruct his child-wife in Sanskrit, an undertaking strongly protested by fellow Brahmans in the vicinity. So Ananta Shatri moved away to the edge of a forest near Mysore and there planted fields, taught his wife Sanskrit, and fathered three children—a son and two daughters, to whom he also taught the sacred language. Ramabai was the youngest child.

The family lost its property by the forest in one of India's periodic economic depressions and, being a priest, Ananta Shatri set out with his wife and children on a pilgrimage, earning a pittance by reciting religious verse at temples. Many pilgrims died in the famine of 1876–77, among them Ramabai's parents and her sister. The horror of death by starvation was indelibly imprinted in her mind. She called her mission "Mukti" ("Deliverance") and in times of famine she combed the countryside looking for widows and children with none to care for them. She collected the hungriest, took them home by the thousands, and when the mission's food or water ran short, she prayed, and another shipment of supplies would arrive, or it would rain.

Her lecturing for women's rights caused a sensation in Calcutta, and even reached the ears of Queen Victoria. Describing one of her appearances in 1880, a British colonial official said it was as though "Saraswati, the goddess of eloquence, had come down to visit." Ramabai's crusade for women and children did not, however, solve the immediate problem of how she would live. To her surprise, and pleasure, a young lawyer, a friend of her deceased brother, proposed marriage. She accepted, and moved with Bipin Bihari Medhavi to the Assam region where he practiced. One daughter was born, and nineteenth months after the wedding Ramabai was a widow.

Taking her child, Manorama ("Heart's Joy"), she went to Poona and there resumed her street lecturing, following it up with organizing efforts among high-caste women. Her activism brought an invitation to testify before a colonial commission considering educational possibilities for Indian women; one part of her career was solidly launched.

In Calcutta and during her marriage she had studied Christianity. Ramabai knew she was dissatisfied with Hinduism, but she was not sure she wanted to embrace the faith associated with Western missionaries. She reached no decision until she visited England in 1883 as the guest of an order of Anglican nuns. The kindness and spiritual sincerity of the sisters touched her, and in 1883 she was baptized into the Church of England.

Pandita Ramabai was a church member for eight years, she later said, before she knew what it meant to be a Christian: "I came to know, after eight years . . . that I had found the Christian religion, which was good enough for me; but I had not found Christ, who is the Life of the religion and the Light of every man that cometh into the world."

She compared her awakening to Christ to that of the blind and lame healed by Jesus in the Gospels. She said:

I can give only a faint idea of what I felt when my mental eyes were opened and when I, who was "sitting in the darkness, saw great light," and when I felt sure that to me who, but a few moments ago "sat in the region and shadow of death, light had sprung up." I was very like the man who was told, "In the Name of Jesus Christ of Nazareth rise up and walk." "And he leaping up stood, and walked, and entered with them into the temple, walking and leaping, and praising God." The Holy Spirit made it clear to me from the word of God, that the salvation which God gives through Christ is present, and not something future. I believed it, I received it, and was filled with joy.

Ramabai spent a year and a half in England, teaching Sanskrit at the Cheltenham Ladies' College and studying there herself. Then came three years in America, studying educational methods and building a network of support for the school and home for widows she planned in India. In the United States she wrote a book, *The High Caste Hindu Woman*, that served to popularize her cause. A nondenominational group of individuals pledged to support her work for ten years.

The home and school opened in Bombay in 1889, and the next year, was relocated near Poona and expanded to include a secondary school for girls. Mukti Mission was open to persons of all religions; Hindu girls were never pressured to become Christian, although a fair number did. Pandita Ramabai did not try to hide her love for Christ or to force her faith on others; she did believe that if Indian women were given education and independence they would "naturally adopt" Christianity. She considered herself a "sweeper" removing the difficulties lying in the way of evangelism.

Mukti Mission was enlarged over the years to include a home for unwed mothers, farms, emergency facilities in times of famine, a printing press, and industrial arts. Several normal schools were opened. In 1899 Pandita Ramabai built a church seating two thousand people, and the sanctuary doubled as a relief center in famine crises.

Pandita Ramabai hoped that her daughter, educated in England and the United States, would succeed her at Mukti, a town of its own by the second decade of the present century. Plans were moving in that direction when Manorama died in 1920.

An interesting feature of Ramabai's missionary concept was her insistence that Mukti must not merely receive mission support from Europe and America, but must also be involved in the world Christian mission as a donor. The church at Mukti sent funds to other mission institutions in India, to the China Inland Mission, and to Armenia. The Pandita kept in touch with the Protestant revival movement throughout the world, and devoted herself to prayer for the conversion of the whole human race.

Deafness overcame Ramabai in the early 1900s. She spent increasing spans of time in solitude and in translating the Bible into the Marathi dialect. Her translation, for which she learned Greek and Hebrew, received mixed reviews from linguistic experts and was revised in the 1950s, but it is thought to be the only translation of the Bible made from original sources by a woman.

Hinduism was undergoing a time of renewal in the late nineteenth century, and many Indians resented Pandita Ramabai's defection from the religion of her birth. To such criticism she replied: "While the old Hindu Scriptures have given us some beautiful precepts of living, the New Dispensation of Christ has given us the grace to carry these principles into practice, and that makes all the difference in the world."

The Pandita died the night after she finished reading the last proof of her Marathi translation of the Bible.

Flannery O'Connor (1925–1964)

"Lives lived between the house and the chicken yard do not make exciting copy," she once said of herself.

Stricken in her mid-twenties with lupus, an inherited vascular disease that attacks the bones, Flannery O'Connor lived most of her last thirteen years on a farm near Milledgeville, Georgia. She walked with difficulty among the peacocks, Chinese geese, and Muscovy ducks in her "chicken yard." Yet despite a limited geographic range her artistic imagination encompassed the field where "physical fact" and "spiritual reality" play at mystery.

Flannery O'Connor was a literary genius, and a modern novelist and short story writer of unapologetic Christian reference whose works do not preach at the reader but pursue with an exciting, exacting pace "the terrible speed of mercy" (a line from a novel) in the earthly city of the sleeping children of God. Her "gravest concern," she wrote to a fellow author, was "the conflict between an attraction for the Holy and the disbelief in it we breathe in with the air of the times."

Her literary corpus is relatively slim; two novels, *Wise Blood* and *The Violent Bear It Away;* two story collections, *A Good Man Is Hard to Find* and *Everything that Rises Must Converge;* assorted essays and articles; and, recently, a volume of letters, *The Habit of Being.*

She was emphatic about her Christian reference. In a 1957 statement, O'Connor said:

I see from the standpoint of Christian orthodoxy. This means that for me the meaning of life is centered in our Redemption by Christ and what I see in the world I see in its relation to that. I don't think that this is a position that can be taken halfway or one that is particularly easy in these times to make transparent in fiction.[13]

The transparency of Christianity in her fiction is a question debated by both readers and scholars. When the first novel and collection of stories appeared in the 1950s, some people, especially those conditioned to "Christian fiction" of bright light and sparkling piety, were bewildered, even offended. O'Connor's stories reek with violence (a family murdered on an outing, a child drowned in baptism, a reluctant evangelist raped by the devil parading as a homosexual) and grotesque people (a delinquent with a club foot, a hermaphrodite at a county fair, ugly old people).

Some critics attributed her bizarre characters to a Southern background; "The Misfit" who kills a whole family in the title story of *A Good Man Is Hard to Find* most assuredly was not the sort of protagonist expected from a Roman Catholic writer.

Flannery O'Connor was born and raised Catholic in the predominantly Protestant South. She came into the world in Savannah, Georgia, entered parochial school there, but around age twelve moved with her parents to Milledgeville, her mother's hometown, a small, typical town south of Atlanta that was the Georgia capital in Civil War days. She attended high school and college in public institutions in Milledgeville and, after receiving a bachelor's degree in social science, decided to become a writer. Mary Flannery dropped her first name when she enrolled in the famous Paul Engle's Writers' Workshop at the Univeristy of Iowa in 1945. A master of fine arts from Iowa, she spent a year in a writers' colony in New England, then two years in Connecticut as a boarder in the home of friends, fellow writers. Illness—the beginning of lupus, from which her father had died in 1941, took her home to Georgia, to her mother Regina. Mother and daughter moved out of a rambling home in Milledgeville to a more manageable house on the family farm, "Andalusia," outside town.

She was a Southerner and a Roman Catholic, but never a "Southern writer" or a "Catholic writer" as those terms are commonly used. A woman of gleeful humor, she told author Andrew Lytle, "the only thing that keeps me from being a regional writer is being a Catholic and the only thing that keeps me from being a Catholic writer (in the narrow sense) is being a Southerner."[14] Yet both her region and her religion exerted influence on her fiction and her presentation of Christianity.

O'Connor linked her recognition of the grotesque in life (and, she said, recognizing the grotesque means having some idea of what is not grotesque) to her perception that the South, in her day, had not come under the notorious notion of human perfectibility by human effort. The South, she said, "still believes that man has fallen and that he is only perfectible by God's grace." Her fiction takes sin *and* grace most seriously. The means of grace sometimes seems unusual—for the grandmother in the family killed by "The Misfit," it is recognition that the killer is one of her children—but redemption is never far off in an O'Connor story. The context of her work is not unclear. The collection *A Good Man Is Hard to Find* is prefaced by a quote from Cyril of Jerusalem: "The dragon is by the side of the road, watching those who pass. Beware lest he devour you. We go to the Father of souls, but it is necessary to pass by the dragon."

Her Catholicism gave Flannery O'Connor a sacramental view of life, of nature, and of persons. A Christian sacramentalist puts major theological emphasis on the Incarnation, the righteous God intentionally present in human frailty—really present. The Holy Eucharist (Holy Communion) was no mere symbol to O'Connor. Once at a dinner party, according to her letters, author Mary McCarthy said she had communed as a child but had come to think of the sacrament "as a symbol and implied that it was a pretty good one." O'Connor replied in a shaky voice, "Well, if it's just a symbol, to hell with it."[15]

In her sacramental view, imperfect nature and imperfect, ugly people are loved and can be made beautiful by God. "The trees were full of silver-white sunlight and the meanest of them sparkled," she wrote. And Christians, she believed, have a responsibility to the grotesque and ugly members of the human race. She liked to tell the story of Nathaniel Hawthorne, a "fastidious gentleman," fondling a scurvyed workhouse child who refused to be ignored. "I shall never have forgiven myself if I had repelled its advances," Hawthorne wrote in a notebook published after his death.

The truth of the Christian Gospel to O'Connor is protected by the church (the Catholic church in her mind, though she was a great admirer of several Protestant theologians, including Paul Tillich). With G. K. Chesterton she never thought Catholic dogma restricted her artistic creativity. "Dogma is the guardian of mystery," she said. She did not question the church's authority to define right doctrine; she maintained the right to criticize nondoctrinal Catholicism. O'Connor had less than complimentary opinions of Catholic education, and she could be biting in her criticism of fellow Catholics who expected the church to be institutionally perfect. "The Church," she quipped, "is founded on Peter who denied Christ three times and couldn't walk on water by himself." In another letter she wrote:

I think that the Church is the only thing that is going to make the terrible world we are coming to endurable; the only thing that makes the Church endurable is that it is somehow the body of Christ and that on this we are fed. It seems to be a fact that you have to suffer as much from the Church as for it but if you believe in the divinity of Christ, you endure it.[16]

Flannery O'Connor no doubt counted herself among those who as Christians know the importance of the imitation of Christ; she would have thought it uproariously funny to be included in the company of those whose lives suggest the First Beatitude, poverty of the spirit. "I do not lead a holy life," she wrote. "Not that I can claim any interesting or pleasurable sins (my sense of the devil is strong) but I know all about the garden variety, pride, gluttony, envy and sloth, and what is more to the point, my virtues are as timid as my vices."[17]

She does suggest a model of the poor in spirit in her awareness of sin and grace, her artistic appeal to morality, and her strong sense of truth. O'Connor grieved that "the moral sense has been bred out of certain sections of the population, like the wings have been bred out of certain chickens to produce more white meat on them. This is a generation of wingless chickens, which I suppose is what Nietzsche meant when he said God was dead."[18]

"My audience are the people who think God is dead," she wrote in 1955, before the now happily deceased "death of God" theology, and in that statement she limited herself too much. Her audience also includes people who are trying to rid themselves of the substitutes for faith.

CHAPTER II

Mourners, Not Moaners

"Holy are those who mourn . . ."

LESS THAN A DECADE AGO a Greek Orthodox church in Tarpon Springs, Florida, became an instant attraction when someone claimed to see tears on the face of a saint in one of its paintings. Irrational? Scientifically impossible? Of course. Every "reasonable" mind knows paintings cannot weep.

Reports of weeping likenesses of Jesus, Mary, or a saint are not nearly as common today as in times past. When they do occur they are dismissed as hysteria, superstition, or the condensation of moisture in unusual places. Defending the authenticity of weeping icons (religious pictures) or statues would be pointless, but the theological symbolism of tears on holy faces is right to a point. Weeping holy pictures are invariably interpreted by those who believe in them as signs of divine or saintly grief over the state of the world, and, while piety may be misplaced in the veneration of wet frescos, an awareness that Christianity is a religion of holy mourning, of passionate lamentation, is quite relevant.

The Second Beatitude is hardly a popular sermon text. It sounds morbid: "Holy are those who mourn . . ." Good for a funeral, but for what else? For a great deal more, when Christian grief—when God's grief—is understood. None of the Beatitudes can be fully interpreted apart from the life and ministry of Jesus, and his example makes sense of holy mourning.

Jesus, so Christians believe, was God incarnate (in the flesh) and also a real human being. He knew the joy of living. He had a sense of humor and enjoyed irony, although the Church has often tried to rob

50

him of his playfulness. The riddles he used in response to cagey questions from adversaries were in part jest. He liked a good party, the chatter of children, and fields of wild flowers. At the same time, Jesus had a keen sense of the dark, evil ways of humankind—both the malevolence twisting individuals, and that infecting, disrupting social organization. He wept over the city of Jerusalem, wishing it knew what made for peace, and his tears were human, and they were God's tears—a divine lament over the state of the world.

Jesus established mourning as a quality of Christian holiness, and the mourners blessed in the Second Beatitude are those whose grief is akin to that of Jesus. The Greek word for "mourn" in Matthew 5:4 is the strongest possible term for grief. It implies agony of heart expressed in a flood of tears, a bewailing of a state of affairs. Holy mourning is deep, deep caring about what God loves and cares for.

Christians who exemplify the Second Beatitude are great grievers —mourners, not moaners. Mourners are powerfully, righteously upset over the strength of sin and evil; moaners are complainers. The lips of moaners move while the souls of Christian mourners hurt. Frontier Christianity in the United States understood the sanctity of mourning, and provided a "mourners' bench" in its meeting houses. This special pew was not for members of bereaved families but for persons struggling with sin, usually their own.

Holy Christian mourning, however, is broader than personal grief over personal sin. It also covers those grief-stricken by the sin of others and by the ills of the world. Across the Christian centuries, such mourning has taken two primary forms. One expression is that of the penitents, men or women convinced that their religious calling is to share Christ's agony, his suffering brought on by evil's tirade against divine love. Professional penitents seek to identify with Jesus by helping to bear the sin of the world, and by bearing it, to reduce it; for example, Paul the Simple, a fourth-century Egyptian monk who broke into tears when he saw people languishing in immorality or spiritual despair; or Elizabeth Prentiss, a nineteenth-century American hymn writer and pastor's wife who could think of no greater joy than to spend her life "with those who mourn, to fly to them at once, and join them in their prayers and tears."

Another expression of holy mourning is more action-oriented: weep over the world but also strive to overcome evil and correct ills by social and political means. These are the mourners whose tears become hospitals, orphanages, rescue missions to the destitute, and schools; for example, William and Catherine Booth, who founded the Salvation Army in nineteenth-century England to save souls through the Gospel and to save bodies with food and other physical necessities; or Rose Hawthorne Lathrop, daughter of Nathaniel Hawthorne, whose tears became a ministry of love and care among cancer patients in early twentieth-century America.

No contradiction exists between these two expressions of Christian mourning. Both are motivated by a deep caring for what God cares about, and both share an awareness of the enormous power of evil. The holy task of defeating, at least beating back, the devil is a common theme in the lives of many great Christian mourners. Some of the saints, heroes, and heroines of the faith have even thought of themselves as decoys able to identify the devil and, therefore, have exposed themselves to unusual temptations in order to lure the tempter onto the holy ground that undoes evil. "Say the truth and shame the devil," said sixteenth-century Bishop Hugh Latimer. While it may seem pretentious to act as bait for the devil, it is nevertheless a strong reminder of a fundamental Christian belief: followers of Christ must oppose evil in every loving manner.

Great Christian grief at times appears antithetical to Christianity as a religion of love, joy, and spiritual bliss. The opposite is actually the case. Mourning is in order because evil and troubles keep love, joy, and bliss from being perfected. Christian mourners do not reconcile themselves to tribulation; they point beyond it, try to overcome it in ways spiritual and material. Mourning itself is a positive, forward-looking emotion.

Psychology in recent years has stressed an understanding of grief complementary to the Second Beatitude. That is, grief is a good and necessary process when a person or a people must cope with loss, such as the death of a loved one or some other "goodbye" (as in divorce, retirement, or leaving home). Mourning puts the situation in perspective: "John [or Alice] is gone. What do I do now? How shall I go on as a widow or widower? What is next?" Grief is the self's way of burying the dead, the past, so life can be resumed.

"Holy are those who mourn . . ."—who in William Barclay's word are "brokenhearted" over the way things are, who hurt for a sinful, troubled world, but who wait and work for the full flowering of the reign of God's love. Blessed are those who care enough to be holy mourners.

Mary Magdalene

Mary, the Mary called Magdalene, is an intriguing mourner because of her prominence among the followers of Jesus and because she is one of the most maligned women in Christian history.

This Mary was the woman most prominent in the traveling band Jesus gathered in Galilee. She is mentioned by name fourteen times in the four Gospels, more than any other woman and more than most of the men in Jesus' inner circle. Mary may have been a chief source of financial support for Jesus and his ministry. The Gospel of Luke says she and other women provided for Jesus and his twelve closest disciples.

Mary Magdalene went to Jerusalem for the religious festival (Passover) at which Jesus was arrested, tried, and executed. Unlike some of the male disciples, she and other Galilean women did not go into hiding when their leader was taken. Mary and her sisters watched the crucifixion, mourning for Jesus, mourning for themselves, and lamenting the travesty of justice they were seeing. The women stayed until the end, and they saw where the body of Jesus was laid—in a tomb offered by one Joseph, an Arimathean.

On the second morning after the crucifixion, as soon as they could be out and about without violating Sabbath laws, Mary and her friends went to the tomb to continue their mourning, to properly prepare the body for burial, using herbs and spices as was the custom.

The four Gospels do not tell exactly the same story about the sequence of events at the tomb. John's gospel says Mary first went alone, found the tomb empty, and rushed to tell Peter and the other male disciples, who came, were mystified, and left. Then, John says, Mary went again to the tomb where she encountered the risen Lord. The Gospels of Luke and Matthew have Jesus appearing to Mary and the other women when they first arrived, and the Gospel of Mark has two alternate accounts of Mary's visit to the tomb. One of Mark's endings says Mary's group met a young man in white who told them Jesus had risen and, being frightened, the women told no one. The other account is more like John's, with Mary going alone and becoming the first person to see the resurrected Christ.

Despite variations in the gospels' stories of the first Easter, Mary Magdalene was remembered in the early church as a preeminent mourner at Jesus' passion and as one of, or the very first, follower to know that the cause was not lost. That should have been enough to assure her an honored and honorable place in church history. As it happened, a scheme of misidentifications was to project her across the centuries as a reformed prostitute, at least in the Western branches of Christianity.

Pope Gregory the Great (sixth century A.D.) decided that Mary Magdalene was the same as Mary of Bethany, the sister of Martha and Lazarus, a family close to Jesus, and, what is more, that she was also the unnamed adulterous woman Jesus saved from death and forgave in Luke 7:36–50. Support for the Magdalene's harlotry was found in passages saying Jesus cast seven demons out of this Mary. Her recurring demon, it was decided in the sixth century, was sexual promiscuity.

Gregory's patchwork made a good yarn. Here was a fallen woman, a member of a good family, who reformed, was praised as Mary of Bethany for her attention to Jesus' words and for her anointing of his feet before the crucifixion; who watched the execution, and became the first witness to the resurrection. Good yarns are not always true. Gregory's went too far in merging too many biblical women. The tradition of Mary Magdalene as a harlot was never accepted in the Eastern Orthodox Church. Popular Roman Catholicism and Protestantism to this day consider Mary a prostitute, albeit a reformed one, and a "Magdalene" in English is a repentant whore.

None of the gospels says Mary Magdalene was ever a prostitute. True, none says she was not, but there is little reason to make that conjecture on the sketchy information provided. The "Magdalene" part of her name seems to come from a town north of Tiberius on the Sea of Galilee (far from Bethany, which is near Jerusalem). Tourist guides in modern Israel point to a few ruins in a field as Magdala. Magdala was most likely a Gentile city remembered in the early Middle Ages as a place of revelry, which may have encouraged Pope Gregory to think of Mary as a loose woman.

That Mary was a woman of means is suggested by Luke's statement that she helped support Jesus, and also by the inclusion in the list of her benefactors of one Joanna, the wife of a high official in King Herod's household. When or how Mary met Jesus is unknown. She may have sought him out because of his reputation as a healer; two Gospels, Luke and Mark, report that Mary was possessed of seven demons.

Belief in demon possession was common in the ancient world.

Anyone sick or sinful was thought to be controlled by evil spirits. Was Mary ill? Was she a habitual violater of religious law or moral precept? The New Testament does not say. "Seven demons" does indicate a serious predicament. The number seven represents great quantity or duration, as in the seven seas, meaning all the oceans of earth, or the seven-year itch, meaning a long-term skin problem.

Whatever her trouble, Mary was healed and restored by Jesus, and her gratitude was limitless. Jesus gave Mary a new start in life; she devoted her means, her time, and her tears to him.

Nothing is known of Mary Magdalene after the first Easter. One legend has her going with Mary, the mother of Jesus, to Ephesus (in what is now Turkey). Another has her becoming a missionary in France. She was probably part of the early Christian community in Jerusalem and, if she was still alive, may have fled eastward with Christians escaping the Roman army that destroyed Jerusalem in A.D. 70.

Within that holy company mourning for the sins and ills of the world, Mary Magdalene has a distinction. Her tears were dried, she was comforted, in her own lifetime. Mary's closing line in the Gospel of John is unmatched in all Christian literature: "I have seen the Lord!"

Anthony of Egypt (250–355)

By modern standards Anthony took an unusual way of showing his concern for the sin and trouble of the world. Instead of offering a course on ten easy steps to goodness, instead of organizing a movement to attack the root causes of hunger and injustice, Anthony withdrew to the solitude of the desert, there to spend most of eighty-five years in prayer and vigorous self-discipline.

Anthony of Egypt is the father of Christian *asceticism*, an expression of the Faith that started in the Middle East in the third century A.D. and later swept Europe as *monasticism*. *Ascetic* is a Greek word referring to the use of a particular set of rules and exercises to perfect a skill. Christian asceticism is physical self-denial and mental and emotional discipline for the sake of spiritual goals. It requires vows of poverty, obedience, and chastity.

As asceticism spread it developed several forms, including monastic orders with thousands of members living in established communities. In Anthony's day ascetics were usually singular monks living in caves in the desert, though the idea of communal asceticism arose in his lifetime, and he organized a group of hermits who wanted to imitate him. Anthony was probably not the first Christian to pursue an ascetic life in the Egyptian desert, but he was the first to become well known and to attract a following.

Born in 250 in Coma, an Egyptian village near the Red Sea, Anthony apparently inherited wealth and, as would happen to Francis of Assisi centuries later, he had trouble justifying his worldly fortune in the light of New Testament warnings against riches. Had Jesus not told a prosperous young man to sell his goods and give the proceeds to the poor (Luke 18:22)? And what about Jesus' advice that true disciples must deny themselves, even to the point of forsaking home and kin (Luke 9:23, 14:26)? Anthony interpreted these passages literally. At age twenty he gave away his inheritance to become a monk in the desert near Coma.

For fifteen years Anthony prayed, fasted, engaged in hard physical labor, and contended with the devil, who he believed visited him daily with temptations. Anthony and the other "desert fathers" lived as they did partly for their own souls' salvation. The greatest Christian work, said Anthony, is to always take blame before God for personal sin and "to expect temptation to the last breath." But asceticism is not spiritually self-centered. The monastic ideal from the start saw ascetics as doing service for the world, as individuals deeply troubled by sin and suffering, so troubled that they set out to do something most persons could not do. Anthony's prayer, worship, and physical hardship were undertaken for the whole church. So were his battles with the devil. "Our life and our death is with our neighbor," said the hermit.

Anthony was not pleased with his service to God and to the church during his first fifteen years as a monk. To find greater solitude, he retreated to a mountain called Pispir near the Nile, settling near an old fort. Legend has it that so holy was Anthony the snakes left the area when he arrived. He lived at Pispir for twenty years, rarely seeing anyone except a man who brought bread every six months.

Meanwhile, friends and admirers wanted Anthony to instruct them in the way of asceticism. Their demands became so intense that the recluse finally opened his door. About 305 he organized a set of rules and teachings for other ascetics, putting special emphasis on the monk's role in recognizing and defeating demons.

Twice Anthony left the desert for brief trips to Alexandria. The first came in 311 during the last of the Roman persecutions of Christians (see pages 225–230). Anthony and a band of monks from Pispir went to the city to volunteer for martyrdom. Finding no one interested in burning him at the stake or feeding him to lions, Anthony went home to the wilderness—though not for long—at Pispir, where a sizeable monastic community had gathered. A Daniel Boone of asceticism, Anthony struck out for the desert between the Nile and the Red Sea, finding himself another mountain, on which the monastery of Anthony still stands.

His final trip came in 339, a journey to Alexandria to preach against Arianism, a heresy that caused controversy in Christianity for decades. The Arians (named for a priest, Arius) taught that God the Father and God the Son are different, thereby denying the full unity of the Holy Trinity. Arianism was repudiated in the Nicene Creed (325 A.D.), especially in the part about Jesus Christ "being of one substance with the Father." In Alexandria Anthony had a chance to visit with Bishop Athanasius, the great foe of the Arians, who wrote a biography of the saintly monk.

Anthony was famous throughout the Christian church in his old age—so famous that the Emperor Constantine and his two sons wrote to him asking for his prayers. When his fellow monks were astounded that their leader should get a letter from the emperor, Anthony said, ". . . be astounded that God should have written to us, and that He has spoken to us by His son."

On his last mountain Anthony prayed, fasted, raised a garden, and received a few visitors. For himself he wanted only solitude and the challenge of hardship, but he also seemed to realize that the monastic ideal would move out of the desert into urban life. Christians in any setting, he said, must decide what kind of virtue they will reflect in their lives.

Bridget of Sweden (1303–1373)

Bridget (or Brigitta) had not one but a series of religious careers, most of them arising from happenstance (or providence) rather than deliberate planning, despite her reputation as a prophetess. This fourteenth-century daughter of Sweden possessed a remarkable ability to make the most of every opportunity and disappointment she encountered. Her central motivations were to foster acceptance of the love of Christ and to mend the ways of Christians whose infidelity

abused that love. She mourned and wept profusely over the world
and tried to set it on a holy course.

In her seventy-odd years she was a mother, a nun, an adviser to
the Swedish royal family, the founder of a religious order, a professional cajoler of popes, an organizer of charities, a pilgrim preacher,
and a visionary. Bridget was raised to be a feudal lady, and she was
that too.

The daughter of the governor of the Swedish province of Uppland,
she was married in 1316, when she was thirteen years old, to Ulf
Gudmarsson, five years her senior, the son of another landed family
and later a provincial governor. The couple lived happily together for
twenty-eight years and had eight children.

In keeping with the practice of the day for noble women to serve as
ladies-in-waiting to the Queen of Sweden, Bridget was called to the
royal court in 1335. She was ill at ease as a glorified maid to Queen
Blanche. She soon saw that the new king, Manus II, and his bride
needed guidance, so she proceeded to offer it. Her visions, earlier
concerned with spiritual matters, turned to politics. Stated as messages from God, Bridget instructed the young rulers on how to
conduct affairs of state and to purify their faith in Christ. She
dreamed of model peace plans for the warring armies of England and
France. When her visions became more of a standing joke than a
contribution to policy making, she quit the royal court and went on a
pilgrimage to Spain with her husband. On the way back home, Ulf
became sick. Husband and wife pledged to God that if he should
recover they would retire to the religious life and, indeed, they
returned not to their feudal castle but to a monastery at Alvastra on
Lake Vetter. There Ulf died in 1344, and Bridget stayed for four
years as a penitent. She told frequent visions to a prior, who recorded
and translated them into Latin.

Bridget then decided to found a religious community at Vadstena.
Her Order of the Most Holy Saviour (Brigittines) included women
and men, living in separate enclosures, with the men subject to the
mother superior in temporal affairs and the women subject to the
abbot in spiritual matters. Men and women at Vadstena shared the
same church, and could read books. The Brigittine mother house
became Sweden's literary center in the fifteenth century.

A papal charter was needed for the new order. Bridget set out to
get one, but getting anything from the pope was unduly complex in

the fourteenth century. The succession of pontiffs was headquartered not in Rome but temporarily in Avignon, a city in modern France that belonged then to the kingdom of Naples. Bridget wanted the pope, then Clement VI, to return to Rome, and in the holy year of 1350 she set off for Italy with a double purpose: to get a charter for her order and to entice the papacy home.

Bridget never again returned to Sweden in life. With Rome as her base, she devoted her last twenty years to her twofold mission, and to several new ones. In 1370 the Brigittines finally got a papal charter, but the popes did not abandon Avignon until four years after her death. Meanwhile, she kept busy organizing charities for the poor and trying to strengthen the entire monastic movement. Bridget thought nothing of presenting herself to an abbot in Farfa or Bologna with a plan to reform his house. Bishops, aristocrats, and common folks who seemed to her to abuse Christ were unsparingly denounced. She called one erring pope "a murderer of souls, more unjust than Pilate and more cruel than Judas."

Her life in Rome, where she was attended by her daughter Catherine (also a Catholic saint), was filled with hardship and heartaches. She was often reduced to begging for food. Furthermore, her favorite son, Karl (or Charles), turned out to be an enormous moral disappointment to her. Bridget decided in 1371 to undertake a pilgrimage to Palestine. Her children Catherine, Karl, and Birger were to accompany her. While waiting in Naples for transit, Karl pleased the eye of the notorious Queen Joanna, who after assuring herself of his manhood, decided he would do nicely as her next husband. Despite a wife in Sweden, Karl was more than willing to cooperate; his mother was distraught. Her prayers for divine deliverance of her son were answered after a fashion. Karl died of a fever.

Catherine and her mother continued on the pilgrimage. Their stay in the Holy Land was apparently uneventful, except for a shipwreck near Jaffa. On the return trip, Bridget stopped to mourn over and preach against the wickedness of the Christians on Cyprus and in Naples. She was not well received. While Bridget was later described by a biographer as kind, meek, and smiling, she was seen by some contemporaries as self-righteous and sour in her old age. Given her disappointments, she probably had to be a saint to maintain any compassion.

Bridget died in Rome in 1373. Her body was taken in triumphal procession across Europe for burial at Vadstena. She was canonized less than twenty years later by the Roman Catholic Church and named the patron saint of Sweden.

Lydwina of Schiedam (1380–1433)

Her story as it has come down is hard to take as truth today and, if true, is even harder to accept. Lydwina of Schiedam believed it her part in life to endure constant, agonizing physical pain as a penance for sin—not necessarily her sin, but that of others.

Legend, surely a medieval legend, highly suspect in modern times, when pain is considered a great evil to be exorcised by aspirin, tranquilizer, or a shot of gin. The accounts of Lydwina, who lived in Schiedam, Holland, from 1380 to 1433, no doubt have been embellished, yet she lived, she suffered, and she believed it had spiritual meaning.

Christianity stops short of saying pain is automatically holy. It does support the idea that physical and emotional suffering can be holy when endured for a holy cause. Lydwina's vocation was total identification with the passion of Christ and, through this particular form of the "imitation of Christ," she was a penitent paying the penalty for the world's sin. Her interpretation of almost forty years of pain was based on a doctrine of the Atonement out of vogue today—the belief that God is owed a debt for the dishonor done to divine holiness by sinful people. But that doctrine is one of the classical understandings of the Passion.

Lydwina's vocation is shared by numerous saints, often though not always women, of Roman Catholicism and Eastern Orthodoxy. Some forms of Protestantism, notably those teaching predestination, include the possibility of holy suffering as expiation (paying the debt) for sin. The wife of American Puritan divine Jonathan Edwards (see page 30) is supposed to have been willing to be damned to hell for the glory of God, but very few Protestants today take predestination seriously, and are more apt to interpret suffering as either the result of sin—someone else's—or as an accident of nature.

Professional penitents of Lydwina's sort occur most frequently in contemplative or mystical Christianity, often as nuns taking self-discipline to the point of pain, as was the case with Mary Bartholomea of Florence in the late sixteenth century, Mary Magdalen Dei Pazzi in the seventeenth, and, to a much lesser degree, Thérese of Lisieux in the nineteenth. (Thérese came to distrust blood/pain penitence.)

Lydwina of Schiedam, however, was not a nun, and she did not inflict pain on herself. She was a laywoman, a girl really, who had an accident that left her an invalid racked with pain. She tried to find meaning in her situation—a mark of creativity and human sanctity —and decided she could hurt for others. In this, Lydwina is similar to a more recent Catholic saint, Gemma Galgani, an Italian girl who died in 1903 after a short life of congenital illness. Gemma Galgani is said to have experienced the stigmata—bleeding nail prints in her hands.

The daughter of a Dutch laborer, and the only girl in a family of nine children, Lydwina was apparently a typical teenager before the accident. According to her biographers, who included Thomas à Kempis, at age fifteen she broke a rib in a fall while ice skating. Complications set in, an infection, and perhaps, internal injuries undetected by doctors in that day. Maybe the fracture healed wrong. At any rate, Lydwina was an invalid for the rest of her life—an invalid and worse. She hurt. To get her mind off the pain she began to meditate on the Passion of Christ, and found her vocation. She later added to her discomfort by lying on planks and wearing a horsehair belt.

Grotesque, disfigured, and blind in one eye, Lydwina became the center of a cultus and a matter of controversy. One priest of her parish considered her a nuisance—which she probably was to him —and refused for a time to take Holy Communion to her bedside. For the most part, she was endorsed as a holy woman by local and Dutch church authorities, and according to one unlikely report received no nourishment except the Eucharist for the last nineteen years of her life.

She developed visionary and healing powers. She claimed mystical transportations to holy places, and was reckoned a local saint long before her death. Veneration of Lydwina became widespread in Europe, but she has never been formally canonized by the Roman Catholic Church. Her cultus was recognized by the Vatican only in 1890, though she is regarded as the patron of those who suffer for the sins of others.

The significance of individuals such as Lydwina of Schiedam in the Holy Company is based not so much on what she did as what she was—a woman in an extreme situation who found a reason to be and tried to be something worthwhile. She did suffer, she could suffer, so she did it for selfless reasons.

Camillus of Lellis (1550–1613)

Camillus (or Camillo), the son of an impoverished Italian nobleman, was also a sufferer, though not a perpetual invalid, and his agony over the ills of the world took the form of service to the sick.

The founder of a religious order called the Ministers of the Sick (Camillians) was a pioneer on the frontier of nursing. His era, the late sixteenth and early seventeenth centuries, saw the beginnings of modern medicine in Europe. Seven years before Camillus was born, Andreas Vesalius, a professor at the University of Padua, Italy, scientifically described the human anatomy, preparing the way for modern surgery. The bacterial causes of various infectious diseases were being discovered, and chemical drugs were appearing. Before Camillus' death in 1613, the Englishman William Harvey was nearing his conclusions on the circulation of the blood. The idea that life's quality and length could be positively affected by medicine, sanitation, and trained nurses was taking hold among farsighted individuals, including Camillus of Lellis. But Camillus' pilgrimage to a ministry of healing followed a winding path, and in his early years he seemed an unlikely candidate for either nursing or a religious vocation.

He was a huge man—reportedly six feet, six inches tall—and roguish, a soldier-of-fortune in his youth, and a compulsive gambler tempted all his days by prohibited games of chance. Camillus considered himself a mighty sinner.

Born in Bocchianico, Italy, in 1550, he went with his father at age seventeen to fight with the Venetians against the Turks, who had conquered the last remnant of the old Christian (Byzantine) Empire in the East. On the campaign he contracted a leg infection that troubled him the rest of his life. He also suffered from a rupture. About 1571 Camillus entered Saint James (Giacomo) Hospital for the incurably ill in Rome. He was both a patient and a servant, it being common for hospital nurses and orderlies to have no medical training. Surprisingly, his health improved, but his rough, quarrelsome ways bothered people, so he was dismissed to return to the war.

Camillus succeeded in gambling away even the shirt off his back, and in 1575 was destitute in Naples. He took a job as a day laborer on a new building for a Capuchin community, and contact with the monks reminded him of a vow he had once made to become a Franciscan. Under the guidance of Capuchin friars, the soldier-of-fortune with an aching leg was reintroduced to Christianity. Prevented from entering a religious order because of his disease (orders required a certificate of sound health), he returned to Rome and to Saint James Hospital to work again as a servant. His compassion and assistance were so unusual that he came to the attention of hospital and church officials. Distressed by the slipshod practices and uncaring attitudes of many hospital attendants, Camillus and a small group of other serious-minded servants banded together to improve the service. Believing he would be even more effective if he were a priest, he was ordained in 1584.

An annuity set up by a benefactor at his ordination freed Camillus from financial strain. He and two companions left Saint James with the intention of establishing their own hospital. This plan was opposed by Camillus' spiritual adviser, Philip Neri (canonized in 1622). The three friends set themselves up as a mini–religious community, and for a time did volunteer work in Rome's Holy Ghost Hospital. The community grew, developing as a kind of traveling medical corps pledged to care for sick prisoners, victims of plague, and any other ill people.

In 1591 Pope Gregory XIV recognized Camillus and his group as the Ministers of the Sick. As the badge of the order, the founder chose a large red cross. During the last decade of the sixteenth century, Camillians formed the first field ambulance corps by rescuing the wounded from battlefields in Hungary and Croatia.

Meanwhile, Camillus founded a second house in Naples, where the ministry included care for sailors with plague. Two Camillians died in that labor, becoming the first recorded martyrs to church-related public health service.

Camillus founded fifteen houses of his order and eight hospitals. He labored hard to improve hospital and general medical practices. He particularly opposed the practices of dismissing patients before they were well, and of dispatching bodies for burial before death was certain.

Tired and barely able to walk, the Camillian superior relinquished his leadership in 1607, but until his death six years later assisted at the mother house in Rome. He died shortly after completing a visitation to all of the order's hospitals.

A Father Cicatelli, a companion of Camillus for twenty-five years, wrote a biography of this great Christian in 1625. Cicatelli said:

In the sick Camillus saw the person of Christ. His reverence in their presence was as great as if he were truly in the presence of the Lord. . . . Great and inclusive was his charity. Not alone the sick and dying, but also every other needy or suffering person found a place in his deep, kind concern.

John Vianney (1786–1859)

George Sand and Victor Hugo were his contemporaries, but John Vianney, priest in a small, isolated French village, was more famous than either of them in the 1850s. People by the thousands went to the Curé D'Ars from 1827 until his death in 1859. As many as twenty thousand pilgrims a year made him their confessor. Why?

Born a peasant, Vianney had no physical appeal or power as an orator. The sermons he left neither sparkle with wit nor impress with their style. His knowledge of the world and of theology was slight. He kept mostly to the village of Ars, tending his flock, welcoming pilgrims, and promoting the cult of Saint Philomena, the Roman Catholic saint of doubtful existence to whom healing powers were attributed until recently.

Vianney seems an enigma, almost medieval, in the mid-nineteenth century. Revolution and the Napoleonic episode had loosened the grip of the church on French life and politics; modernity was in flower, the human mind "enlightened," and society increasingly secular. Still, the pilgrims went to the Curé D'Ars.

While he lacked book knowledge and wide experience in the world, John Vianney had a timeless sense of psychology. He had, to quote Clare Boothe Luce, an "exquisite sense of sin. His great apostolic mission was to mitigate the ravages of sin, by making people see sin for what it is—opposition to God, and self-destruction."[1] The pilgrims went to the Curé D'Ars for personal assistance with their lusts, guilts, and ignorances of themselves. "The little curé did not scold or scorn the sinners who came to him. He showed them, in Christlike charity, where they were against God—in short, in what respect they were being their own worst enemies."[2]

Vianney knew things more important than Latin or the latest trend in Paris. He knew Christ; he knew people, but few people who knew him in his youth would have guessed he possessed unusual talents. He almost did not become a priest, because the French Revolution and family duties delayed his schooling, because he deserted Napoleon's army, and because he was such a poor student once he got to seminary.

His family lived at Dardilly, near Lyons, where he was born in 1786, his childhood corresponding to the years of the revolution. A call to the priesthood at age eighteen could not be answered; his large farm family needed his labor. Two years later he was able to begin studies in a small seminary in the nearby village of Ecully. Vianney was a wretched student. Latin, a requirement for the priestly vocation, evaded him.

To complicate his situation, the academically slow youth was drafted into the army, his name being absent from the list of exempt seminarians. He reported to an induction center in Lyons in October, 1809, expecting to go with the Napoleonic forces to Spain. But he became ill and his unit departed without him. Three months later he was ordered to Roanne where another company was being formed. The spiritual Vianney paused in a church to pray, and prayed too long (or just long enough). He missed the convoy. Catch up on foot, he was told.

Vianney walked as slowly as he learned Latin. Along the way he met a stranger who convinced him that since he was technically AWOL he might as well make a fact of it. He lived for more than a year with a farm family, hiding when necessary in a hayloft. Had Napoleon not declared a general amnesty to deserters when he married Marie-Louise of Austria, Vianney might have been forced to live incognito until Waterloo.

He went home, received his tonsure (hair cut), and resumed his studies, first in Verrieres, then in Lyons. Again, he did poorly, although some of his instructors recognized in him the beginning of pastoral gifts. Allowances were made for his paucity of academic skills, but Vianney still failed his first examination for priestly orders. "The most unlearned but the most devout seminarian in Lyons," said church officials.

Finally, because of his devotion, and on the insistence of Abbé Balley, his mentor from Ecully, he was given minor orders. In 1815, after becoming a deacon, he was named curate (assistant) to Abbé Balley, and was ordained priest later that year. His common sense was evident as soon as he sat down behind the confessional screen. Vianney had a talent for getting to the heart of what was bothering people.

While he predated psychiatry, Vianney knew the value of talk therapy. The Christian church at its pastoral best has always used basic psychological truths, which in essence are spiritual truths; the shame of the Church is that it has often not trained its pastors to use what it knows. Vianney had the gift of listening, but that was not all. He also had a visionary's intuition about people, and he loved them.

Ordained he was, but Vianney would find no cathedrals in his future. After three years in Ecully he was dispatched to Ars-en-Dombes, a small village of some two hundred religiously neglected people. Church attendance and the observation of other Catholic practices were spotty. Vianney set about to revitalize Ars spiritually, although meeting with no immediate positive response. He decided that if the people would not pray and fast for themselves he would pray and fast for them.[3]

He also visited every home, introduced religious classes for children, preached plain sermons, attacked moral vice, and to show the virtue of Christian service, opened a shelter for orphans in 1824. Ars became a model parish. For his work, Vianney won respect and, as his fame spread, he naturally provoked jealousy among fellow priests in the area. When one critic called him "mad," the bishop of Balley said, "I wish all my clergy had a small grain of the same madness."

John Vianney demonstrated a quality common among Christian saints, heroes, and heroines who agonize over the sin and trouble of the world. He had a personal, running battle with the devil. To mortify the flesh—one way to overcome temptation and thereby undo the devil—he ate simply and slept on straw, a fact to remember in assessing reports that the devil repeatedly set fire to his bed.

Once pilgrims started to arrive in large numbers around 1837, the curé (actually a priest but always called the Curé D'Ars) spent ten to twelve hours a day in winter and up to sixteen hours in summer in the confessional. From the early 1840s until his death he gave a daily talk to the visiting penitents. These homilies were simple, short, and spontaneous.

Along with his talent for listening, Vianney also knew how to encourage people to bring a sense of devotion into their daily lives. He advised frequent private prayer. "Private prayer," he said, "is like straw scattered here and there: if you set it on fire it makes a lot of little flames. But gather these straws into a bundle and light them, and you get a mighty fire."

The priest was knighted by the emperor of France in the early

1850s. Looking at the imperial cross, which he refused to wear, Vianney said, "I can't think why the emperor has sent it to me, unless it is because I was once a deserter." He disliked and discouraged the veneration heaped upon him by pilgrims. "What misguided devotion," he said.

Vianney declined larger, wealthier parishes, but the years and the pace took their toll, and late in life he admitted he would have preferred the monastic vocation. Three times he quit Ars, returning each time with renewed dedication to his task as pastor to souls in a sinful world. When the curé was canonized in 1925, he was made patron saint of Roman Catholic parochial clergy.

The Curé D'Ars died quietly on August 4, 1859. Earlier, a village schoolmaster had applied to Vianney a comment first made about Bernard of Clairvaux: "The most difficult, extraordinary and amazing work he did was his own life."

Sarah Grimké (1792–1873)
Angelina Grimké Weld (1805–1879)

They first scandalized South Carolina's Episcopalians by joining the Society of Friends (Quakers); then, without chaperone, they traveled in the North; and finally, they committed the worst sin of all: the Grimké sisters from Charleston became abolitionists. And they stirred rancor among Philadelphia's Quakers and Boston's Congregationalists by taking the public platform to do penance as former slaveholders and, with no ecclesiastical sanction, to condemn slavery as a sin against God.

Sarah and Angelina Grimké were the most notorious sisters in the United States in the 1830s. Abolition had not become a popular movement anywhere in the country. "Proper" young women did not lecture or write pamphlets urging wives and mothers to demand their rights at the polls and, lacking political power, to use their natural gifts in persuading their men to free the slaves.

The Grimkés were considered so dangerous in New England that with them in mind the Massachusetts General Association of Congregational Ministers issued a pastoral letter denouncing all women lecturers. Such women, said the letter, "threaten the female character with widespread and permanent injury"; women who assume the role and tone of men as public reformers become "unnatural." The two renegade "southern belles" thought themselves the most natural of Christians, announcing the truth and mourning for the unrepentant who heaped indignity on the backs and souls of God's black children.

Sarah, the eldest by thirteen years, was less aggressive than Angelina, but it was she who first spurned the comfortable, aristocratic life to which the sisters were born. Their father, Judge John Faucheraud Grimké, owned a large plantation and many slaves. One brother was a justice of the Ohio Supreme Court; another was a Philadelphia lawyer. Mrs. Grimké was from a fine Charleston family. The Grimkés grew up in the laps of luxury and slave women.

Their pilgrimage to the abolitionist cause apparently began when Sarah was a teenager and Angelina a mere child; just how is unclear. Sarah recalled waiting until night to defy the state law against teaching slaves to read. She and her maid, her pupil, would lie before the fire "with the spelling book under our eyes." The sisters' reading of the Bible may have influenced them to respect human equality, although the Bible was also a mainstay of the proslavery forces. Both Grimkés were conscientious with Scripture as adults, and worked with Theodore Weld, the prominent abolitionist, in setting forth biblical arguments against slavery. Another likely influence was their brother, Thomas, the lawyer in Philadelphia, who was active in the American Peace Society, an organization with abolitionist roots in David Low Dodge's (see page 208) New York Peace Society.

Sarah moved to Philadelphia in the 1820s and there joined the Quakers. The home folks, Episcopalian by class, were horror-struck, except for Angelina, who proceeded to affiliate with the small Quaker meeting in Charleston. By 1829 Angelina was also in Philadelphia, and she took the lead as the abolitionist in the family. Angelina was impatient with the lack of Quaker activism in support of the movement represented by William Lloyd Garrison. Philadelphia Quakers opposed slavery and helped on the underground railroad, but were not given to political crusading. Risking expulsion from the Friends, Angelina joined the local Female Anti-Slavery Society in 1835.

The younger of the Grimké sisters was a smart tactician. She calculated that she could get public attention as a white Southern woman against slavery. She calculated right and, after much prayer, wrote to Garrison saying, "the ground upon which you stand is holy ground." Her letter appeared promptly in *The Liberator*, the major newspaper of the abolitionist movement. Charleston gasped, and Angelina had only begun. She followed with a tract, *Appeal to the*

Christian Women of the Southern States, urging women to pressure their husbands and sons to work for emancipation of the slaves. The postmaster in Charleston publicly burned the pamphlet, and the sheriff let it be known where Angelina Grimké would sleep and eat if she set foot in the city again.

Meanwhile, Sarah, to catch up with her sister, wrote *An Epistle to the Clergy of the Southern States*—a second explosion followed among the Southern gentry and Northern proslavery advocates. To back up their appeals, the women persuaded their mother (Judge Grimké was dead) to free the family slaves.

Abolitionists seized upon the publicity value of two charming southern women with a religious grievance against slavery. Managed by Theodore Weld, the sisters became a feature on the abolitionist lecture circuit. Angelina, the more forceful speaker of the two, sometimes identified herself as a "repentant slaveholder" with a debt of freedom to pay to "the suffering slave and to the deluded master."

The Grimkés drew larger and larger audiences in the Northeast, to the distress of the clergy, a bastion of the status quo in early nineteenth century America, especially when it came to the role of women in public affairs. Abolitionists themselves were divided on the morality of the sisters' lecturing in public.

Sarah and Angelina quickly made a connection between the forced servitude of blacks in the South and the forced silence of women throughout the nation. Sarah wrote a series of articles on "The Province of Women" for the *New England Spectator*. Later collected in a booklet called *The Equality of the Sexes and the Condition of Women*, the articles cogently argued against a literal interpretation of biblical passages making women inferior to men, and, the author said, if women were allowed to study Greek and Hebrew the translations themselves would be different. The male, wrote Sarah Grimké, will always use the woman as a means to his own welfare "without regard to her own happiness, and the glory of God, as the end of her creation." Her feminist message had a modern ring:

I ask no favors for my sex. I surrender not our claim to equality. All I ask of our brethren is that they take their feet off our necks, and permit us to stand upright on the ground which God has designed us to occupy.

As the Grimkés increasingly identified with the women's suffrage movement, some abolitionists feared they were doing more harm than good to the antislavery cause; women, after all, could not vote for lawmakers. Weld shared that fear to a degree. He encouraged the sisters to give primary focus to abolition, and he had a chance to manage affairs quite closely after he married Angelina in May, 1838. The wedding party was interracial and, to show his goodwill on women's rights, the groom attacked the "unrighteous power vested in husbands over their wives."

Angelina returned to the lecture platform only briefly after her marriage. She collapsed in Boston, and was unable to speak coherently for several years. The sisters retired from public crusading. Sarah made her home with the Welds, first in the New York area, and for many years in Hyde Park, Massachusetts. Celebrities for a relatively short time, the Grimké sisters collaborated in the 1850s with Weld on articles favorable to both the emancipation of slaves and women's rights. One of their favorite passages of Scripture is the motto of all who mourn over inequality in the life of the church:

There is neither Jew nor Greek, there is neither bond nor free, there is neither male nor female; for all are one in Christ Jesus (Galatians 3:28).

Simone Weil (1909–1943)

When she died in England on August 24, 1943, local newspapers in Kent reported Simone Weil a suicide by starvation. They also quoted the attending physician as saying she "had a curious religious outlook, and would say that she had no religion at all." That the young Frenchwoman deliberately starved herself to death is debatable; that she had a "curious religious outlook" judged by common standards is not.

Simone Weil, writer, social philosopher, and mystic, was one of the great Christian penitents of the twentieth century. Her personal identification with human suffering, with ills caused by the sins of greed and power, is almost beyond the comprehension of modern minds. In solidarity with the inmates of Hitler's concentration camps, she did limit her intake of food, thereby contributing to her death from tuberculosis.

She may well have told her physician in her final days that she had no religion, because in a formal sense—in terms of membership in an organization—that was true. But religion is more than membership, and however curious it may have seemed, Simone Weil was possessed of a religious outlook as intense as her ability to suffer with the suffering. Of Jewish ancestry, she was strongly drawn to Catholic mysticism but, like Anglican mystic Evelyn Underhill (see page 192), was put off by the rigidity of Roman Catholic church administration, especially the papacy. At some point she ceased thinking of herself as Jewish. She considered Christian baptism but was reluctant to seek formal entry into the church, partly because she appreciated other religions and felt that institutional Christianity was narrow-minded in its claims to an exclusive corner on truth.

Simone Weil certainly thought of herself as a Christian, as a Catholic outside the church. She told an acquaintance in 1942: "I adhere totally to the mysteries of the Christian faith, with the only kind of adherence that seems to me appropriate for mysteries. This adherence is love, not affirmation. Certainly I belong to Christ—or so I hope and believe. But I am kept outside the Church by philosophical difficulties that I fear are irreducible. They do not concern the mysteries themselves but the accretions of definitions with which the Church has seen fit to clothe them in the course of centuries."[4] She was bothered, for example, by the Roman Church's claim to know precisely what is and is not acceptable Christian teaching.

Her decision not to seek baptism was in part a protest against theological legalism. In this her attitude was similar to that of the nineteenth-century Danish theologian Søren Kierkegaard (see page 34), a Lutheran critic of rigid Protestant doctrine. Like Paul Tillich, the twentieth-century German-American theologian influenced by Kierkegaard, Weil was concerned with the God above, beyond, and beneath the God of organized Christianity.

Simone Weil was born in Paris in early 1909. She and her older brother André were precocious children in a family of intellectuals and scientists. Their father was a physician. Both children were well educated, introduced at an early age to the best literature and art. Simone was as frail as she was bright in childhood, and she was pampered.

Stories about her childhood intellectual accomplishments and her humanitarian instincts sound like legend. At the age of three, she is supposed to have rejected the gift of a ring by declaring, "I do not like luxury"; at age five she is said to have refused sugar because the French soldiers fighting in World War I had none. Such stories may be true, but literal or embellished, they give her the aura of a medieval saint.

She was a good, though not the best, student in her class at the Ecole Normale, where she devoured philosophy, the natural and social sciences, and classical languages. Her intention was to teach. From 1931 through 1938 Weil taught philosophy in no less than five different schools, usually spending no more than a year at each. She was often unhappy with the situations, and school boards were unhappy with her because of her support of the French labor movement and other causes considered radical. She took a year off from teaching in 1934–35 to work in a factory in order to learn about the conditions of industrial laborers. This experience deflated a romantic idea of the noble worker and depressed her hopes for social revolution as a welling-up from the masses, among whom she found little commitment to fraternity and few shared social goals. Also, the year in the factory almost literally killed her. On one assembly line she constantly burned her hands; she suffered anemia and caught an ear infection. Of factory work, she said, "It's inhuman."

Another year, 1936–37, she devoted to the Spanish civil war. Like many other idealistic young people, Simone Weil was drawn to the anti-Franco cause in Spain. She went officially as a journalist, but was soon caught up in a workers' movement involved in military operations. Although a pacifist by nature, she insisted on going on a field campaign. Assigned to help the cook, the near-sighted young woman stepped in a pan of scalding oil, badly burning her leg. Shortly after, her parents came to Spain looking for her and finally persuaded Simone to return to France with them.

The Weil family, including Simone, moved from Paris to Marseilles when the Nazi-inspired Vichy government came to power in 1940. She worked on a farm, studied Sanskrit, worked for the French resistance, and continued to write. She had earlier started to write—journals, essays, and poems dealing with politics, philosophy, religion, and social theory and in Marseilles began a series of works that would later establish her reputation as a great writer. Simone Weil during her life was not a widely or well-known author. None of her works appeared in English translation until 1945.

Although she said she was not Jewish, Simone Weil could not stay in France if she wanted to live, as the Nazis strengthened their hold on the country. She accompanied her parents to New York in 1942 but decided she was too far away from her work in the resistance movement. "I cannot stand this life," she said of exile in America. In England she found work with the French Resistance and was crestfallen when her colleagues refused her request to be parachuted behind the lines in France. Along with her duties with the movement

—mostly analysis of routine reports—she found time to write a great deal in her last months. Her topics were political and religious, and to friends she confided agony of the spirit. When she surveyed the suffering and injustice in the world, she felt herself to be a coward in combatting it. Perhaps, she thought at times, God should make her a slave, and she had periods of self-hatred.

Simone Weil collapsed in mid-April, 1943. The diagnosis was tuberculosis of a type the doctors thought would respond to treatment. Confined to a London hospital, she never really cooperated with the recovery program. She ate too little, wrote too much, and tortured herself with remorse for having left France. On August 17 she was transferred to a sanitarium in Ashford where she died a week later. Burial was in the section reserved for Catholics in an Ashford cemetery. Some sources say she was informally baptized in the London hospital; others say she was not.

Of her books published after her death, the best known and perhaps most important is *Gravity and Grace*, (in English), a personal testimony to the lordship of Christ. The theme is simple: everything in life is brought down just as gravity pulls objects to the ground; everything in life is lifted only by the grace of God.

She considered herself a heretic, wanted to be nothing more than a slave, and none wept more Christlike tears over the suffering world. She looked for children of God willing to bear the suffering with people and with Christ, and, finding few, she bore what she could: "The world needs saints who have genius, just as a plague-stricken town needs doctors. Where there is a need, there is also an obligation."[5]

CHAPTER III

Beware: Tamed Christians

"Holy are the gentle . . ."

Antoine de Saint Exupéry in his fable *The Little Prince* tells about taming. A fox asks the little prince to tame him. The child agrees but does not know how, so the fox explains the process of boy and animal getting acquainted, steadily moving closer until they can relax as companions. Taming, says the fox, means making ties, and something more: one is forever responsible for what one tames.[1]

In his poetic way, Saint-Exupéry deals with a basic Christian theme. The faithful believe God has made ties with humanity in Jesus Christ, ties intended to bestow beauty and to tame the wild lusts, vicious pride, and terrible cruelty of men and women. Furthermore, God never abandons those tamed in Christ's love. To accept the ties God offers, to realize God's presence as an indestructible reality, is rarely easy for anyone. To be tamed in love changes the way one thinks and acts; it brings responsibilities, fidelity to the tamer, and a concern for the untamed. At the same time, lives tamed by, tied to, God are amazingly free, delivered from fear and liberated from the clutter of daily uncertainty.

Tamed Christians are free to be gentle and taming. This makes them dangerous to any who think human freedom equals self-indulgence, personal power, or wealth. To persons who worship the world's idols, gentle, God-controlled Christians are revolutionaries.

The Third Beatitude points to the holiness of the gentle revolutionaries of love, mighty as the tamed of God. That, however, is not the way the verse, Matthew 5:5, is usually translated. "Blessed are the meek" is the more familiar reading, and this is both pyschologically

74

and linguistically unfortunate. Making a model of the meek gives the impression of the Christian life as a plate of squishy humble pie. Meekness is hardly an attractive quality in its contemporary meanings: mild, spineless, spiritless, excessively submissive. Humility, as in the First Beatitude, is a virtue—but spinelessness?

"Meek" is a questionable translation of the Greek noun in Matthew 5:5. Though the word was stronger, more positive in the seventeenth century, when the standard English versions of Scripture were made, some scholars say it never should have been used in the Third Beatitude. "Gentle" is a better literal reading, but even that does not capture the full range of the quality of life being highlighted. *Praus*, the term in question, had a variety of meanings in first-century Greek, and the Third Beatitude makes direct reference to Psalm 37:11. The verse in Matthew is not at all simple.

Psalm 37:11, from which the Third Beatitude is drawn, assures the poor and oppressed that they shall possess the land and know prosperity. The obvious connection between the Psalm and Matthew 5:5 leads some biblical scholars to conclude that the Third Beatitude should appear as verse 4, as it does in a few ancient manuscripts, where it would be a poetic parallel to the first, "holy are the poor in spirit," instead of a separate blessing. This argument has merit, and was accepted by the translators of *The Jerusalem Bible*, the very fine version published in English in 1966.

Other scholars and committees of translators prefer the more familiar order of the Beatitudes, partly because *praus* has meanings not influenced by Psalm 37:11. For example, the ancient Greek philosopher Aristotle used a form of the word to mean the median between too much and too little anger. It could also mean humility as a quality of mind among persons aware of their need to learn, and it could refer to tamed animals.

The late William Barclay insisted that the Third Beatitude would need a lengthy translation to be fully explained. He said it recognizes the bliss of one "who is always angry at the right time and never angry at the wrong time, who has every instinct, and impulse, and passion under control because he himself is God-controlled, who has the humility to realise his own ignorance and his own weakness."[2]

Matthew 5:5, the Third Beatitude, in this chapter on the Holy Company is understood in Barclay's broad interpretation. Saints, heroes, and heroines of holy gentleness are never spineless or spiritless. They are willingly tamed in the love of Christ. Their passions are holy passions controlled by God's passionate wooing of wild souls; their indignation is Christ's anger, their impulses Christ's will, and their ignorance and weakness are offered to God for transformation into wisdom and strength.

Tamed, gentle Christians are remarkably free and spirited as they live in the presence of God. Their greatness is in what Brother Lawrence called the "practice of the presence of God," but they can also move the world with deeds. They can take to heart the dictum, "Love God and do what you please," since they are pleased to please God, and in their pleasure accomplish mighty acts confounding, threatening common human habit.

Ahead are tamed Christians. Beware: they come armed with the Gospel.

Mary and Joseph

Mary, the mother of Jesus, and Joseph, her husband, are without doubt the most famous couple in all of history, equaled, perhaps, only by Adam and Eve. Their unique places in the Holy Company are not threatened in the least by the shortage of biographical facts about them. Individually and together they represent supreme gentleness, supreme human obedience to God, but considering them as real human beings is not easy for two reasons: Christians disagree on the interpretation of the sketchy biographical data available, and they disagree even more on the place of Mary in piety.

To Roman Catholics and Greek Orthodox, and to some Anglicans, Mary is queen of heaven, the first of all the saints, the ever-virginal "mother of God." Most Protestants do not venerate Mary as a mediator with God. They understand her as the epitome of womanhood, of motherhood, and tend to think of her primarily as a figure in sentimental Christmas scenes. To speak or write of Mary is to run the risk of bruising someone's piety. The risk must be taken, because both Mary and Joseph belong in the company of real women and men whose lives reflect Christian holiness.

The New Testament is the sole source of information on Mary and Joseph as historical characters, and two of the four Gospels contain most of what the early church knew, or remembered, of them. The Gospels of Mark and John, thought to be respectively the earliest and latest of the four, are not interested in Joseph at all, and deal fleetingly with Mary. Mark names Mary only once. John puts her in two major scenes, one (a wedding) at the start of Jesus' public ministry, and the second (at the cross) at the end. The Gospels of Matthew and Luke are the primary sources on Mary and Joseph, because each tells a nativity story.

Matthew's and Luke's Christmas stories differ significantly in detail, while they agree in essence. The Lukan account is told from Mary's point of view, the Matthean from Joseph's; they are complementary, and both emphasize obedience to God in an unusual situation.

The two nativity stories agree that Mary was a virgin betrothed (engaged) to Joseph when she became pregnant. A betrothal period of about a year, during which the chaste bride-to-be lived at her own home, was typical Jewish practice in the first century B.C. Luke and Matthew further agree that the pregnancy was the work of God, not of any man. The couple was married, and the two Gospels say Jesus was born in Bethlehem, a town in southern Palestine, in the reign of King Herod (the one called "the Great") and grew up in Nazareth, a town in the north. Jesus' contemporaries apparently assumed he was the natural son of Joseph. Astonished folks in Matthew 13:55 call him the "son of the carpenter," from which it is taken that Joseph was a carpenter. Genealogies in Luke and Matthew trace the ancestry of Jesus through Joseph, though Luke adds a parenthesis saying Joseph was the father "as was supposed," and Matthew carefully identifies Joseph not as Jesus' father but as the husband of Mary.

The age of neither Mary nor Joseph at the time of Jesus' birth is known. Mary would most likely have been a teenager, since women in her day married young. Christian art and literature have traditionally portrayed Joseph as older, maybe an old man, but this is speculation serving a theological purpose. The Gospels occasionally refer to the "brothers" or the "brothers and sisters" of Jesus, references that came to bother Christians who had decided Mary was a perpetual virgin. A convenient way to deal with Jesus' siblings was to make them half-brothers and half-sisters, the children of an older Joseph by a former marriage. The theory finds slim support in the Gospels, but married before or not, Joseph may have been an old man when Jesus was born. He evidently died between Jesus' twelfth birthday, when he took the boy to Jerusalem, and the start of Jesus' ministry some eighteen years later. He is simply not present in the Gospels. Joseph, of course, could have died young.

Nativity stories in Luke and Matthew agree on basics but diverge

on other points, such as where Joseph and Mary lived before Jesus
was born. Luke says they were residents of Nazareth who went to
Bethlehem for a census because Joseph was of the house of David,
meaning the Jewish tribe of Judah. Matthew implies that the couple
grew up in Bethlehem and went to Nazareth, after a trip to Egypt,
because northern Palestine was a safer place for the child Jesus.
(Galilee was not ruled by Herod the Great who, according to Matthew, wanted to kill the Christ-child.) Matthew has nothing of crowded inns, the nativity in a stable, or of shepherds visiting the child.
Matthew has "wise men"—Persian priests—coming to Mary and the
babe in a house at a date when Jesus could have been as much as two
years old.

Luke's Christmas account has shaped Christian conceptions of
Mary. Here is the beautiful "Magnificat," a poem combining themes
from the Psalms and other parts of the Old Testament into a hymn of
grateful obedience to God. Mary's song begins:

> My soul magnifies the Lord,
> and my spirit rejoices in God my Savior,
> for he has regarded the low estate of
>   his handmaiden.
> For behold, henceforth all generations
>   will call me blessed;
> For he who is mighty has done great things
>   for me,
> and holy is his name.
>
> (Luke 1:46b–49 RSV)

Mary in Luke understands the purpose and mission of the child she
bears, and is willing to accept the social risk of pregnancy before
marriage in order to accomplish God's will. The Gospel of Mark, one
of Luke's sources of information, has a less elevated opinion of Mary.
Mark suggests (Chapter Three) that Mary did not understand Jesus'
mission and may have thought her adult son "beside himself." Luke
omits the Marcan hostility to Mary and in his second book (the Acts
of the Apostles) places the mother of Jesus among the faithful in the
early church in Jerusalem. Luke's materials supply the portrait of
Mary as the ideal mother and symbol of Christian womanhood, and
the church has been well-advised to emphasize this positive interpretation. Mary acquitted herself well in raising her son, even if she
might not always have understood everything he said or did.

Joseph is the chief actor in Matthew's nativity sequence. A man of honor, he was naturally upset when his fiancée became pregnant. He thought to break the engagement quietly until, the Gospel says, he had a dream in which the pregnancy was explained as divinely initiated. Accepting the explanation, Joseph in Matthew is chief protector of Mary and the child, undertaking a flight to Egypt when the young Jesus is threatened by Herod, then resettling in a safe haven, Nazareth.

The author of Matthew goes to great lengths to counteract first-century rumors that Jesus was illegitimate. He does this in part with Joseph, a man of moral purity who accepts the virginal conception. Matthew also prepares his readers, most of whom were probably Jewish, to accept God's sometimes unorthodox way of doing things. The preparation is subtle and clever. Matthew's genealogy of Jesus, unlike Luke's, includes the names of four women (in addition to Mary): Tamar, Rahab, Ruth, and Bathsheba. Now a fascinating thing about each of these women is her suspect reputation in her own time. Tamar (Genesis 38:24) seduced her father-in-law; Rahab (Joshua 2:1) was a harlot who assisted the Israelities in conquering Jericho; Ruth was a Moabite woman (a foreigner) who may well have seduced Boaz, her second husband; and Bathsheba committed adultery with King David before the ruler dispatched her husband so he could marry her.

Why did Matthew include these and only these four women from the Old Testament in his genealogy of Jesus? Was he trying to say that Mary was morally stained but that this was acceptable because God had precedent for using loose women to accomplish divine purpose? This seems unlikely. Why would a Gospel writer intent on asserting Mary's virginity mention these women of questionable reputation? Better to cite wholly upright ancestors, such as Sarah and Rachel.

Matthew's reason for naming the four women was probably defensive; defensive not for sexual license, but for the acceptance of the extraordinary in God's plan for a messiah.[3] The unusual in Mary's situation was virginity. Tamar, Rahab, Bathsheba, and maybe even Ruth were "bad women" who served as links in God's chain of salvation; how much greater then Mary, totally pure, the mother of Christ.

By any measure, Mary and Joseph had an unusual marriage. They had possible slander to resist, remarkable experiences to ponder, and a unique child to raise. Both of them accepted heavy responsibilities, more than once-in-a-lifetime responsibilities. Theirs were once-in-a-world responsibilities, and their obedience to God has never been excelled except by the Son.

Polycarp (70–156?)

He was the gentlest and the strongest of men. Polycarp is a case study in Christian humility, but there was nothing spineless, spiritless, or retiring about this second-century bishop of Smyrna (modern Izmir, Turkey). He was courageous, forthright, and submissive only to God.

Polycarp was one of the earliest Christian martyrs. He could be discussed just as well in Chapter Eight, on persons persecuted for their faith, but he also fits under the Third Beatitude because of his commanding servanthood and the manner in which he faced execution. Missing facts about his long life are more than made up by the strength of character shown in his writings and in comments made about him by contemporaries.

When and how Polycarp became a Christian and then a bishop are matters of speculation. Some sources say he personally knew the Apostle John, who appointed him to lead the church at Smyrna. That may or may not be true. Polycarp was eighty-six years old when he died about A.D. 155 or 156, so he may have known persons who knew Jesus. The Christians of Smyrna may have elected him bishop; the procedures for selecting church leaders in Polycarp's day are clouded in uncertainty. That he was the bishop and greatly loved by Smyrna's Christians is not in doubt.

Christianity in the first half of the second century was a rather small movement, growing, and occasionally worrying the government of the Roman Empire. Its communities were scattered, and kept in touch by letters and reports carried by traveling evangelists. Polycarp was a letter writer. He lent encouragement to congregations undergoing persecution and, like the Apostle Paul, sometimes answered questions about the meaning and application of the Faith. Only one of his letters still exists, and it contains important information about its author. In this letter to the church at Philippi in Greece, Polycarp described what was expected of Christian ministers (presbyters). He said:

. . . The presbyters must be compassionate, merciful to all, turning back those who have gone astray, looking after the sick, not neglecting widows or orphans or one that is poor; but always taking thought for what is honorable in the sight of God and of men; refraining from all anger, partiality, unjust judgment, keeping far from the love of money, not hastily believing evil of anyone, not being severe in judgment, knowing that we all owe the debt of sin.[4]

These qualities of an ideal priest and pastor are a good description of Polycarp himself. The Christians in Smyrna adored their bishop. This is obvious in a letter they wrote to another church describing his execution and announcing their plans to annually observe the anniversary of his martyrdom.

Smyrna's letter on the martyrdom of Polycarp paints a word picture of a real man of Christlike gentleness and strength caught in a web of intrigue. The letter draws several comparisons between the treatment of Jesus and that of Polycarp.

For reasons unclear, the civil authorities in Smyrna decided to kill a few Christians. As the roundup progressed, believers in the city became worried about their bishop—an obvious target. They persuaded Polycarp to take refuge in the country with a Christian family, but the soldiers found his trail and, after torturing a farm servant, learned that Polycarp was hiding in a hayloft.

After his arrest, the bishop asked permission to pray and proceeded to spend two hours loudly commending to God everyone he had ever known and the entire church. The soldiers were impressed but took him back to town anyway. Interesting in the letter is the passing observation that Polycarp did not want to be martyred, that he did not voluntarily surrender to be killed for his faith. The idea that martyrdom is a good thing, the one sure ticket to heaven, came to be popular later in the Western, or Roman, church; it never prevailed in Eastern, or Greek, Christianity. The East generally saw martyrdom as an opportunity of last resort, yet to be embraced if living meant a denial of faith.

Polycarp was brought up for a hearing and asked to denounce his religion by cursing Christ and taking an oath to Caesar. "I have served him [Christ] eighty-six years, and he never did me any wrong," the bishop replied. "How can I blaspheme my King who saved me?" The judge threatened to throw him to wild beasts. "Call them, for repentance from what is better to what is worse is not permitted us who are Christian." The judge threatened him with fire. "The fire will burn for only an hour . . . come, do whatever you want."

The local arena having closed for the day, the sentence was fire—

burning at the stake. Polycarp was resolved. As he had been led to the hearing a voice had given him courage: "Be strong, Polycarp; play the man."

Polycarp played the man—the man of Christ.

His first obedience was to the one he praised at the stake as "the beloved Servant."

Dominic (1170–1221)

The journey began as a regular sort of diplomatic mission. Domingo de Guzman (Dominic) was accompanying Bishop Diego d'Azevedo of Osma, Spain, to Copenhagen, where the latter was to negotiate the marriage of the son of the king of Castile to a Danish princess. The thirty-four-year-old monk and his superior spent a night in Toulouse, and a conversation with their host that lasted until dawn changed the course of Dominic's life.

While calling himself Christian, the host gave an interpretation of the faith strange and terrifying to Dominic. The physical world, said the Frenchman, is entirely evil, absolutely opposed to goodness and God, that is, the world of the spirit. People, he said, are trapped in the evil material sphere, and the purpose of life is to free the soul to return to God; to do this, great personal purity is necessary, and believers must not marry, or bear children, or find any enjoyment in physical existence.

Dominic was hearing an explanation of an old Christian heresy, the doctrine of dualism, that, in effect, makes God the Lord of only half the world and also denies the need for grace in this life. Not only was Dominic's host a follower of this teaching, but so were many people in southern France in the early thirteenth century. The movement was called by two names, Albigensian (for the city of Albi) or Cathari (a word meaning "pure").

Rather than reject the host, Dominic tried to explain the orthodox understanding of Christianity, including the truth of God as creator and sustainer of the whole world. The Spanish monk decided that his work must be to preach the true faith to the Cathari and others who did not know it. The idea of a new religious order of preaching friars was born in his mind.

Dominic encountered the Cathari in 1204, and it took several years to launch the Order of Friars Preachers (Dominicans). His concept of wandering preachers living on alms was revolutionary, although others were having similar thoughts, including Francis of Assisi, his contemporary.

Both Dominic and Francis felt called to serve God in the world rather than from behind monastery walls. Each—and they met at least briefly—founded socially based orders of mendicants (monks living on alms), and each shared the ideal of simplicity and the goal of personal Christian holiness. Their orders, however, took different tasks in the world. The early Franciscans devoted themselves primarily to service among the poor; the Dominicans were preachers, evangelists to Christians and non-Christians alike.

Compared with Francis, and the comparison is inevitably made, Dominic suffers. His personality was less winning, though he was described by a contemporary as "beautiful . . . radiant . . . pleasant," and quick to compassion. Poets, dramatists, and moviemakers today are not drawn to Dominic as to Francis, but the saint of Assisi is in a class of his own and to pale beside Francis is not a great criticism of any person. Dominic was unquestionably a great Christian light of his day, a zealous but gentle servant of Christ in a chaotic world.

His sermons were moving; his person was plain. Dominic had a motto that best describes him as a mighty man tamed by divine love: "The man who governs his passions is the master of the world. We must either rule them, or be ruled by them. It is better to be the hammer than the anvil."

Dominic was born in modern Caleruega in what was the kingdom of Castile, Spain, in 1170. His father was a minor feudal lord. Young Domingo received a good education and in 1196 entered a monastic community attached to the cathedral at Osma. He rose rapidly in the community (becoming either superior or assistant superior) and numbered among his close friends Bishop Diego, a man of foresight and creativity.

At the end of the diplomatic mission to Denmark in 1204, Dominic remained in southern France to make plans for preaching missions to the Cathari. This work was complicated by a number of factors, at least two bearing on the general situation of the church in Europe. First, the church was in great need of reform to deepen spiritual life; the ideas of the Cathari spread in part because church officials and priests neglected their responsibilities to instruct the people. Second, the Vatican was ill-disposed to charter new religious orders.

Dominic's initial requests for permission to send preachers to the

Cathari were denied, though he did establish a convent in Prouille for women converted from the heresy by his personal efforts. The monk was a barefoot firebrand for orthodoxy, and a bit of a laughingstock in Cathari country. To understand his zeal for orthodoxy, it is important to remember his background. Spain in his day was not Christian from the Pyrenees to Gibraltar. The southern lands were under Muslim control, and Dominic had no doubt observed the infiltration of Islamic thought into Christianity. Mixing Christianity with other religions or with heretical notions, such as the Cathari did, troubled him deeply.

Whether Dominic could have converted the Cathari by preaching is a moot question; he had little chance to prove the power of the word in that situation. In 1208 a representative of the pope was killed by an official of the count of Toulouse, the major political defender of the Cathari. The Roman Church decided the time had come to wipe out the heretics, so a "crusade" against them was organized. Even if they were heretical, the Cathari were mercilessly treated; while they were not pacifists and fought back, they were no match for the pope's army led by Simon de Montfort, the Earl of Leicester.

During the civil war, Dominic dropped out of sight and may have continued his preaching in regions relatively unaffected by the military conflict. Contrary to some assertions, he neither took part in the crusade nor did he approve the use of force in combating unorthodox theology.

Dominic's plan was to overcome the heretics by setting an example of orthodox spirituality purer than the most perfect Cathari. For that reason he and six monks who joined him in Prouille went as begging, barefoot preachers. Once the war was over, Dominic and his group went to Toulouse, where he organized mendicant diocesan preachers to work among the ordinary people. He envisioned preachers fanning out across Europe.

Pierre Cella, a rich citizen of Toulouse, and Bishop Foulques of that city became the patrons of the young movement, but Pope Innocent III was not interested in the dreams of Domingo de Guzman. Bishop Foulques took Dominic with him to Rome to the Fourth Lateran Council in 1215, and though that council decreed against the forming of new orders, Innocent's successor, Honorius III, confirmed the Dominicans, who took the Rule of St. Augustine as their pattern and so were not technically new. The Order of Friars Preachers had sixteen members in 1216; sixty communities existed when the founder died in 1221.

Dominic insisted on education for the preachers, and Dominican houses flourished around the great medieval universities. The combined emphasis on orthodoxy and learning would also make the order a natural choice to oversee the Inquisition, established in 1231 to root out heretics. The Dominicans were put in charge of the Inquisition by the Vatican in 1232 and smeared their name in the eyes of later centuries by the use of torture and execution to enforce orthodoxy. Dominic had nothing to do with the order's role in the Inquisition, which was perhaps most intense in Spain.

From 1217 until his death, Dominic made his headquarters in Rome and made long journeys visiting the houses of the order and preaching. He died with his mendicants in Bologna. His bequest to the monks was threefold: "Have charity among you, hold to humility, keep willing poverty."

Brother Lawrence (1611–1691)

Nicholas Herman—Brother Lawrence—is one of those quiet, gentle Christians history almost forgot to record, and if there had been no record he would not have cared, though the world would be spiritually poorer without his example of "the practice of the presence of God." In one of the few letters he wrote, Brother Lawrence said:

Were I a preacher, I should preach above all other things, the practice of the presence of God: Were I a teacher, I should advise all the world to it; so necessary do I think it, and so easy.

He was neither preacher nor teacher. Nicholas Herman was a lay brother assigned to kitchen duties in a Carmelite monastery in Paris. He spent forty years among pots and pans, wine kegs, and vegetables. Most of all he was in God's presence, for Brother Lawrence learned to make his thoughts and actions, his whole life, a constant prayer. He was no less aware of the presence of God when he peeled carrots than when he received Holy Communion.

A life totally devoted to God was to Brother Lawrence a total joy, and this quality is no doubt the reason anything is known of him. The joyful brother in the kitchen came to the attention of an official on the staff of the cardinal of Paris. This official, M. de Beaufort, made records of four conversations with Brother Lawrence. These conversations were summarized in short publications on the life and character of Nicholas Herman after his death in 1691. Additional information on Brother Lawrence's thought, but little on his life, comes from sixteen letters and from a collection of maxims found among his modest possessions.

Nicholas Herman was born in 1611 in Lorraine. His parents were peasants. Nothing else is known of his early life. In his first conversation with de Beaufort he told of an experience that was for him his real birth, his spiritual birth. He was eighteen years old at the time, and the experience was nothing more than seeing a tree stripped of its leaves in winter and realizing it would in a short time be filled with flowers and fruit. De Beaufort wrote that young Herman "received a high view of the providence and power of God, which has never since been effaced from his soul. That this view had perfectly set him loose from the world, and kindled in him such a love of God that he could not tell whether it had increased during the more than forty years he had lived since."

The peasant lad with a high view of the providence and power of God served briefly as a footman. He was unsuccessful because "he was a great awkward fellow, who broke everything." He also fought in the Thirty Years War, part of the conflict dividing and devastating Germany in the wake of the Reformation. Herman was once captured and accused of spying, and might have been hanged had his singular indifference to the charges not convinced his captors of his innocence. A wound suffered in a campaign against Sweden left him with a permanent limp.

Back home, determined to war no more, Nicholas Herman vowed to enter the religious life. He first tried being a solitary hermit. That was not for him. With the sponsorship of an uncle who was a monk, he became a lay member of a Carmelite community in Paris. Brother Lawrence had been in the kitchen fifteen years when de Beaufort interviewed him in 1666, and remained there another twenty-five years. Founded in the thirteenth century in Palestine and named for Mount Carmel, the Carmelites formed one of the four major mendicant orders of the late Middle Ages. Poverty was a requirement, but the order grew fat and in the sixteenth century underwent reforms to restore the original severity of life. The monastery Nicholas Herman joined was strict.

Brother Lawrence wanted nothing for himself. He did not like to be about in society, finding himself troubled when he had to deal with merchants who supplied the monastery. His only desire was to cook, clean, and experience the presence of God. De Beaufort wrote: "As he proceeded in his work he continued his familiar conversation with his Maker, imploring His grace, and offering to Him all his actions. When he had finished, he examined himself how he had discharged his duty; if he found well, he returned thanks to God; if otherwise, he asked pardon, and, without being discouraged, he set his mind right again, and continued his exercise of the presence of God as if he had never deviated from it."

The lay brother recommended the practice of the presence of God to other people. All it required, he explained, was to live each minute with an awareness of the love of God. His words of admonition to others, according to de Beaufort, were not as effective as his own example. "His very countenance was edifying, such a sweet and calm devotion, appearing in it as could not but affect the beholder." Brother Lawrence was never impatient, frustrated, or hasty in the kitchen. He told de Beaufort:

> That time of business does not with me differ from the time of prayer, and in the noise and clatter of my kitchen, while several persons are at the same time calling for different things, I possess God in as great tranquility as if I were upon knees at the blessed sacrament.

Elizabeth Bayley Seton (1774–1821)

Elizabeth Seton is known primarily these days as the first native-born American citizen declared a saint by the Roman Catholic Church. Since she was canonized recently (1975), her name and a few facts about her, notably her conversion to Catholicism after her husband's death, are rather widely known. The woman herself as a real participant in post-Revolutionary American religion, education, and charitable work tends to be seen through the window of legend.

Mrs. Seton could be used as a case study of the often unintentional application of subtle exaggeration to religious heroes and heroines; in this case, exaggeration not of her piety so much as of her singlehanded accomplishments. She is given sole credit for social institutions and ideas she made no pretense to have initiated. For example, she is put forth as the founder in 1797 of a pioneering agency for widows and children in her native New York City. This assertion comes especially from Protestants who like to identify with her in her Anglican period.

Actually, Mrs. Seton was only one of a group of women fostering the Society for Relief of Poor Widows with Small Children. A Mrs. Isabella Graham was the guiding spirit behind the society.

Likewise, Elizabeth Seton is called the "mother of the U.S. parochial school system" and founder of the first free parochial school, both debatable claims. Who first did what in American Catholic education is as difficult to determine as who set up the first American Protestant Sunday school.

What she did found, with the help of others, was the American Sisters of Charity, but her greatness was not her ability to organize; her greatness was of the spirit, a gentle, trusting spirit fixed on Christ and on children. Elizabeth Seton embodied Jesus' command, "Let the children come to me," and her life can be read as one long preparation to be mother of the Sisters of Charity and of the youngsters—poor and rich, Catholic and Protestant—she brooded over at Emmitsburg, Maryland, from 1810 to 1821. In her brood were five children of her own.

She was born Elizabeth Ann Bayley, daughter of a surgeon and a frail mother who died when she was three years old. She and a sister were raised partly by relatives. Elizabeth Ann was a happy, alert child. At one point she thought of becoming a Quaker because she liked the hats the women wore. As a young adult she dallied with Deism, the idea that God created the world, then left it to run itself, a philosophy in vogue in the young American nation.

Family connections provided entry into New York City's very Protestant late eighteenth-century social world, and in that rarefied environment she met William Magee Seton, scion of an illustrious mercantile family. Elizabeth Bayley and William Seton married for love in 1794 and settled into a life as comfortable as life could be in a city periodically ravaged by diseases, including yellow fever. They lived for a time at 27 Wall Street, then a fashionable residential address, and summered in the distant village of Bloomingdale, located about where 79th Street now crosses Manhattan Island.

Elizabeth Seton might well have spent her whole life as a contented New York matron active in Trinity Episcopal Church had it not been for her husband's health. Mr. Seton probably had tuberculosis. His physical condition worsened, and so did the family business. In 1803, Elizabeth, William, and their oldest child, Anna, set sail for Italy, where they had business associates, in a hopeless attempt to find a healthier climate for Mr. Seton. He died before the year's end.

Widow and child stayed in Italy for several months awaiting passage back to New York. Her serious introduction to Catholicism is believed to have come in Italy, especially through the members of the Filicchi family. Once home, Mrs. Seton went through economic and spiritual hell. She was hard pressed to support herself and three daughters and two sons, and she was in a quandary over her religious direction. Her friends were of more help in feeding her than in calming her soul. She was religiously pushed and pulled from one side by Protestant friends and from the other primarily by Antonio Filicchi, who was in America on business.

Mrs. Seton made profession of faith and received Holy Communion as a Catholic in March, 1805. Her decision was very personal. Mother Seton had little interest in formal theological matters; she was no Christian intellectual. Late in life she confided to a friend that she had changed church affiliations less from conviction than because she was tired of religious inquiry having to do with the safety of her soul. She wrote: "How often I argued to my fearful uncertain heart: at all events Catholics must be as safe as any other religion, they say none are safe but themselves—*perhaps it is true*. If not, at all events I shall be as safe with them as any."[5] In saying this, she was probably too hard on herself. Elizabeth Seton had a strong attachment to Catholic sacramental practice. At the same time, her shift to Catholicism was no doubt motivated in some degree by a desire to find a meaningful life away from the social and religious involvements reminding her of the happy days with William Seton. She was also sick of the "endless salutations" and "dissipated dress" at Trinity Church.

To pay the bills, she tried running a boarding house. She failed; she failed also in a private school she opened with friends. Antonio Filicchi pressured her to join a Catholic community devoted to education in Canada. She was more responsive to the suggestion of a priest who proposed Maryland, a state founded by Catholics, as a place for her to begin an American teaching sisterhood. In 1809, she relocated adjacent to Saint Mary's Seminary in Baltimore, and there began what would become the American branch of the Sisters of Charity of Saint Vincent de Paul.

The next year Mrs. Seton and a small community of women, including her daughters (the sons were in boarding school), moved to Emmitsburg. Her idea was to establish a free, coeducational school for poor rural children, but that dream never fully materialized. Funds were too limited. To survive financially, paying students—

girls—from the cities were needed. The school had some local and some poor children; its bread and butter came with the daughters of rich families in New York, Philadelphia, and Baltimore. Mother Seton would remark that her hope of "a nursery only for our Saviour's poor country children" had given way to a school "forming city girls to faith and piety as wives and mothers."

The school at Emmitsburg was strict but humane. Teachers were well trained and supervised. Rich or poor, children were drawn to Mother Seton as much as she was drawn to them. Mrs. Seton's gift for mothering extended individually to the girls, and also to the boys at the nearby Mount Saint Mary's School. She wrote glowingly of watching youngsters skipping across the fields.

The early years at Emmitsburg were hard. The sisterhood, first called the Society of Saint Joseph, had trouble finding its direction. Mother Seton's position as superior was not secure until 1812, and her work was interrupted in 1812 and again in 1816 by the deaths of her oldest and youngest daughters. Mother Seton had able assistance from her nuns in expanding the order beyond Emmitsburg, first to an orphanage in Philadelphia, and before her death to another in New York and to schools in those cities. The American Sisters of Charity had some fifty members in 1821, a good number considering that the Catholic population of the United States was only 200,000 out of 7.2 million people.

To read the biographies of Elizabeth Seton is to meet a woman of considerable emotional dependence on men, though men had a way of unduly complicating her life and goals. Confusion during the initial years at Emmitsburg resulted in the main from priests trying to decide what the sisterhood would do without consulting the women. Her sons disappointed her. Neither William nor Richard were interested in religion, and the youngest failed in business. On her deathbed, Mother Seton was engaged in getting Richard out of a legal scrape.

In the decades following their founder's death at Emmitsburg, the Sisters of Charity became a major force in organizing schools, orphanages, hospitals, and universities serving the whole of American society. The seeds of the harvest of service were planted by Mother Seton, who wrote of her role in Emmitsburg:

You know I am as a Mother encompassed by many children of different dispositions—not equally amiable or congenial but bound to love, instruct and provide for the happiness of all, to give the example of cheerfulness, peace, resignation and consider the individual as proceeding from the same origin and tending to the same end than in the different shades of merit or demerit.[6]

Mary Slessor (1848–1915)

Like Elizabeth Seton, Mary Slessor was a woman of personal, practical faith whose love of Christ was expressed in large measure through her care of children—African children. Mary Slessor was a Scottish factory worker who became the Christian "Ma of Calabar" (modern Nigeria). She labored for thirty-nine years along the Calabar River and its tributaries in a day when many Europeans could not survive in fever-infested West Africa.

Missionaries such as Mary Slessor are today embarrassments to some sophisticated Christians who see the nineteenth-century missionary movement as a handmaiden to European and American colonialism in the so-called Third World (Africa, Asia, and Latin America). In retrospect, the missionary enterprise of the last century did at times and places align itself so closely with political and economic interests that it seemed to baptize colonialism. That unfortunate reality, however, does not cancel the Christian validity of the movement as a whole or of individual missionaries. Women and men of Mary Slessor's ilk were in many cases more deeply committed to Christ and to human welfare than are their modern critics.

Miss Slessor was, of course, a woman of her age. A loyal subject of Queen Victoria and her heirs, she never questioned the British right to set up a white-controlled government along the Calabar River. She considered Africans "heathens" until they converted to Christianity, and taught the women to iron their skirts as proper Presbyterians in Scotland would do. She abhorred various African practices, including black complicity in the slave trade, forms of infanticide, and live burials, but at heart she was a missionary after the model of Saint Patrick, who wholly identified with the people he sought to change. Furthermore, Mary Slessor tried to counteract some of the offenses of colonialism, such as trading guns and liquor to the Africans.

She was born in Aberdeen, Scotland, in 1848. Mary, her six brothers and sisters, and her mother were victims of a drunken father and husband. A move to Dundee when she was eight years old did not mend Mr. Slessor's ways. Mother and children were forced to go to work in the local mills. Mary joined the child labor force at age eleven and spent fourteen years as a factory girl. She had little formal education, what little she had coming from her mother and her Presbyterian parish. Mary volunteered to work in a slum mission set up by her church, and dreamed of someday being a missionary to a distant land.

People of the 1980s have no idea of the romance of the missionary movement in nineteenth-century Europe and America. Tales of heroic missionaries could move young people like the Rolling Stones do today. The death of David Livingstone, the explorer and missionary-physician in Africa, set off a wave of missionary zeal in the mid-1870s. Mary Slessor offered herself and despite her weak educational background was accepted by the foreign mission agency of the Church of Scotland (Presbyterian). High in hopes to convert West Africa in a hurry, she set sail in 1876. One of her first lessons in Old Calabar was that mission work is slow work.

Twelve years she labored in the settled towns near the mouth of the river, gaining a reputation for efficiency, care in learning the native languages, and, most of all, love for the Africans. Then she set off on a series of moves taking her farther and farther into the interior, into uncharted territory. She preached, built hutlike churches, and exhorted the Africans to give up alcohol, and to stop abandoning unwanted children, especially twins, who were considered a bad omen. Mary Slessor took orphan after orphan into her own home and gave her name to at least five African daughters.

Her skill as an arbiter of disputes came to the attention of the colonial government. Twice, in different places, she agreed against her will to serve as the local consul, or judge. Mary Slessor's "court" was one of the sights of Calabar in the 1890s. There sat a short Scotswoman listening to Africans argue their cases as she rocked a black child in her arms. Her decisions had less to do with law than with justice, tempered by mercy. If a man found guilty of owing a debt was penniless, she found him a job. One reason she agreed to represent the British crown was her sense that she understood the African sense of justice better than some outsider who might be sent in.

By the end of the century, Mary Slessor was famous in Calabar and Britain. She thought nothing of fame; she did not consider herself in any way extraordinary for a person who loved Christ and cared about people. "Ma" was aghast when in 1912 she received the Cross of Saint John of Jerusalem from King George V. She hid the letter announcing the honor, but could not avoid public notice when the cross itself arrived via diplomatic channels for presentation. To her friends' relief, she showed up at the ceremony wearing an old cotton dress, a straw hat, and shoes—the latter being a European fashion she had abandoned. The whole business of the Cross of Saint John she dismissed as a batch of "blarney."

Mary Slessor died upriver among her daughters on January 13, 1915. Her last months were filled with distress over the outbreak of World War I. When her body arrived for burial at Duke Town, one of the settlements on the Calabar near the ocean, an old woman is supposed to have shouted: "Do not cry, do not cry. Praise God from whom all blessings flow. Ma was a great blessing."[7]

Mary McLeod Bethune (1875–1955)

She was the fifteenth of seventeen children, and from the start seemed different to her parents, poor black owners of five acres near Mayesville, South Carolina. Young Mary was not different physically. Her special quality was deeper, more mysterious, and, of course, there was a major difference in circumstance. Unlike her parents and the oldest of her brothers and sisters, she was never a slave. The Emancipation Proclamation was a dozen years old when she was born in 1875.

The greatest difference about Mary McLeod (Bethune after 1898) was her talent for freedom. She encountered Jim Crow laws, racial bigotry of the heart, and endless social obstacles weighed against her people; she raised banners of freedom, and could hold them high because she was free. She was free to dream, free to defy the conventions of discrimination, free to be direct in demanding justice and opportunity for blacks, and free to proclaim her total dependence on God.

The girl from the South Carolina cotton patch accomplished remarkable things in her eighty years. She built a college and hospital for blacks in Daytona Beach, Florida. She mothered the influential National Council of Negro Women. Mrs. Bethune advised presidents, had a hand in shaping the Charter of the United Nations, and worked for voting rights for all American women.

God, she said, "is the Guide of all that I do." She believed in herself and her work because she believed in a loving God of love, justice, and mercy. Mary McLeod Bethune was a great twentieth-century

American social reformer, and she was also a Christian mystic. "As I grew I knew what it meant to absorb my will into the will of God," she wrote in a brief "spiritual autobiography."

To love God and to value freedom she learned from her parents, Samuel and Patsy McLeod. She also learned generosity from them. She learned to read and write in a Presbyterian school for black children in Mayesville. After graduation from the elementary school, she returned to the cotton field, assuming her career in education was over—then a kind of miracle happened. Mary Crissman, a Quaker in Colorado, had a little money she wanted to invest in the education of a black girl. She made her offer known to Scotia Seminary, a secondary school in Concord, North Carolina, where young Mary's teacher in Mayesville had studied. By the hand of providence, the scholarship came to Mary McLeod.

Miss Crissman helped to pay the black girl's way through Scotia and the Moody Bible Institute in Chicago, where she studied to become a missionary in Africa. She expected assignment through a Presbyterian mission agency, but upon graduating from Moody in the mid-1890s was told there were no openings for black missionaries in Africa. Dejected, she returned to Mayesville to teach in the school she had attended. She spent a year in each of two schools for blacks, one in Atlanta and the other in Sumpter, South Carolina. Meanwhile, Mary McLeod married Albertus Bethune and became the mother of a son.

Denied the mission field, Mary Bethune turned to education. But not just to teaching; she would found a school herself. Then living in Florida, she selected Daytona Beach as the site of her Literary and Industrial School for Training Negro Girls. Daytona was picked because it was on the verge of a tourist boom and because expansion was bringing in black workers whose children had no educational opportunities. The school opened in 1904 in a barnlike old house she rented with her last few dollars. Five girls enrolled. For equipment, Mary Bethune scavenged a dump next door; to raise money she sold sweet potato pies to guests at a new resort hotel. As she had hoped, her pie stand provided contacts with potential benefactors. Sweet potato pie was the first mutual interest she shared with James Gamble, the soap maker, who along with Thomas White, of sewing machines, made possible the expansion of the school.

The move to Daytona meant separation from her husband. Albertus Bethune was himself a teacher but thought his wife dreamed too big. He wanted a less hectic life and never settled in Daytona, though he visited and they stayed in touch until his death.

With Mr. Gamble as chairman of the trustees, the Daytona school grew rapidly after 1906. New buildings sprang up; enrollment climbed. Twenty years into her venture, Mrs. Bethune realized that her institutional child needed a more secure future than she could provide by her own fund-raising efforts. A broader organizational affiliation was needed, preferably with a Christian denomination, to protect the private status of the school. Her choice was the Board of Education of the Methodist Episcopal Church, an agency with a good record in providing education for black youths. She also consented to a Methodist proposal to merge her school in Daytona with a boys' school, Cookman Institute, in Jacksonville. Bethune-Cookman College was established in 1923 with Mrs. Bethune as president.

Although she had long considered herself a Presbyterian, Mary McLeod Bethune had attended a Methodist church as a child, and with her school she entered the Methodist denomination. Her membership was more than formal. She devoted enormous energy to Methodism for the remainder of her life, and was especially active in the national Methodist women's organization.

Her civic activities were legion: the Red Cross, the NAACP, the National Urban League, the Association of Negro Life and History, the National Council of Negro Women, the National Committee on Atomic Education, and many others. She received ten honorary degrees from colleges, along with other awards, including the Star of Africa from the Republic of Liberia. Mrs. Bethune was President Franklin D. Roosevelt's special adviser on minority affairs and, during World War II, was assigned to monitor the treatment of blacks in the United States armed forces. In the 1940s her national activities were so demanding that she stepped down as president of Bethune-Cookman, becoming president emeritus for life.

Much of her last decade was spent living in a cottage on the campus she loved. She strolled the grounds leaning on a cane that had belonged to President Roosevelt. One day in 1954 she forgot the need for the cane: the U.S. Supreme Court had outlawed racial segregation in public schools. Fairly dancing, waving the cane in the air, she moved across the campus telling the students, "Sing . . . 'Rise and shine and give God the glory . . .'"

As her life drew to a close, Mary McLeod Bethune wondered what she had to leave her people—certainly no worldly possessions. Her last will and testament was a written legacy of seven bequests, the first being the quality Saint Paul said was the greatest of all: "I leave you love. Injuries quickly forgotten quickly pass away. Personally and racially, our enemies must be forgiven. Our aim must be to create a world of fellowship and justice where no man's color or religion is held against him. 'Love thy neighbor' is a precept which could transform the world if it were universally practiced . . ."[8]

Toyohiko Kagawa (1888–1960)

He was hailed as a modern Saint Francis, favorably compared with Mohandas Gandhi, and in America and Europe he was named in the same breath with Albert Schweitzer as a great Christian hero of the twentieth century. That was only thirty-to-forty years ago. Today, Toyohiko Kagawa is an unfamiliar name, at least in the United States, except to the elderly; few of his more than one hundred fifty books are available except in dusty church libraries.

Great personalities sometimes go out of vogue when they grow old or die, even with good reason to keep them in active memory. That happened to Kagawa, a Japanese social reformer, preacher, and champion of peace who died in 1960. Why is not clear. His ideas were not irrelevant to the 1960s and 1970s; just the opposite, in fact. His opposition to war and nuclear weapons, his philosophy of international economic justice, his advocacy of economic cooperatives to help the poor help themselves, his attacks on urban problems, his support of women's rights—all this and more would have proposed him as a natural mentor to idealistic causes of the world's young and oppressed peoples across the last two decades. Yet few reformers, even in the churches, turned to his example or his voluminous writings for guidance. They preferred Marx, Herbert Marcuse, and Ché Guevara. Perhaps Kagawa had been around too long, been too lionized; perhaps he was too Christian. Whatever, twenty years after his death, Koyohiko Kagawa deserves rediscovery by Christians concerned for a gentler world of peace, justice, and respect for human dignity.

Despite the fame he achieved in his lifetime, Kagawa was a self-effacing man of enormous generosity and an incredible supply of energy. "He put his religion in his shoes," said one of his eulogists.

His religion was also in his heart. "Jesus Keep Me Near the Cross" was his favorite hymn.

Kagawa was born in 1888 in the industrial city of Kobe. His father was a nobleman; his mother a concubine. Both parents died before his fifth year, and he lived for a time with his father's legal wife, a woman who despised him. He was sent to a brother, then an uncle. His family permitted him at age fourteen to enroll in an English class taught by an American Presbyterian missionary. The lad had strict instructions to learn English, not Christianity, but he was converted anyway, a fact he withheld from his guardian until he was ready for college. He was instantly disinherited.

Following a near-fatal bout with tuberculosis—an experience that led to his first autobiographical novel, *Crossing the Death-line*—he entered Kobe Theological Seminary. That was 1909, and Kagawa's understanding of the social implications of Christianity was already well-formed. He could not live in a bright, clean Presbyterian dormitory and look out upon his city's notorious slum, Shinkawa. He moved to the slum, living in a six-by-six room he came to share with derelicts and drunks who needed to know, as he had learned, that God cares for them. After his marriage in 1914, he and his wife, Haruko, continued to minister in Shinkawa. While he studied at Princeton Theological Seminary in the United States from 1913 to 1915, Mrs. Kagawa studied in a Toyko Bible institute. The couple would have three children.

The Princeton graduate, back home, became active in the embryonic Japanese labor movement. He organized the Japanese Federation of Labor. His first arrest came in connection with the Kobe shipyard strike of 1921. Kagawa wanted to keep Marxism and violence out of the labor movement, but was nevertheless marked as a radical. The Imperial government's view of him softened in 1923, when he organized the massive reconstruction effort to put Japan on its feet following a devastating earthquake.

Across the 1920s and 1930s Kagawa was both social reformer and evangelist. He organized Tokyo's social bureau, championed the right of universal suffrage (granted to men in 1925), set up credit and farm cooperatives, founded settlement houses in urban slums, and created nutrition services. By 1936 the Kagawa Fellowship supported thirty-six social institutions. Most of the funds came from royalties on Kagawa's books and from donations he solicited.

Toyohiko Kagawa had little patience with piecemeal, Band-Aid approaches to social justice. He was convinced the entire economic order, the international economic order, must be reformed. He called his concept "brotherhood economics."

He traveled and spoke all over Japan, the Philippines, Australia, New Zealand, and the United States. The 1928 Jerusalem Missionary Conference, which he attended, inspired him to launch a coordinated evangelistic ministry in Japan. Never large, the Japanese Christian population increased significantly under his leadership.

The winds of war were blowing in Japan in the 1930s. Kagawa knew it. The Christian with his religion in his shoes walked and talked peace. He stepped up the efforts of the National Anti-War League he had founded in 1928. All to no avail. When Japan invaded China in 1940, Kagawa apologized to the Chinese people, an act bringing reprisals. The next year he was part of a Japanese Christian peace delegation to the United States.

Pearl Harbor was a great personal blow to Kagawa; the ensuing war ended much of the social work he had begun. He resumed his labors in 1945, reopening churches and helping to guide Japan's National Council of Churches. The gentle pacifist again traveled, preached, and wrote. He was welcomed to London in 1949 as a second Saint Francis of Assisi; Christians in Europe and America called him the "conscience of the world." But as the 1950s unfolded he was more symbol than organizer.

That Kagawa was a social prophet is not to be doubted. In the 1930s he told the church and the world which issues needed attention to forestall the growth of communism and fascism. He named the issues clearly: overpopulation, competition for raw materials and markets, transportation, and an international monetary system. It is the world's agenda today.

He asked nothing for himself. Kagawa only asked the world to consider and accept his motto:

> Everything comes to life by love,
> Love bears, breeds, and guides,
> Love is eternal.
> Love makes the whole world,
> And the world is one.[9]

Clarence Jordan (1912–1969)

As the men shoveled the soil onto the old packing crate containing his earthly remains, Faith Fuller stepped to the graveside and in her two-year-old voice sang a verse of "Happy birthday . . . dear Clarence." Jordan would have loved it, found it fitting too, had he been around to comment, that he died just as the Christian community he started and saw flicker was being reborn. He knew all about ironies and paradoxes, about seed having to die to sprout.

Clarence Jordan was a farmer—a planter of corn and pecan trees and a sower of the Word of God. The soil he tilled was in Sumter County, Georgia, near Americus and Plains; the field he sowed with the seeds of love, fertilized with the hope of interracial peace, was the whole of the American South in the 1940s, 1950s, and 1960s. He knew drought and pestilence—especially human pestilence—and almost despaired at times of any harvest except from the pecans. But he believed the Bible, believed Jesus was alive in the world, even in Sumter County, and he kept his hand to the Gospel plow.

Jordan, his wife, Florence, and a few friends in 1942 established Koinonia Farm, an experiment in Christian communal living. (*Koinonia* in Greek means "community" or "fellowship.") In their minds the farm would be a model for the rural poor; it would be open to people of all races who shared its philosophy, including disavowal of all personal possessions, and temporary hospitality would extend to all. Jordan believed Christianity is a religion for this life as well as for eternity, and he believed Christians serve Jesus by serving one another and strangers. He said: "The resurrection places Jesus on this side of the grave, here and now, in the midst of life. The Good News of the resurrection is not that we shall die and go home with him but that he is risen and comes home with us, bringing all his hungry, naked, thirsty, sick, prisoner brothers with him."[10]

Jordan grew up in Georgia, in Talbottom, where he was born in 1912. His family's bank and store crashed in 1933. The idea for Koinonia Farm developed while he was a graduate student (studying Greek) at the Southern Baptist Theological Seminary, Louisville, Kentucky in the late 1930s. A sharp awareness of the need to reconcile white and black Christians was honed through work with Baptist groups in Louisville. He had taken a degree in agriculture at the University of Georgia before attending seminary, and Jordan decided to combine his call to the land, his call to the pulpit, and his call to practice Christian brotherhood.

The Koinonia experiment in its first incarnation, from 1942 to the mid-1960s, was not a notable economic or communal success, except that it touched the lives of individuals and it survived. Survival was no small accomplishment. It was locally suspect from the start because it was "different." Black people ate at the dinner table with whites. Some early members were conscientious objectors. In 1950 the Koinonia residents were expelled from the nearby Baptist church for being radical in general and, specifically, for taking a student from India—he looked black—to worship.

Violence against the community erupted in 1956 as efforts were underway in Georgia to implement the U.S. Supreme Court ruling against segregated schools. Koinonia had experienced a spurt of growth; the economic future looked good. Though it did not have, never had in those days, many black members, it was a symbol in Sumter County of change in the social and racial status quo. Crops were ravaged, equipment destroyed, a roadside market burned, and the farmhouses sprayed with machine gun fire. Law enforcement officials were too busy to investigate.

Would the small community of forty people leave, as the chamber of commerce requested, or stay? Stay! Koinonia Farm weathered an economic boycott by area merchants (who refused to sell supplies to the community or buy its produce) by expanding its mail-order sale of pecans. Forgiveness was the only defense the community had against the injustice it experienced.

When the violence subsided and the boycott wore down, recovery was slow and never complete. Many members moved away, not so much because of the troubles but because the community seemed to lose its unity as persecution ebbed. Jordan was despondent about Koinonia's future. In the early 1960s he undertook a new project —the translation of the New Testament into what he called the "cotton patch version," a rendering of Scripture with a Southern accent. He fervently believed that the Bible should never be frozen in formal language. "Cotton patch" was greeted with both praise and disdain. Some folks did and some folks did not like his style—for example, Matthew 2:1–2: "When Jesus was born in Gainesville, Georgia, during the time that Herod was governor, some scholars from the Orient came to Atlanta and inquired, 'Where is the one who was born to be governor of Georgia? . . .' "[11]

Meanwhile, the community continued to dwindle. By 1967 only the Jordans, their four children, and one other family called the farm home. Jordan decided the only option was to sell the farm. But new life was to come from the experiment. In a chance encounter, Jordan met Millard Fuller, the father of the two-year-old who sang "Happy

Birthday" at his grave. They, together with friends from across the country, conceived the idea of "Koinonia Partners," a plan to help people obtain jobs and homes on and beyond the Koinonia farm.

The new idea moved away from the strict communal pattern. People would own their own houses and work in partnership. This plan worked. By late nineteen seventy-nine, Koinonia Partners had built eighty-six houses on the farm and in Americus. The agricultural and craft businesses of this thoroughly interracial community flourish. Volunteers flock to it.

Clarence Jordan died in 1969 in the shack he used for a study. He was working on the "cotton patch" version of the Gospel of John. The Sumter County medical examiner refused to come to the farm to sign the death certificate. So Millard Fuller, not wanting the expense of an ambulance, propped the body in the car and drove it to town. Jordan would have loved that.

In his "cotton patch" version of Matthew, Jordan translated the Third Beatitude as follows: "They who are gentle are his people, for they will be his partners across the land."[12]

Clarence Jordan was a gentle partner of God.

CHAPTER IV

Whetted for Truth

"Holy are those who hunger and thirst for righteousness . . ."

"PLEASE, SIR, I WANT SOME MORE."

"What!" gasped Bumble, faint with disbelief.

"Please sir, I want some more," said Oliver Twist, holding out his plate.

Hunger makes people bold—"desperate" and "reckless" like Dickens' poorhouse lad.

Hunger and thirst can change the course of lives and of history. Whole nations have moved to escape famine and drought; wars caused by shortage of bread; wars lost for lack of water. Esau in the Old Testament sold his birthright for a bowl of pottage.

"Hunger" and "thirst" are strong nouns—and even stronger verbs. The reason is simple; Homer said it all in Achilles' words, "Now I think no riches can compare with being alive."

Remembering the intense human drive for food and water is helpful in understanding the Fourth Beatitude, "Holy are those who hunger and thirst for righteousness . . ." The verbs are as strong as exist for expressing human desire. They are words at the core of physical life: "And the people spoke against God and Moses . . . 'there is no food and water' " (Numbers 21:4b–5).

The linguistic and emotional strength of hunger and thirst as applied to the drive for bodily sustenance are in this Beatitude (Matthew 5:6). Furthermore, the hungering and thirsting is of an intensity difficult to show in the English translation of the Greek text. In the original, Matthew 5:6 is constructed in a way that assigns a consummate appetite to those who hunger and thirst. The special grammatical structures cannot be translated literally without a peculiar combination of prepositions, but the sense can be expressed. Hunger and thirst in the Fourth Beatitude express a desire for the whole of the object, as though, in physical images, a hungry woman asks for the whole loaf of bread instead of a piece, or a thirsty man for the whole pitcher of water. The hunger and thirst in Matthew 5:6 are for the entirety of the object.

This consummate appetite is saved from gluttony by the nature of the object—righteousness—and here the analogy to food and water ends. Righteousness is not subject to shortage at the source or to overconsumption. But what is righteousness?

Several recent translations of the Bible do not use "righteousness" in Matthew 5:6 but simpler words or phrases, such as "justice" or "what is right." These terms, easier on modern eyes and ears— righteousness is a word to stumble over—represent valid linguistic possibilities, but they may misrepresent the meaning of the Fourth Beatitude by limiting the object to ethical behavior. Righteousness involves ethics; ethics is not the whole of righteousness, and Matthew 5:6 concerns an object wholly desired. The word may be long and uncommon, but righteousness is a good translation here.

Righteousness, like most major biblical words, has a variety of uses in the Old and New Testaments, and is applied to both God and persons. As a description of God, especially in the Jewish Scripture, it is almost a synonym for holiness; for example, the holy and righteous God is a recurring theme in the Psalms. Righteousness is slightly different in that it does have specifically ethical overtones, so that it can mean, and is sometimes translated, "the justice of God." The righteous God is especially concerned with the poor and helpless —the God of goodness contrasted with the evil of human ways. At the same time, the righteous God is strength, contrasted with human weakness.

The term is often relational, used in the vocabulary of covenant —the steadfast God expecting steadfast obedience from the people of covenant. As applied to individuals, righteousness is relational in that it compares a person with God, the norm of righteousness, and in this use has strong ethical implications. In various places in the New Testament the Greek term in the Fourth Beatitude is translated "just," "justice," "right," or "rightness."

Matthew 5:6 can correctly be read as commending those with a hunger and thirst for justice, or for what is right in an ethical sense.

The problem with such translations is not their linguistic accuracy but their scope, given the fragility of words and the difficulty of understanding biblical righteousness. To identify the object in this Beatitude as justice or rightness is to run the risk of confining it to contemporary concepts of personal and social morality as something people can achieve by individual or political efforts.

From other passages it is clear that the author of Matthew (and almost all other biblical writers) understood righteousness as a God-ward condition. Matthew often links righteousness with God's kingdom, or reign. Moreover, in the Gospels and the letters of Paul righteousness originates in God: God is making a new, righteous relationship possible through Jesus Christ. Ethical considerations among persons come into play within the new relationship with God.

Righteousness in the Fourth Beatitude is best understood as right relationship with God in all spiritual and ethical dimensions —individual and communal. This understanding includes rightness and justice, and it includes more. A consummate hunger and thirst for righteousness covers ethics and also a passion for truth—God's truth, to know it and be guided by it. The desire in Matthew 5:6 is for nothing less than God's truth and way in all things. The Psalmist described the outcome of the right relationship: "Mercy and truth are met together; righteousness and peace have kissed each other." (Psalm 85:10 KJV).

Righteousness personified is Flavia Domitilla, a first-century Roman matron, defying her uncle, the Emperor Domitian, in organizing her life around her Christian prayers, her Christian charity, and burial of the Christian dead. It is the thirteenth-century Belgian mystic Jan Van Ruysbroeck, ascending the ladder of spiritual love, addressing his guests when he had something to say and remaining silent when he did not. Righteousness is Muriel Lester serving the poor in London's slums during World War II—serving not out of a sense of benevolence but because she was following the "divine Lover." And righteousness is twentieth-century Swiss theologian Karl Barth, spending his life reviewing and refining the church's theology.

A passion for God's way also is grappling in large and small ways with relentless questions such as those raised by the Grand Inquisitor in Dostoevsky's *The Brothers Karamazov*. In the story embedded in the novel, the Inquisitor has Jesus arrested and sentenced to the stake for disturbing the peace by restoring sight to the blind and giving life to

WHETTED FOR TRUTH 105

the dead. The old prelate lectures the imprisoned Lord on his mistakes, especially his failure to provide tangible proofs of God.

Human souls and bodies, says the Inquisitor, are controlled by miracle, mystery, and authority people can see. The resurrected Christ, he complains, performs the miracle of faith by resorting to invisible mystery and authority. How much better for mankind and the church had Jesus accepted the devil's offers—agreed to turn stones into bread, to show power by jumping from the temple steeple, and to assume the government of this world. As it is, according to the Inquisitor, Jesus' hands are empty except for "freedom," a problematic gift providing no guarantees that God exists, and requiring a leap of faith in the dark. The church has found it necessary to "improve on" Christ's work and, therefore, will not have the Lord coming around to tamper with the system.

Passion for righteousness means a willingness to take risks in making systems appropriate to miracle, mystery, and authority, a willingness also to scrutinize those systems by the norm of righteousness. Hunger and thirst for God's way is willingness to accept paradoxical freedom, to leap in faith beliving that God is the catcher.

Finally, for Christians, righteousness is Jesus Christ—the Way, the Truth, and the Life in the Gospel of John. Those who hunger and thirst for righteousness have a holy passion to know and imitate the Lord.

Paul of Tarsus (?–65?)

The compiler of a recent list of history's most influential figures declined to put Jesus in the top spot because, he said, Christianity had a cofounder—Paul of Tarsus.

While the best word to describe his role could be debated, Paul was the pivotal personality in the first generation of Christians. Jesus announced the Gospel, but the church was not merely to repeat what he said. Christianity came proclaiming Jesus Christ himself as its content, and Paul was foremost in establishing that message and in asserting it as a universal religion.

Though born about the same time, Jesus of Nazareth and Paul of Tarsus never met. Paul encountered his Lord Jesus Christ around A.D. 35 in a searing revelation on the road from Jerusalem to Damascus. He considered the experience his call to an apostleship as valid as that of any who had walked with Jesus. And of the apostles he was the first to realize the contrast between the Gospel of Christ and the Jewish world from which it came, and also the first to understand that the church could not be ethnically restricted. A Jew who never rejected his Jewish heritage, Paul was the apostle to the Gentiles.

To Paul, Jesus Christ is the Gospel, the living revelation of God's goodness, love, and grace—righteousness—to those of faith. In Christ, he taught, God is making right the relationship not only between God and people but also among people. Paul had a relentless hunger that Jew and Gentile alike hear and believe this good news.

That was Paul the Christian missionary, author of a substantial part and the oldest books of the New Testament. Before his conversion, he breathed "threats and murder' (Acts 9:1) against the young Christian sect. Reliable information on the life of Paul comes only from his own letters and from the Acts of the Apostles. These two sources, each apparently independent of the other, are not always in agreement, but both say that Saul (his Jewish name) opposed the embryonic church; Acts reports him as present and "consenting" to the stoning of Stephen, the first Christian martyr. Neither source explains whether Saul/Paul the persecutor acted officially or was personally motivated. Paul in Galatians simply says he "was advanced in Judaism beyond many of my own age among my people, so extremely zealous was I for the traditions of my father" (1:14).

Data is also fragmentary on Paul's career before he "persecuted the church of God violently and tried to destroy it" (Galatians 1:13). He was born near the start of the first century A.D. in Tarsus, a Greek-Roman city on the southern coast of what is now Turkey. His father may have been well-to-do, since Paul was a Roman citizen, a privileged status often inherited. His primary language was Greek, though Tarsus had a synagogue and Paul most certainly was raised in strict Jewish belief and practice. Intending to be a rabbi, he learned a trade, as was customary for young scholars. His "tentmaking" or "leatherworking" (Acts 18:3) was a skill by which he evidently supported himself on his preaching tours.

Acts states that Paul went to Jerusalem at a young age to study the Jewish law "at the feet of Gamaliel" (22:3). Paul's letters say nothing of his studying with the famed Rabbi Gamaliel; perhaps he did, and perhaps in Jerusalem he learned of and was offended by the Christians. Another open question is how much time Paul spent in Jerusalem. The city was not his base of operations after he became a missionary, and both the letters and Acts clearly indicate theological tension, though not necessarily personal animosity, between Paul and the leaders of the Jerusalem church. The tension had to do with the spread of the Gospel among the Gentiles.

A precise chronology of Paul's residences and travels is impossible to set. It is clear that Damascus, and later Antioch, were his early headquarters, and he did not consider himself under the jurisdiction of Peter, James the brother of Jesus, or the other leaders of the Jerusalem church. He did not request a commission for his missionary journeys, the first taking him to Cyprus and cities of Asia Minor, the second extending his work into Greece, and the third a long swing revisiting many churches established in both Asia and Europe.

The early missionaries (Paul and others) to the Gentiles worried some of the Jerusalem leaders (Peter least of all, it seems). Christianity was still viewed as the fulfillment of Jewish messianic expectations. Should Christians not also observe Jewish religious laws, such as those on clean and unclean foods and circumcision? Paul believed that Jewish Christians should follow the Jewish law (to a point, anyway, although not to the point of refusing to eat with Gentiles), but that Gentile Christians need not become Jews. Faith, not the letter of law, he said, is what matters:

For we hold that a man is justified by faith apart from works of law. Or is God the God of Jews only? Is he not the God of Gentiles also? Yes, of Gentiles also, since God is one; and he will justify the circumcised on the ground of their faith and the uncircumcised through their faith. (Romans 3:28–30 RSV)

Right relation to God, according to Paul, is based entirely on the initiative of God, the giver of law and of grace in Jesus Christ. Law and the human inability to keep it, he said, shows the depth of human pride and sin; grace in Jesus Christ vanquishes sin and establishes peace between God and humanity. Christ he presented as the "new Adam" replacing the old, fallen one from whose nature persons are saved by God's gifts of faith and obedience. That, to Paul, is justification, or righteousness.

Acts reports that tension over the mixture of Jews and Gentiles in the church became so intense that all the major leaders gathered in Jerusalem to consider the issue. At the conference Peter made the primary speech against imposing Jewish law on Gentile believers. Acts 15:12 says Paul and his colleague Barnabas were present and spoke. With the opinions in, James proposed a compromise: Gentiles should not trouble themselves with Jewish observances, except that they should abstain from meat sacrificed to pagan idols, from pagan worship involving sex, and from eating anything containing blood (prohibited to Jews) and, some manuscripts add, from "what is strangled."

If Paul was party to the so-called "apostolic decree" from the Jerusalem conference, he did not promote it as such, at least not the dietary provisions. He would have automatically endorsed the warning against sexual immorality, but on eating meat from animals slaughtered in pagan temples he took a more flexible view in I Corinthians 8. Christians, he said, have liberty to eat what they want, but if going to a pagan temple for meat causes other people to think a believer is honoring an idol, refrain from the practice. On dietary rules in general, Paul was emphatic: "Food will not commend us to God" (I Corinthians 8:8). The position of Paul on the Jewish law would eventually prevail in most of the Christian church (not in all; the Ethiopian Orthodox Church, for example, still observes some Old Testament dietary laws.)

A physical description of Paul in an early fictional writing has enjoyed some popularity across the centuries and has influenced artistic portrayals of the apostle to the Gentiles. He was, says the "Acts of Paul," a short man, "thin-haired upon the head, crooked in the legs, of good state of body, with eyebrows joining, and nose somewhat hooked, full of grace: for sometimes he appeared like a man, and sometimes he had the face of an angel." What he looked like, of course, no one really knows, but by Paul's own admission (II Corinthians 12:7) he had an ailment or deformity that pained him. He called it his "thorn in the flesh." Speculation on the nature of the thorn is endless and none of it conclusive; anyone's guess is as good as anyone else's.

In addition to the bodily discomfort of the "thorn in the flesh," Paul experienced suffering and deprivation in the course of his missionary trips. His own words summarize it best:

Five times I have received at the hands of the Jews the forty lashes less one. Three times I have been beaten with rods; once I was stoned. Three times I have been shipwrecked; a night and a day I have been adrift at sea; on frequent journeys, in danger from rivers, danger from robbers, danger from my own people, danger from Gentiles, danger in the city, danger in the wilderness, danger at sea, danger from false brethren; in toil and hardship, through many a sleepless night, in hunger and thirst, often without food, in cold and exposure. And, apart from other things, there is the daily pressure upon me of my anxiety for all the churches. (II Corinthians 11:2–28 RSV)

Anxiety over the churches he had founded or nurtured was one motivation for most of the letters of Paul found in the New Testament. These documents are real letters, often written in response to questions or to resolve controversies in the young congregations. The occasional nature of the letters (and others that were lost) keeps Pauline theology from having a systematic flow, but it also keeps the writings lively. His most systematic statement of faith is found in the Epistle to the Romans, a letter of self-introduction to a church he did not found. Paul kept meaning to go to Rome—he did, finally, in chains.

His last and longest ordeal began in that old controversy involving Jews and Gentiles. Paul went to Jerusalem to deliver a contribution made by the young Gentile congregations. Acts, the only source of the story, says he was set upon in the Temple by Jews aroused by reports that he had taken Greeks into the inner court (forbidden to non-Jews). Rescued by Roman soldiers who learned he was a Roman citizen, Paul was held in a sort of protective custody, and later transferred to Caesarea when a plot against him was discovered. He had two choices as a Roman citizen in his predicament: one, have the Jewish charges against him heard by the Roman governor in Jerusalem or, two, appeal to Caesar in Rome. Paul took the second option.

Shipwrecked off Malta, he was transferred to another boat, which reached Italy intact. There Paul lived restricted but not confined, awaiting his hearing before Caesar, probably Nero. He wrote some of his most important letters in Rome. Acts leaves him there: "And there he lived two whole years at his own expense, and welcomed all who came to him, preaching the kingdom of God and teaching about the Lord Jesus Christ quite openly and unhindered" (28:30).

One tradition says Nero finally dismissed the charges and Paul resumed his career, perhaps going to preach in Spain. This theory arose in part to account for the three Pastoral Epistles (Titus and First and Second Timothy), letters of obvious late date compared to other Pauline writings. This theory has Paul seized a second time and executed. Since many scholars have concluded that the Pastorals are not from Paul's hand (but by a Paulinist using bits of original material) another theory has Paul executed by Nero about A.D. 65. That seems likely, but there is a third, almost never mentioned possibility. Paul may have died a natural death in Rome.

When or how Paul of Tarsus died is not nearly as important as his life and writings. He took the Christian faith into the Roman world, gave the church its enduring theological direction, and forced succeeding generations to look for truth in the cross of an obscure Nazarene: "For the foolishness of God is wiser than men, and the weakness of God is stronger than men" (I Corinthians 1:25).

Augustine of Hippo (354–430)

Hunger and thirst for righteousness, he taught, is a gift of God setting souls on a quest toward being found by God.

A riddle? Not to Augustine, whose mature thought was bounded on every side by God's grace. God, to him, initiates and finishes the human pilgrimage toward truth, love, and salvation. He saw his own life as a God-directed pilgrimage from dry ground to the waters of faith and wisdom flowing both to and from God. He understood history as moving to and from the city of God, and, for better or worse, what Augustine thought mattered in the fifth century, and matters still.

Aurelius Augustine is to Western Christianity what the Sears, Roebuck building is to Chicago's skyline—a dominant presence. His influence is surpassed only by that of Jesus and Paul of Tarsus, and is twofold in nature. First, his mind was the channel that shaped and transmitted classical Western orthodoxy. Augustinian theology provided Europe's religious and social framework for almost a thousand years after the fall of Imperial Rome. Second, renewal movements in church and theology often hark back to Augustine. For example, the Protestant Reformation was in large part a reassertion of his ideas, and twentieth-century Christian thought has turned to him in its attempts to fathom evil.

His own earthly pilgrimage in grace began in the North African village of Tagaste (now Souk-Ahras, Algeria) in 354, and ended seventy-five years later in nearby Hippo (Annaba), where for thirty-five years he was bishop. His life spanned decades of political upheaval and theological controversy. In his youth adherents of heretical Christian sects probably outnumbered orthodox believers in North

Africa, and as he died the Germanic Vandals, Christians of a heretical variety, were besieging Hippo.

For thirty-two years Augustine's own quest for truth proceeded outside the church. His mother Monica was a devout, uneducated Christian; his father Patricius, a poor Roman freeman, remained unbaptized until shortly before his death in 371. Augustine (like his brother and sister) was instructed in Monica's faith as a child; baptism was delayed, a common practice in the late fourth century. The sacrament and church membership were thought to be appropriate only for persons settled in life. (Ambrose, the great preacher of Milan, was not baptized until after he was elected bishop.)

Augustine apparently cared little for the church. Monica cried and prayed for the conversion of husband and son, but avoided nagging and recognized Augustine's natural talents for learning whether he was baptized or pagan. At age eleven the boy was sent to school at Madaura where he perfected his taste for fleshly recreation as much as he developed the mind. In his *Confessions*, written when the author was forty-five years old and intended to praise grace and depreciate himself, Augustine portrays himself as a youthful liar, thief, and fornicator: "Behold with what companions I walked the streets of Babylon, and wallowed in the mire thereof, as if in a bed of spices, and precious ointments."

The middle-aged bishop probably exaggerated his adolescent sins, but the youth from Tagaste did have a sexual urgency. After Madaura he went to Carthage where there sang around him "a cauldron of unholy loves": by age eighteen he had a mistress and a son, Adeodatus. How much indiscriminate dipping he did in the cauldron is open to question, since he loved the mistress, kept her for fourteen years, and might have married her had social custom permitted the union of a teacher and a prostitute.

While he may have philandered, Augustine became a serious student of philosophy in Carthage, and while reading a now lost book by Cicero turned to the love of truth, to thoughts of God. He felt an inner longing that his "unholy loves" and his professional ambition did not satisfy, but the Christian Scripture his mother urged him to read bored him. The first step in an intellectual pilgrimage that would bring him back to the Bible took him to a group called the Manichees.

Manicheaism teaches—it is still found in several forms— materialistic dualism which, among other things, denies the unity of

God. Originating in Persia, the classical form Augustine encountered and embraced posited an eternal civil war between good and evil, light and darkness. The material world in this scheme is part of the realm of evil; individual souls are sparks of light trapped in darkness, and God sent Jesus to free the sparks. Liberation requires special knowledge and strict asceticism in Manichean philosophy.

Augustine ate the Manichees' "empty husks" for nine years, initially finding in dualism an explanation of his internal struggles. He attributed his physical lust and drive for fame to his material self, but he kept his mistress, and therefore could be only a low-level Manichee. "O God, give me chastity, but not yet," he prayed.

Looking back on his Manichean interlude, Augustine lamented his ignorance of the image of God in persons and his blindness to "true inward righteousness." Nine years of Manichean ignorance proved enough. His continuing spiritual dissatisfaction, the death of a close friend, and unruly students in Carthage (where he had become a teacher) led him to Rome.

In Rome he fell in with a group of skeptics who helped free him from Manicheaism without pointing him to Christ. He planned to open a school of rhetoric, but changed his mind when he found that Roman students never paid their teachers, so he left the city in 384 to teach in Milan, and he later saw the move as providential.

Augustine's life began to come together in northern Italy. Milan was the home of Bishop Ambrose, great preacher and foe of the remnant of organized Roman paganism. The new teacher of rhetoric went to hear Ambrose's elocution and stayed to listen to the sermon's message. He began to read the Bible, and at the same time discovered Plato as reintroduced to the West in the writings of the Neoplatonists. Augustine found answers in Greek philosophy to some of his theological problems. For example, he had been unable to think of God in non-material terms. From Neoplatonism he learned to contemplate God as pure, changeless light and spiritual unity; evil as nothingness. He would include Neoplatonic elements in his later theological writings and, in fact, Augustine melded biblical religion and Neoplatonic philosophy.

Meanwhile, his body continued to complicate this life. His mistress and son were in Milan with him; then Monica appeared with a plan to marry him to a young woman whose connections could foster his career. Augustine agreed to the engagement and reluctantly sent the mistress home to Africa (Adeodatus stayed), but since the wait for the bride was two years he took an interim mistress.

Problems of marriage, mistresses, and lust were settled before two years passed. Augustine was introduced to the monastic ideal, just entering the West from the Eastern Church. If Anthony of Egypt (see page 55) could overcome temptations of the flesh, could he not also? He arrived at an answer in the summer of 386 while sitting in a garden:

I heard from a neighboring house a voice, as of boy or girl, I know not, chanting, and oft repeating, "Take up and read; Take up and read." . . . I arose; interpreting it to be no other than a command from God, to open the book, and read the first chapter I should find. . . . Eagerly then I returned to the place where . . . I laid the volume of the Apostle . . . I seized, opened, and in silence read that section on which my eyes first fell: *Not in rioting and drunkenness, not in chambering and wantonness, not in strife and envying: but put ye on the Lord Jesus Christ, and make not provision for the flesh* (Romans 13:13).[1]

Augustine's "chambering" days were over. He diligently prepared for baptism, performed by Ambrose on Easter, 387. The incident in the garden is recorded as Augustine's conversion, and it indeed was a turning point; however, he was not immediately transformed into a theologian. That would come gradually, and his theology would take an extremely negative view of sexual activity—even within marriage. For this he is sometimes accused of hypocrisy: all those years of promiscuity followed by prudishness. The value or damage of Augustine's teaching on sexuality, including his linking of conception and original sin, continues to be debated, and that debate must not be allowed to cloud the fact that his sexual behavior in young manhood was a grave problem to him. He felt guilty and slovenly; *for him* celibacy was the way to quiet the guilt, thus allowing his creative genius to flow into his writings and his pastorate at Hippo. Augustine was a model pastor when it came to the spiritual and physical welfare of the people. "I do not propose," he said, "to spend my time in the empty enjoyment of ecclesiastical dignity, but I propose to act as mindful of this—that I must give an account of the sheep committed unto me."

After Augustine's baptism in Milan, Monica wanted to return to Tagaste. Her son resolved to go with her, taking Adeodatus, and there establish a retreat house for Christian study and devotion. The party set out, but at Ostia, the port of Rome, Monica fell sick and died. Augustine tarried in Rome for a year, then returned to his place of birth where he gathered a small ascetic community (the beginning of the Augustinian Order), and where Adeodatus died about 389.

Augustine prayed and wrote in relative seclusion for three years. In 391 he chanced to attend church in Hippo and, to his amazement, emerged a priest. Hippo's bishop (a sort of senior pastor in those days) was Greek, one Valerius, and needed an assistant who could speak Latin and the local Punic language. Recognizing Augustine in the congregation, Valerius incited the worshippers to thrust the visitor forward as a candidate for ordination. More or less trapped, Augustine agreed, and five years later succeeded Valerius as bishop.

Hippo was a small, unimportant town, but for thirty-four years it was the theological center of the Western Church. It was Augustine who defended orthodox authority against a series of strong heretical movements, including the Manichees. His writings and the doctrinal issues he addressed are too many to enumerate. Two challenges must suffice as examples. First, the debate over free will and sin; second, the occasion of *The City of God*.

One of the celebrities of the early fifth-century church was a British monk named Pelagius who inspired a large following by teaching that persons are free to choose good or evil. Pelagius denied original sin; the sin of Adam, he said, had nothing to do with anyone but Adam, though most people follow his example and, therefore, need the saving work of Christ to be set afresh on the road to righteousness.

Now original sin was not an official doctrine of the church in the early 400s. Pelagius said he taught nothing except what Christians already believed. Pope Zosimus tended to agree until Augustine had hold of him. To believe human will is free to choose good or evil is to deny the need of God's grace, declared the bishop of Hippo. Adam fell into sin by pride and the human race fell with him; cleansing, restoring grace is a free, undeserved gift that cannot be earned and is distributed as God desires.

Augustine prevailed over Pelagius in that the monk was condemned by the Council of Ephesus in 431, even though controversy over free will and original sin has continued. To Augustine, the will belongs to God who puts into persons the will to be drawn to God: "Forasmuch as He begins his influence by working in us that we may have the will, and completes it by working within us when we have the will."

The City of God can not be divorced from an event that shook the ancient world. In 410 the Visigoths, a Germanic tribe, captured the city of Rome. The dwindling pagan aristocracy blamed the Christians: if the old gods had been honored the tragedy would not have happened. Augustine's masterpiece was started to refute the pagans, and in the thirteen years of its writing developed into a theology of history. One theme warns people against too much trust in real cities, but the central theme is invisible cities, two of them, the "earthly city" and the "city of God"—the city of the damned and the city of the saved. "The earthly city is determined by self-love, whereas the city of God is constituted by the love of God," he wrote. To Augustine, the church can be considered the city of God in "essence and intent," but not literally, since "it is mixed with much earthly evil."

Augustine's book on the two cities was the sociological and political primer of the medieval West. It can be soundly criticized today; fifteen centuries ago it offered a framework for a society in chaos as Rome and the ancient world vanished.

Late medieval and modern Europe broke out of the mold of *The City of God*. The book's sociology and politics and symbolism seemed irrelevant, yet from a Christian perspective the basic theological argument is difficult to ignore. In all ages there seems to be the earthly city "making false gods as she chose, from anywhere or even out of man, to serve by sacrifice." And hope endures in church and Christian hearts for the other city which "makes no false gods but herself is made by the true God."

Augustine hungered and thirsted for that city of righteousness.

Desiderius Erasmus (1466–1536)

The ghost of Erasmus surely nodded in agreement when modern ecumenical pioneers such as Nathan Söderblom (see page 214) called not only for a spirit of unity among divided Protestants but also for Protestant–Roman Catholic dialogue. And the ghost of the Dutchman surely smiled broadly when Pope John XXIII created a Vatican department to promote Christian unity.

Desiderius Erasmus, scholar and wit, wanted an ecumenical movement instead of a tumult when Catholic and Protestant first paced their differences. He agonized as the fabric of Western Christianity tore in the sixteenth century; he hungered and thirsted for a peaceful, united church saying its prayers in humility, adoring God without superstition, and allowing diverse ideas to coexist.

His agony was not, however, that of an innocent caught between opposing forces. Erasmus agonized as a participant, a major intellectual combatant unsure as the Reformation dawned of where he stood, or could stand.

"I laid the egg that Luther hatched," he once said in a burst of poetic overstatement and, in truth, none of his day surpassed Erasmus as critic of the degenerate church Martin Luther set out to reform. He lampooned scholastic theology preoccupied with questions such as whether God could incarnate himself in a mule; lambasted priests who never said Mass and popes who sold tickets to heaven, and caustically observed that "if elephants can be trained to dance, lions to play, and leopards to hunt, surely preachers can be taught to preach."

But the chick out of the shell looked a monster of turmoil to Erasmus. He may have helped to produce it, but he would not step into schism, and, while criticizing Lutheran "excesses", he never stopped urging both sides to work for resolution: "Let us not devour each other like fish. . . . The world is full of rage, hate, and wars."

Erasmus agreed with many Reformation ideas. For example, he had little disagreement with Luther's insistence that a right relation with God (justification) proceeds from divine grace, not human works. What he disliked was violent arguments over doctrine. He considered it righteous for church and individuals to follow the example of Jesus, and he wanted dogmas—articles of required belief—kept to a minimum; after all, he said, Jesus used few words in summarizing his own doctrine when he said, "Love the Lord your God with your whole heart and your neighbor as yourself."

Simplicity was beyond the capacity of the sixteenth century, and Erasmus, the leading intellectual of his day, found himself embattled and embittered by the complexities. As he leaned away from the Reformation, the Protestants said, "traitor"; many Catholics, remembering his stinging criticism of the church, said, "shame." He died in religious limbo, technically a Roman Catholic, given sanctuary in Protestant Basel, Switzerland.

Erasmus was born in Rotterdam, or perhaps Gouda, in 1466, or 1469; he was indifferent to such details. From inauspicious beginnings he became a foremost Renaissance humanist. Renaissance humanism is a much misunderstood movement often assumed synonymous with secularity and the idea that "man is the measure of all things." Some humanists were pagan; not Erasmus and a group of colleagues best exemplifying "northern" humanism. One common mark of Renaissance humanists was a passion for antiquity, especially for classical (Greek and Roman) literature more or less forgotten during the Middle Ages. The use to which humanists put the classics varied, and in Erasmus, secular and religious interests coalesced.

Well versed in Greek and Latin literature, Erasmus, who made wise use of the movable type printing press, wrote popular satires spoofing his age through characters borrowed from the distant past. His most enduring popular book is *The Praise of Folly*, in which Dame Folly ridicules human ambiguities, then does a metamorphosis into the fool for Christ, saying, "Christ himself became a fool when he found in fashion as a man that he might bring healing by the foolishness of the cross. 'For God has chosen the foolish things of the world to confound the wise, and the weak things of the world to confound the mighty.'"

Erasmus' passion also covered Christian antiquity—the Scripture and writings of the Church Fathers. He believed a return to the sources of faith necessary to revitalize the church and reconstitute Christian society. His scholarly works included a text of the New Testament in the original Greek and new editions of the writings of such early theologians as Origen, Jerome, and Augustine.

The inauspicious beginnings mentioned were not incidental in starting Erasmus on the road to Christian humanism. The popular story of his advent is a high Renaissance romance, perhaps or perhaps not originally told by Erasmus, and immortalized in Charles Reade's novel *The Cloister and the Hearth*. According to this tale, his father, Roger Gerhard, loved Margaret, the daughter of a physician, and was living with her, planning marriage, when his family decided he should enter the priesthood. To escape the hounding, Gerhard fled to Rome, leaving Margaret pregnant; later, informed by his family that his beloved had died in childbirth, he sought priestly orders, but returned to Holland to find Margaret and child alive. True to his vow to the church, Gerhard nevertheless provided for his son—Erasmus. (The name Erasmus is Gerhard, "the beloved," in Greek; Desiderius is the same word in Latin.)

Despite its charm, the romance of Erasmus' birth does not accord with the facts; namely, the existence of an older brother, Peter, by the same Gerhard and Margaret. It seems most likely that his parents were simply a philandering priest and a receptive doctor's daughter.

Unable to raise their sons themselves, father and mother wished to find a good boarding school. Their choice was an institution at Deventer run by the Brethren of the Common Life, and this was good fortune to Erasmus.

The Brethren of the Common Life (wiped out by upheavals of the Reformation) began in Holland in the late fourteenth century to foster the mutual goals of spiritual meditation and social service, especially the education of children. It produced the otherwise unknown Thomas à Kempis, author of the *Imitation of Christ*. In Erasmus' day, some Brethren schools, including Deventer, were open to the concern for scholarship associated with the Renaissance. Erasmus and Peter spent about eight years at Deventer learning both the way of Christ-centered devotion and the classics. They could have stayed longer except that both parents died of plague. Gerhard's estate, left to the boys, was quite small.

Guardians named by Gerhard decided that the only future for two illegitimate orphans was in the monastery. They went to another Brethren school for two years. Peter then entered a monastery near Delft, and Erasmus went to an Augustinian house at Steyn where, still a teenager, he was ordained in 1492. Historians debate the motivation of the ordination: was it voluntary or forced? Whichever, it was a mistake. Erasmus had no vocation within a religious order; besides, he was physically frail, and his stomach would not tolerate fish.

Realizing that the bright child belonged elsewhere, his superior arranged for him to become secretary to the bishop of Cambrai, himself one of thirty-six illegitimate children sired by John of Bergen. Erasmus did not care for the work. He next showed up at the University of Paris enrolled in a school for indigents; he liked that less. Withdrawing from the university for a time, he reentered under different circumstances, paying his own way by working as a tutor. Among his first written works were manuals for his students.

In Paris Erasmus met William Blount, Britain's Lord Mountjoy, and in 1499 accompanied his friend to England. His career as a humanist flowered in England as he came to know such persons as Thomas More, for whom he would write *The Praise of Folly*, and John Colet, dean of Saint Paul's. He would return to England on later occasions, and he found his most receptive audience there.

Erasmus never really settled down to live in any one place. Between 1500 and the start of the Reformation in 1517 he was in France,

Holland, Italy, England, Switzerland, and Belgium, often living in a place while he worked with a printer on one of his numerous books. He wrote both for himself and on request. The "Dagger of the Christian Soldier" ("Enchiridion"), his most comprehensive statement of his religious faith, originated when one Mrs. Johann Poppenruyter asked him to write something to persuade her husband, an arms maker, to mend his moral ways.

His travels underscored Erasmus' conclusion that the church and the papacy had fallen on evil days. Italy, he said, was virtually pagan. Pope Julius II (1503–1513), more likely found on the battlefield than saying Mass, disgusted the peace-loving scholar. When Julius died, there appeared an anonymous, strongly Erasmanian manuscript describing an interview between Saint Peter and the late pontiff:

Peter: What did you do?
Julius: Revamped the finances, increased the revenue, annexed Bologna, beat Venice, harassed Ferrara, expelled the French, and would have expelled the Spaniards if I hadn't come up here. I killed some thousands of the French, broke treaties, celebrated gorgeous triumphs, built sumptuous edifices, and left 500,000 ducats in the treasury. . . . At Rome I was regarded as more a god than a man.
Peter: Well now, what is this rabble along with you?
Julius: Soldiers who died fighting for me. I promised them heaven if they did.
Peter: So these are the ones who tried to crash the gate a while ago?
Julius: And you didn't let them in?
Peter: I admit only those who clothe the naked, feed the hungry, give drink to the thirsty, visit the sick and those in prison . . .[2]

Most of Erasmus' books reflect a passion to purify the church of excessive legalism, paganism, and what historian Roland Bainton terms obscurantism, that is, the tendency to be deliberately vague and to oppose the enlightenment of the mind. Erasmus did not think reason can lead to God or knowledge produce salvation. "Only a few can be learned, but no one is prevented from becoming a Christian, no one is prevented from being devout," he said, adding that "no one is prevented from becoming a theologian," meaning that the mind is a gift of God to be used productively. He wanted the Church to open itself to God's gifts, to let the Holy Spirit carry away worldly pretensions and doubtful dogmas, and he wanted the Church to stop electing popes such as Julius II.

Because of this attitude, the Reformers expected Erasmus to endorse and adopt their cause. He did have an affinity with Luther, for example, "I highly approve of Luther when he calls us away from frail confidence in ourselves to the most safe harbor of trust in evangelical grace . . ." He withstood initial papal invitations to write against Luther ("I shall not write . . . to please the Pharisees," he said). As a counselor to the German Emperor Charles V, who represented Rome's case against Luther, he tried to mediate between the parties.

But as the Reformation unfolded Erasmus became nervous. He saw social chaos, even if Luther did not intend it and opposed radical change for its own sake. "The Lutherans are worse than Luther," quipped Erasmus. The humanist finally challenged Luther on a single theological point—the freedom of the will. The debate continued for years in print with both men misunderstanding the other, and continues still: Is the human will free or totally directed by the omnipotent God?

Of all the places he had lived, Erasmus liked Basel best, and to Switzerland he returned to die although the city was under the Protestant flag. His body hurt; his dream of a golden age for the church was dashed. Bitter at times, resolute at others, he left the whole church a great deal to ponder. He wrote in a paraphrase of Psalm 86:

"[God] invited all to the wedding and desires His house to be filled. They come from the shades of ignorance to the light of the gospel, to the worship of the true God, to a life of holiness, to the home of Him who invited them, that is to the Church. Here they are reborn in sacred laver.[3]

Elizabeth Gurney Fry (1780–1845)

London's "greatest curiosity" in the 1820s, wrote John Randolph of Roanoke, the United States congressman, was not the Tower, Westminster Abbey, or the British Museum; the most interesting sight was Elizabeth Gurney Fry. "I have seen . . . Elizabeth Fry in Newgate," he said, "and I have witnessed there . . . miraculous effects of true Christianity."

Newgate was the infamous prison; Elizabeth Fry was a Quaker who had taken it upon herself to bring the love of Christ and righteousness of God to the women inmates and, as long as she was about on a Gospel errand, she reformed the British prison system. And that was only one small part of her response to a hunger and thirst for righteousness, taking as one of her texts Psalm 27:13: "I believe that I shall see the goodness of the Lord in the land of the living."

How Elizabeth Fry did what she did in one lifetime is a mystery best explained by Evelyn Underhill (see page 192) who said of her, "She found in the silence that mysterious power which loves the unlovely into lovableness." She went in search of persons in whom to invest her love, her time, and her means, and she found so many: the sick and dying, women oppressed by centuries of male-imposed social rules, and prisoners—women prisoners hidden in holes behind the facade of proper eighteenth- and nineteenth-century British society.

Not that she did not have anyone to care for at home. Elizabeth Fry and her husband, a London merchant, had eleven children.

She was born in 1780 into the fine and fashionable Gurney family of Earlham Hall, Norwich. Nominally Quaker, she and her brothers and sisters thought the Friends dull and old-fashioned and their silent meetings disgusting. Young Elizabeth enjoyed a colorful and frivolous life until her seventeenth year, when the meaning of the Quaker way was brought home to her by a visiting American preacher. A "plain friend," a young woman in Norwich, also had a religious influence on her. After an evening with Deborah Darby, Elizabeth wrote in her diary, "My heart felt really light and as I walked home by starlight, I looked through nature up to nature's God." She did not know, she said, "what the mountain is I have to climb; I am to be a Quaker." In 1800, she married, moved to London, and in small ways began her remarkable career.

As a young mother she strolled the streets looking for persons in need, offering sometimes medicine, or clothing, or encouragement, and always a Bible. Soon her eyes fell upon notorious Newgate. Socially well placed, she went to the prison governor: "Sir, if thee kindly allows me to pray with the women, I will go inside." Inside she went, into a world no Earlham Hall girl could have imagined.

She found three hundred women prisoners and their children trying to exist in four rooms with no beds, no activities, and only one adult attendant. The inmates seemed to her more like wild beasts than people. What was she to do, in addition to praying? Her first task was to convince the women she came not in judgment but in friendship.

Elizabeth Fry and a group of Quaker associates in 1816 founded the Association for the Improvement of the Female Prisoners in Newgate, and with it a sweeping prison reform movement that would touch most of Europe, America, and Australia. The original goals were modest: to provide the women with clothing, prison employment, and instruction, notably instruction in Scripture. Mrs. Fry personally assumed responsibility for the latter.

In her Newgate classes, the woman who was the greatest curiosity in London introduced the prisoners to a sense of their dignity as human beings created in God's image and to an awareness of God's love for every person regardless of station or crime. She would read the "Suffering Servant" passages in Isaiah, such as: "All we like sheep have gone astray: we have everyone turned to his own way; and the Lord hath laid on him the iniquity of us all" (Isaiah 53:6), and the "him," the servant, she interpreted as Jesus Christ. Mrs. Fry read and taught Psalms in which the writer praises God in times of affliction and New Testament parables pointing to the abundance of God's grace.

Whether the women in Newgate responded to Elizabeth Fry's evangelism or were simply anxious to learn to read cannot be known for certain, but they pressed about her and asked for more of what she brought to them. Perhaps they did, as one biographer says, "begin to understand that courage, holiness, justice and strength are from God."[4]

Within a few years, Mrs. Fry persuaded British authorities to hire a woman matron for Newgate, to provide prison jobs and craft programs, and to view imprisonment as rehabilitation as much as punishment. The Newgate reform underway, she insisted that the government build homes in Australia to receive woman shipped out to that penal colony. And she ranged over England, Scotland, and Ireland visiting other prisons and asylums. France invited her to consult with its prison officials on reform measures. She went to Switzerland, Germany, Belgium, Holland, and Denmark to push for better facilities and more humane treatment of prisoners.

If prisoners were her concern, so were "free" persons locked into poverty and the grip of disease. She raised the money to set up shelters for the destitute who might freeze on cold London nights; she established the Nursing Sisters of Devonshire Square to train hospital personnel. She found jobs for the unemployed and opened an orphanage.

Elizabeth Fry based her activism in part on England's claim in her day to status as a "Christian kingdom"—officially Christian. If Christian, a nation must act Christian, promote social righteousness, she reasoned. But in all her activity, she never forgot that God is the source of righteousness. Her trust in God was as plain as it was profound. "O Lord," she prayed, "may I be directed what to do and what to leave undone; and then may I humbly trust that a blessing will be with me in my various engagements."

When Elizabeth Fry began her public ministry—and she was a Quaker minister—she was a wealthy woman; her husband, Joseph, was a successful merchant who provided two splendid homes for his family. The money and the social position it afforded assisted her in launching the crusade for prison reform. Later, long before her death in 1845, her husband's business failed; the fine houses were sold, and they settled into a modest cottage. The change of status was fine with Mrs. Fry: luxuries, she told her children, were dangers to the spirit better to be avoided.

She cared not a whit for the honors heaped on her in old age, and if kings and princes came to Newgate to see the great "curiosity" they knelt to pray when she and the women inmates knelt.

On her deathbed Elizabeth Fry reflected on a life spent in the quest for inward and outward righteousness:

I can say one thing—since my heart was touched at seventeen years old I believe I never have awakened from sleep, in sickness or in health, by day or night, without my first waking thought being how best I might serve my Lord.

Charles G. Finney (1792–1875)

Boston's Marborough Motel had a different feel in the autumn of 1843. Guests came and went, but the place was more like a church than an inn; indeed, its public hall was a church of sorts, temporarily —Marborough Chapel. Charles Grandison Finney was holding a revival and needed the largest space around.

Not all Bostonians were happy about Finney's presence. Old-guard Protestant divines distrusted the methods and message of the fiery preacher. Unitarians, then in their New England flowering, had a distaste for his zealous, often successful efforts to convert them. But few people could ignore Finney—in Boston or wherever he was. He was an event, a grandstand religious attraction.

Thousands of persons came to Christianity at his revivals, which could last weeks, even months, in the same city. (He spent more than a year in Philadelphia.) Finney preached personal faith in response to soul-saving grace, but unlike some of the great revivalists of more recent times he did not hesitate to attack social ills. His condemnation of slavery was no less forceful than his crusade against sinful hearts.

Persuasive of tongue, audacious in demand, Finney had a gnawing hunger and an unquenchable thirst for humanity's right relationship with God. He hungered for persons to experience the joy of salvation, thirsted for the psychological and social "reformation of mankind." And he wanted the church to be alive and wide awake in the world. "The natural and habitual state of the church has always been that of sleep," he said.

Charles G. Finney was a product of the "Second Great Awakening," a spreading revival that began in Kentucky around 1800. The emotional fervor that went with the awakening was slowest in reaching the Northeast, partly because religious leaders there discouraged enthusiasm threatening the orderliness of the Episcopalians and the staid ways of the Presbyterians and Congregationalists. (Those three groups dominated American religion in the early decades.) Finney brought the "Great Awakening" to the cities of the Northeast with more force than any before him.

He was born in Warren, Connecticut, in 1792, grew up in small towns in western New York, went to school in his native state, and became an apprentice in a law firm in Adams (Jefferson County), New York. Finney's family was not in the least religious. In Adams the promising barrister agreed to direct the choir at the Presbyterian Church, although he had no persuasion to faith. "When I went to Adams . . . I was almost as ignorant of religion as a heathen," he later said. He often did not understand the Sunday sermons, and when he did understand he disagreed.

Involvement in the church plus his study of Mosaic law had their effect. Finney's mind came to focus on the question of salvation. He bought a Bible; he read it. One October day in 1821 he decided to put his work aside and come to grips with his soul. Salvation, he concluded, was not so difficult *if* he could consent to give up his sins and accept Christ. He prayed in the woods, felt the overwhelming presence of Christ, but did not feel converted as he returned to his office.

That night Finney was gripped by what he took to be the Holy Spirit: "I wept aloud with joy and love . . . I literally bellowed out the unutterable gushings of my heart." The next morning a church deacon whose case he had agreed to argue in court came to the office.

"Deacon," he said, "I have a retainer from the Lord Jesus Christ to plead his cause and I cannot plead yours."

Finney gave up the law, studied theology with the local pastor, and began preaching in the towns of upstate New York. His public appeal was electric. The Presbyterians in the area reluctantly ordained him in 1824. Presbyterian reluctance to own Finney continued for the remainder of his life, and in the 1830s he moved to the Congregationalists. He was suspect on two major grounds. First, his methods of evangelism seemed extreme. Finney in his early days resorted to theatrics, such as pretending to shoot a gospel arrow into the sinful heart of a hearer. Second, he did not accept the idea of total human depravity, a tenet important in Presbyterian belief that God has elected only certain persons for salvation. Finney was more inclined to free will as a chief factor in election; in other words, accept God's offer of salvation and election takes place.

Preaching judgment and grace, Finney "captured" town after town of upstate New York for righteousness. His reputation spread. In 1827 he was off to Wilmington, Delaware, then Philadelphia and New York City. A proposal that he preach in Boston in the early 1830s was stoutly opposed by the established clergy of the Bay area. Lyman Beecher, a prominent Boston minister and himself an evangelist, but not of Finney's ilk, threatened to meet Finney at the state line with the militia. (Sensing fate, Beecher finally extended the invitation to Finney.)

Finney had married in 1824 (the first of three marriages—two wives died), and New York City was home for a few years. In 1835 he accepted a professorship at Oberlin, a newly formed seminary in Ohio, on the condition that the school observe no color line. His pattern thereafter was to divide his time between Oberlin (serving as president from 1851 to 1866) and his revival work. Before leaving New York he had pastored a Congregational church, and would do the same in Ohio.

Oberlin was in large part the creation of abolitionists, and Finney was quite at home. The revivalist never minced words in opposing slavery. Christian support for the enslavement of other human beings agonized him. "One of the reasons for the low state of religion at the present time," he said, "is that many churches have taken the wrong side on the subject of slavery, have suffered prejudice to prevail over principle, and have feared to call this abomination by its true name." He considered it scandalous in general that Christians and their churches left social reform to secular institutions and nonreligious people. To him, having Christ in the heart automatically meant doing good works with the hands, and he saw Abolition and other efforts to uplift the downtrodden as very good works.

His revivals took Finney to England in 1849 and 1851. He converted Rochester (New York) in 1855–56. As he grew older, his theatrics declined, but his persuasiveness did not, though he was less on what would later be called "the sawdust trail" as Oberlin claimed his attention.

Charles Finney practiced direct communication with God, and his familiarity with the Divine had its humorous side. At a revival in Ohio in 1853 he decided to take up with God the matter of local drought. He prayed:

We want rain. We do not propose to dictate unto thee, but our pastures are dry, and the earth is gaping open for rain. The cattle are wandering about and lowing in search of water. Even the little squirrels in the woods are suffering from thirst. Unless thou givest us rain, our cattle will die and our harvests will come to naught. O Lord, send us rain, and send it now! Although to us there is no sign of it, it is an easy thing for thee to do. *Send it now*, for Christ's sake. Amen.

According to the story, the drops started as Finney preached. He stopped and led the congregation in a hymn of praise.

Finney firmly believed the righteous God fills the hungry with good things and sends the rain.

Gilbert Keith Chesterton (1874–1936)
Frances Blogg Chesterton (18??–1938)

G. K. Chesterton in 1894 knew people who proclaimed religion, analyzed, and argued it; Frances Blogg he found astoundingly different. She "practiced a religion" much as she practiced gardening, he later said, and "that anyone could regard religion as a practical thing" was entirely new to the aspiring British writer.

He was the more astounded that the young woman practicing the truths of Christianity was the product (as was he) of "fussy" middle-class Victorian culture. Miss Blogg, he said, was neither influenced by her surroundings nor beholden to any poet or philosopher. She loved literature, especially Robert Louis Stevenson, "but if Stevenson had walked into the room and explained his doubts about personal immortality, she would have regretted that he should be wrong upon the point; but would otherwise have been utterly unaffected."[5]

Chesterton wisely fell in love with the imperturbable Frances Blogg, and wisely married her in 1901—wisely for the history of romance, and for two other reasons. First, she had a positive influence on his development as a major twentieth-century voice for Christianity. Second, while she did not inspire his vast literary output across the next thirty-five years, she mobilized and organized his genius. Slow to decision, he was forced to resign as an underpaid book editor and strike out on his own as a writer to earn enough to afford marriage. Once his career was in motion, "G.K.C.," as he is known, had to be managed emotionally and financially. Frances did it.

Although a victim of arthritis of the spine and perhaps sexually distant (she could not bear children, to both their disappointment), Frances Chesterton's love provided the domestic stability and coddling her husband needed. Of necessity, she managed the money, ran the household, read proof (until a professional assistant was hired a decade before G.K.C. died), and acted as a visible anchor to her rotund mate, whose ego was as big as his girth. Once at a picnic, Chesterton asked Frances' whereabouts. "Do you want her?" asked a friend. "I don't want her now but I may want her at any minute," he replied.

Frances also introduced Chesterton to the practice of Christianity within the church, in contrast to personal analysis of and public argument about religion, the expressions of faith he already knew. G.K.C. was a convinced Christian when he was introduced to his future wife. He had come to orthodox faith along a personal path marked by apparent contradictions.

An agnostic around age sixteen, Chesterton underwent a dark night of the soul—a "meaningless fit of depression"—in his late teens. He emerged with both a keen awareness of the reality of evil and an exuberance for life. "Are we all dust? What a beautiful thing dust is," he wrote to a friend. He came to doubt the doubters—the sophisticated skeptics peopling the political and literary circles he frequented. Orthodox Christianity symbolized in the Apostles' Creed became his truth; *the* truth. He would write, "Orthodoxy makes us jump by the sudden brink of hell; it is only afterwards that we realise that jumping was an athletic exercise highly beneficial to our health."[6] His own experience influenced his use of paradox in his writing.

Frances, then a member of the Church of England and Anglo-Catholic in persuasion, showed Chesterton the historic community of faith. G.K.C.'s early books meant less to Frances than the day in 1905 when he mounted the pulpit in Saint Paul's, Covent Garden, to preach to the Christian Social Union. Chesterton quickly realized the importance of the church in the Christian experience. "A man can no more possess a private religion than he can possess a private sun and moon," he wrote in the preface to an edition of the Book of Job.

Chesterton entered the Roman Catholic church in 1922 and Frances, somewhat reluctantly, followed four years later. He had long contemplated the move, which for him was undoubtedly correct. Published in 1908, *Orthodoxy*, his major statement of beliefs, presents a man most spiritually at home in a Catholic context. His religious language was not that of the heart or of individualism (though he was certainly an individualist), but of the mind imbued with the objective truth represented, to him, in the Catholic tradition. Within the parameters of historically accepted teachings, he found liberty and joy. The international character of the Roman Catholic church also appealed to him.

His decision to become Catholic may also have been indirectly influenced by the fact that his two closest friends, writers Hilaire Belloc and Maurice Baring were members of that church, Belloc a born Catholic and Baring a former Protestant—though this is conjecture since neither man encouraged G.K.C. to convert, and Belloc actively discouraged it. More to the point was his brother Cecil's entry into Catholicism about 1912.

Gilbert K. and Cecil Chesterton argued constantly but loved each other passionately. In the first decade of this century both were involved in liberal-to-radical politics and letters in London. By 1912 Cecil, the younger, had his own publication, *New Witness*, and launched what Americans could call a "muckracking" crusade against corruption in the ruling Liberal Party. He went too far, was charged with libel, and lost the case in Old Bailey. Fined but not imprisoned, Cecil continued *New Witness*, turning it over to G.K.C. when he joined the army during World War I. Cecil Chesterton died in France in 1917; his brother was devastated, and vowed to keep the publication alive—at considerable cost to his health and pocketbook—as a memorial to Cecil. It is quite conceivable that Cecil's affinity for the Catholic church had both conscious and subconscious impact on his older brother.

Born and educated in London, G.K.C. aspired to be an artist but abandoned the smock, for which he was ill fitted, for the pen. He had published little when he met Frances Blogg. By the start of World War I he was a leading British writer, of the same literary generation as H. G. Wells, George Orwell, and George Bernard Shaw, the latter a close friend with whom he conducted a running public debate, chiefly on religion.

Chesterton is still read today, but his name is not as widely known as those of Wells and Shaw, partly because his forte was journalism, which dates easily, though he wrote poetry, biography, and fiction (including the "Father Brown" detective series). Also, Shaw's religious humanism and Wells's social idealism were more in vogue than G.K.C.'s Christian orthodoxy following World War I. Further, Chesterton was seized upon late in his life and after his death by a group of Roman Catholic writers who squeezed much of the life out of him for sectarian purposes, instead of sharing his essential Christianity with the world.

G.K.C. belongs to the whole of the church because, Anglican or Catholic, he understood that decadent Western civilization can only be saved from greater decadence by encounter with the paradoxes of Christianity, "the wild truth reeling but erect."

"One must somehow find a way of loving the world without being worldly," he said. That to Chesterton, and in her practical, garden-variety way, to Frances, was righteousness. He hungered and thirsted for Christians to realize that what is required to be of God and to live lovingly is ready at hand—at least he found it so.

Chesterton compared his own discovery of ageless truth to a yachtsman "who slightly miscalculated his course and discovered England under the impression that it was a new island in the South Seas," and thinking it a pagan temple, planted the Union Jack on the pavilion at Brighton. In the pursuit of the obvious, he said, he tried to found a heresy of his own, "and when I had put the last touches to it, I discovered that it was orthodoxy."

The Chestertons did not always have an easy life (though tales of serious sexual incompatibility told by his sister-in-law are discounted by informed biographers). G.K.C. often drank too much and worked too hard, even after Frances moved him to a country place. He collapsed mentally and physically in 1914, lying in semi-coma from Christmas until the following Easter. A new paper launched when *New Witness* folded in 1922 was a constant financial drain. Frances collapsed in Chattanooga, Tennessee, during her husband's 1930–31 speaking tour in America. Chesterton disturbed people in the 1930s by seeming to go soft on Mussolini (G.K.C. did not approve of Fascism); he sometimes sounded unsympathetic to Jews, though he said all Christians should be Zionists.

Chesterton said he always liked to know where he was going; he did not always know. He was one of God's paradoxes.

He died in 1936 at his home outside London; Frances practiced gardening for two more summers before she followed him.

Dietrich Bonhoeffer (1906–1945)

Berlin, July 27, 1945: Dr. and Mrs. Karl Bonhoeffer switched on the radio for the nightly broadcast of the BBC. A service of worship from London's Holy Trinity Church was in progress. The hymn "For All the Saints" with its line, "we feebly struggle, they in glory shine," was heard, then the voice of the German translator: "We are gathered here in the presence of God to make thankful remembrance of the life and work of his servant Dietrich Bonhoeffer, who gave his life . . ."

The aging couple had suspected the worst; they now knew what other members of their scattered family had already learned. The son for whom they had waited since Germany surrendered to the Allies on May 7 was not coming home. That made two sons and two sons-in-law killed by the Gestapo. Pastor Dietrich Bonhoeffer, a rising Lutheran theologian, had been hanged April 9 at the Flossenbürg concentration camp.

In London the service continued with a eulogy by Anglican Bishop G. K. A. Bell of Chichester. Bonhoeffer in life and death, said the bishop, marked the "deepest value" in the witness of the "Confessing Church," that part of German Protestantism refusing to cooperate with Nazism. He was called a martyr, resisting in God's name the assault of evil, and revolting in human conscience against injustice. Bishop Bell saw hope for the world if God pleased in the future to lead church and nations through brave persons such as Bonhoeffer.

As a remembrance of Bonhoeffer's life the memorial service was fitting; as a farewell it was premature. The martyr's thirty-nine years were only the first chapter of his work. Unexpected by anyone in 1945 was the impact he would have on the modern church and theology through his writings, letters, and papers scribbled during a two-year imprisonment and then unpublished books written before his arrest in 1943. Abused as well as used creatively, Bonhoeffer's writings were in the theological avant-garde in the 1960s, and today are staples read by seminarians of every church. His significance rests mainly in the questions his works pose about the relationship of God and humanity, faith and everyday reality. Bonhoeffer lived in the worst of times politically and spiritually, but his basic question also would apply to the best of times; that is, "How can we live the Christian life in the modern world?"

He asked that question in *The Cost of Discipleship*, a book-length meditation on the Sermon on the Mount begun in the early 1930s, when he was pastor of two small Lutheran congregations in London, and finished later that decade when he was director of a clandestine "Confessing Church" seminary near the Baltic Sea. In this book, his only published work at his death, Bonhoeffer made a distinction between "cheap" and "costly" grace, the first being the church preaching forgiveness without repentance, the cross, and the living Christ; the second giving rise to Christian discipleship that could cost a believer his or her life.

Bonhoeffer chose to respond in faith to costly grace, and the course he took is illumined by his understanding of the Beatitude on hunger and thirst for righteousness. He wrote of the Fifth Beatitude in *The Cost of Discipleship*, "Not only do followers of Jesus renounce their rights, they *renounce their own righteousness* too. They get no praise for their achievements or sacrifices. They cannot have righteousness except by hungering and thirsting for it . . . but they cannot establish it themselves."[7]

Renunciation of righteousness in the pursuit of a righteousness one cannot establish has the making of paradox—the paradox of righteousness—and so was Dietrich Bonhoeffer's life a paradox, particularly in relation to the reason for his martyrdom. Never fooled by Hitler, Bonhoeffer began the Nazi period as a pacifist. He along with many other German Christians resisted passively, but as time passed he came to believe active resistance was necessary to remove Hitler. Together with several members of his family he joined a plot, planned inside the *Abwehr* (German Military Intelligence Department), to assassinate Hitler; the conspiracy was discovered.

Was Bonhoeffer's decision to help foster a plot against Hitler a part of the history of righteousness or an act of political resistance? Bishop Bell in his July 27, 1945, eulogy called Bonhoeffer a Christian martyr for both his religious and his political resistance. The postwar church in Germany was less sure at first that hanging for political resistance constitutes Christian martyrdom. Today, Bonhoeffer is almost universally honored as a saint and martyr, and his own theology provides a rationale for such recognition.

Christian ethics, according to Bonhoeffer, emerge from the cross of Christ rather than from human wisdom; people do not make themselves righteous even when they hunger and thirst for it; people do not work up to being God, but because of the Incarnation and cross persons can be persons ("man can be man"), taking responsibility for their maturity. As a Christian man renouncing rights, reward, and righteousness, Bonhoeffer made the conscious decision to adopt a violent course in the assault on evil.

"In the almost fifty years that I worked as a doctor, I have hardly ever seen a man die so entirely submissive to the will of God," said the prison physician who saw Dietrich Bonhoeffer hanged.

This remarkably devout theologian was born in Breslau in 1906. He and his twin sister, Sabine, were the seventh and eighth children of Karl and Paula Bonhoeffer; the family was financially well off, his father being a psychiatrist and neurologist who from 1912 headed the University Hospital in Berlin. Dietrich announced his intention to become a theologian at an early age, and told by his brothers and sisters that the church was a "poor, feeble, boring, petty bourgeois institution" gave a pure Lutheran reply, "I shall reform it."

He studied at the University of Tübingen, electing to write his dissertation on the nature of the church, a theme to which he would return frequently; Christianity to Bonhoeffer was not a matter of free-lance spirituality. Licensed in theology, he spent a year (1928–29) as a Lutheran curate in Barcelona, Spain, and the 1930–31 academic year was devoted to postgraduate work at Union Theological Seminary in the City of New York. Bonhoeffer was deeply moved by the religious vitality of the black churches of Harlem.

Back in Germany he joined the faculty at Berlin University and was ordained in 1931. As Nazism engulfed his homeland in the early 1930s he took part in the formation of the "Confessing Church," and won the animosity of Nazi officials for his criticism of Hitler's Aryan policy. (His sister Sabine had married a Jew.)

When it became expedient that he leave Germany, Bonhoeffer pastored Lutheran congregations in London for eighteen months, but he did not want to continue apart from the "Confessing Church," and he would make a similar decision in 1939 when, briefly in New York, he declined a teaching post in America. For almost five years he was involved in a clandestine Preachers' Seminary first operating at centers in Zingthof and later Finkenwalde, and finally decentralized in an attempt to escape detection. Twenty-seven students were arrested in 1937, and the program was impossible to continue after March, 1940. Out of the seminary experience Bonhoeffer wrote what may be his most practical book, *Life Together*, a study on Christian community.

Bonhoeffer had been denied the right to lecture at Berlin University in 1936; in 1940 he was forbidden to speak in public. Having no work, he faced the possibility of being drafted into military service; somehow, despite his record as a subversive, friends managed to have him named to the *Abwehr*, the locus of the conspiracy against Hitler. Bonhoeffer had been in touch with the conspirators since 1938. The military intelligence agency was able to pursue its plot because the nature of its work provided a shield of secrecy difficult for the Gestapo to pierce.

As an *Abwehr* agent, Bonhoeffer was occasionally able to leave Germany, and it was he who acted as courier in delicate but unsuccessful overtures to the British government. The conspirators wanted the Allies to stop the war at the moment Hitler was killed, thereby saving Germany from total destruction. Bonhoeffer conveyed the plan to Bishop Bell, whom he met in Sweden, and the Anglican prelate, the last in British history to have the slightest political influence, transmitted it to the Foreign Office. The Allies said "no"; they had set a course for the total defeat and surrender of Germany. The plotters pushed ahead, but the Gestapo was pushing the *Abwehr*, which had become suspect; an outline of conspiracy was discovered. On April 5, 1943, Bonhoeffer, two brothers-in-law, and two sisters were arrested (the sisters were later released).

The eighteen months Bonhoeffer spent in Berlin's Tegel Prison were consumed with protecting others in the conspiracy and in writing a never completed book on *Ethics* and many letters and incidental papers published as *Letters and Papers from Prison*. He remained in touch with his family during that period. The attempt on Hitler's life in July, 1944, failed. Documents found in the ensuing investigation implicated Bonhoeffer as a primary conspirator. In October, 1944, he was moved to the basement of the Gestapo prison in Prinz Albrecht Strasse and there weathered the Allied bombing of Berlin.

In early 1945, the Russian army was advancing in East Prussia

Nazi Germany was falling; Hitler refused to recognize it. Heinrich Himmler was plotting against the Führer. Bonhoeffer, still considered a dangerous threat to the state, was transferred in February to the Buchenwald concentration camp, on April 3 to Regensburg, April 6 to Schönberg, and April 8 to Flössenburg. Subject to military law as an *Abwehr* agent, he and five colleagues were court-martialed following an all-night "trial" in a laundry house.

The next morning the men were executed near the bottom of a flight of steps still visible at the deteriorating camp, symbol of the devil's own game.

The Bonhoeffer family had no idea what had happened to Dietrich as the war ended. They knew his brother Klaus had been executed in Berlin on April 23. Maria von Wedemeyer-Weller, a young woman to whom Bonhoeffer had become engaged in January, 1943, traversed Germany looking for him. Fellow prisoners took the news of his death to Switzerland to the offices of what in 1948 would become the World Council of Churches; from there it reached England, and finally Berlin.

In prison Dietrich Bonhoeffer wrote: "The immanent righteousness of history only rewards and punishes the deeds of men, the eternal righteousness of God tries and judges their hearts."[8]

Martin Luther King, Jr. (1929–1968)

History has coincidences too wholesome to be coincidental: the Dexter Avenue Baptist Church in Montgomery is a stone's throw from the spot where the Southern Confederacy was born, and from that church next door to the Alabama Capitol came the man to lead the United States in a giant step toward racial justice.

But to identify Martin Luther King, Jr. only as "civil rights leader," as is commonly done, is to miss the meaning of the man; to trace his philosophy of nonviolent social change only to Monhandas K. Gandhi, or his passion for justice to African religion, is to ignore reality. He was first and always in his remarkable career a Christian pastor and theologian, schooled by black Christianity and the color-blind theology grown from the Bible.

King was of the church, pained when white Christians failed to hear the "deep groans and passionate yearnings" of oppressed black people, but ever *of* the church. "I have been disappointed with the church," he wrote from a jail cell in Birmingham. "I do not say that as one of those negative critics who can always find something wrong with the church. I say it as a minister of the gospel, who loves the church; who was nurtured in its bosom; who has been sustained by its spiritual blessings and who will remain true to it as long as the cord of life shall lengthen."[9]

He called himself a "drum major" for righteousness, and his hunger and thirst for right human relations, for justice, was fed by faith in a God of righteousness. Martin King was possessed by the dream of American democracy; he wanted his country to fulfill the promises of the Declaration of Independence and the Constitution yet he was more than a true patriot. He wanted humanity to cleave to a moral law higher and fairer than any legislation; his greatest dream was for the community of love at the foot of the cross. "Jesus made love the mark of sovereignty," he said.

"Martin Luther King was thrust into leadership under the most unpropitious circumstances possible,"[10] says sociologist C. Eric Lincoln. Montgomery, Alabama, "cradle of the Confederacy," was not in 1954 the ideal place to commence a crusade against decades of Jim Crow treatment of black Americans, and King was new in town, just married, and by objective standards an unlikely candidate to lead the crusade.

He had grown up in Atlanta's segregated but substantial black middle class—"black puritanism," Lincoln calls it. He graduated from Atlanta's black middle-class Morehouse College, then went North to Crozier Theological Seminary, a Baptist school then in Chester, Pennsylvania, and on to Boston where he met his wife, Coretta Scott, a voice student from Alabama. In 1953 he received a Ph.D. in theology from Boston University. He was well read in the thinking of Hegel, Thoreau, Tillich, and indeed Gandhi; an intellectual, he knew that neither he nor his people could continue to bear the yoke of segregation, but he did not arrive at Dexter Avenue Church with a liberator's standard.

King was, as Lincoln says, "thrust" into leadership; he did not personally trigger the modern American civil rights struggle. The trigger was the arrest of a seamstress, Mrs. Rosa Parks, for refusing to move so a driver could enlarge the white seating area on a segregated public bus. This brought festering black grievances to a head in Montgomery. Black leaders formed an Improvement Association and elected King president. It became his job to motivate, organize, and protect black citizens pledged to boycott segregated buses. A successful year-long boycott made him a national figure, eloquent of tongue and unyielding for right despite bombs and the seething hate of white racists who threatened him and his young family (the Kings had four children at the time of his death).

To continue and expand the momentum begun by Mrs. Parks's defiance of segregation laws, King in 1957 founded the Southern Christian Leadership Conference (SCLC), with its headquarters in Atlanta. In 1960 he returned to his hometown to oversee SCLC and to serve as copastor with his father at the Ebenezer Baptist Church. SCLC was not the only new civil rights organization in the making in the late 1950s, but it was to become the most effective, in large measure because it found its strength in the black churches and because it insisted on the total nonviolence of protesters.

King was well aware of the social tension created by nonviolent protesters singing and praying outside a city hall; he intended the tension as a means of opening interracial negotiations for social change. From the Birmingham jail he wrote: "Non-violent direct action seeks to create such a crisis and establish such creative tension that a community that has consistently refused to negotiate is forced to confront the issue. . . . This may sound rather shocking. But I must confess that I am not afraid of the word 'tension.' I have earnestly worked and preached against violent tension, but there is a type of constructive non-violence that is necessary for growth."[11]

SCLC did not initiate the nonviolent student sit-in demonstrations that swept the South in the early 1960s, but King welcomed them and joined in (often going to jail for his involvement). He had targeted all segregation laws for abolition. Segregated buses, public facilities, schools, entertainment, and drinking fountains had to go. He was determined that no longer would black parents find their tongues twisted in trying to explain to a six-year-old "why she can't go to the public amusement park that has just been advertised on television, and see tears welling up in her little eyes when she is told that Funtown is closed to colored children, and see the depressing clouds of inferiority begin to form in her little mental sky, and see her begin to distort her little personality by unconsciously developing a bitterness toward white people."

"Love thy neighbor" was an interracial commandment to King; hatred of white racists could never be in his message: "pray for those who abuse you," Jesus said.

A King-led black improvement movement in Albany, Georgia was less successful than the Montgomery boycott. Federal legislation, he saw, was necessary to overcome state segregation provisions; the road to Washington—to a massive march in 1963—went through Birmingham.

Birmingham, Alabama, in 1979 elected a black mayor; in 1963 it was, in King's words, "the most segregated city in America." A relatively young city of heavy industry, Birmingham was a companies' town with few major institutions of higher education and a small black middle class. Jim Crow lived the good life there; anyone who suggested the equality of the races had to be prepared to run. The local SCLC invited King to Birmingham; he went, and would not run. Firehoses and police dogs were turned on the nonviolent demonstrators; King was arrested, and in his cell wrote the most memorable document of the civil rights movement, "Letter from Birmingham Jail" in reply to eight area clergymen (including four bishops, three Protestant and one Catholic) who had criticized the demonstrations as "unwise and untimely." In his letter King set forth his rationale for violating the unjust laws of segregation. "A just law," he said, "is a man-made code that squares with the moral law or the law of God. An unjust law is a code that is out of harmony with the moral law."[12] To support his reasoning he could quote both Saint Augustine and Thomas Aquinas.

Events in Birmingham and the 1963 March on Washington, were the prelude to the 1964 Civil Rights Act outlawing discrimination in voting, public accommodations and facilities, public education, publicly assisted programs, and employment. In late 1964 King went to Norway to receive the Nobel Peace Prize.

The riots in urban black ghettos and new student militants in the mid-1960s challenged King's nonviolent philosophy. SCLC held firm. King did not think nonviolence was a panacea for social ills, but as he said in his Nobel lecture, humanity suffers from three interrelated forms of "ethical infantilism"—racial injustice, poverty, and war —and he could never adopt the tactics of one form—war—to achieve the elimination of injustice.

Urban upheavals combined with King's growing awareness of poverty's role in racial oppression turned SCLC increasingly toward the plight of black Americans in Northern cities. Chicago was the first place outside the South where King engaged in systematic demonstrations (Washington, D.C. is part of the South). His attention in early 1965 was again in Alabama—in Selma, organizing a march to Montgomery to protest continuing state barriers to voter registration.

Selma was both a low and a high point for the civil rights movement of the 1960s; preparation was skimpy, the crowd of marchers large and philosophically diverse. It rose to the high point partly because of virulent opposition. Attempted marches were blocked, clubs flew, and martyrs fell to sniper fire along the highways. Selma became the Mecca of social righteousness in March, 1965, as clergy and laity rallied to a sweeping cause boosted nationally by the antagonism of Alabama Governor George Wallace, and by King's ability to whet in others an appetite for righteousness. The nation was as aroused over civil rights as it would ever become in the 1960s. Postponed by legal suits, the march was finally cleared by a federal judge, and President Lyndon Johnson provided guards.

On March 25, the vanguard of the Selma-to-Montgomery march approached the "cradle of the Confederacy" singing, "Mine eyes have seen the glory of the coming of the Lord."

The Lord had not come, but a new Voting Rights Act was passed in Washington.

King lent his persuasive voice to the anti–Vietnam war movement in 1967, and the next year was engaged in planning a massive nonviolent action in Washington on behalf of all the nation's poor. He took time out in the spring to go to Memphis where the SCLC chapter was supporting a strike of sanitation workers. On April 3, he spoke in Memphis: "Like anybody, I would like to live a long life; longevity has its grace. But I'm not concerned about that now. I just want to do God's will. And he's allowed me to go up to the mountain. And I've looked over, and I've seen the promised land."

An old cotton wagon pulled by two mules bore the coffin of Martin Luther King through the streets of Atlanta on April 9. The day after the speech, he was shot to death as he stood on a Memphis motel balcony.

Russian poet Yevgeny Yevtushenko, visiting in Mexico on April 4, 1968, wrote:

> When I received this news
> that same bullet entered me.
> That bullet killed him,
> but by that bullet I was reborn,
> and I was reborn a Negro. [13]

CHAPTER V

Going Beyond Justice

"Holy are the merciful . . ."

"SHOWERS OF BLESSING" and "pennies from heaven" are hardly the same things, but people wish they were—divine grace in tangible form. Though who today wants pennies? Janis Joplin came closer to it in her song titled, "O Lord, won't you buy me a Mercedes Benz."

Comedy, sometimes pathos, likes to toy with the idea of the good things of life lowered from on high. Fairy tales and songs relish the theme, and it has been taken to serious extremes by religious cults. Melanesian "cargo cults," getting Christianity confused with the affluence of missionaries, expect a new age to dawn with the arrival of a heaven-sent bounty of provisions.

Visions of a supernatural free store can be explained as fantasy, greed, or misunderstanding, as with the "cargo cults," but in any society influenced by Christian or Jewish thought even whimsical or selfish notions of God generous beyond limit suggest a fundamental attribute of the holy: mercy.

Mercy has many current and historical definitions and is often used in the same breath with *justice*. The two words have complex interplay in the language of law and theology, but each has distinctions. Justice usually means "fairness," and in legal and political terms fairness is the goal when justice is put forth as a human right. Justice also has the religious meaning of "righteousness," which is not the exercising of a right but the condition of being and doing right. God in both Judaism and Christianity is the very essence of righteousness, therefore, of justice. For example, the just God separates the sheep from the goats, and demands justice among people and nations.

As an English term translating one set of Hebrew and Greek words in the Bible, mercy is a quality of God going beyond justice. It is justice plus special consideration, a concept also found in law, as when an offender fairly convicted appeals to the mercy of the court. In theology, which is more than heavenly jurisprudence, mercy is first God's grace and forgiveness freely given to a humanity that does not measure up to the standards of divine righteousness. Mercy in this sense is neither owed by God (it is no human right) nor can it be earned; rather it is a divine bonus springing from a divine decision to love sinners. Mercy is also God's special identification with the poor and oppressed, those who are victims of human injustice.

Jesus Christ in Christian theology is the fullest expression of God's mercy understood both as the divine will to forgive and as special endorsement of the value of the downtrodden. The merciful Christ is at once the sign of God's love and forgiveness and the way, through faith, toward a new relationship to the just God. And Christ is healer and uplifter of the broken and despised.

In the Gospels Jesus is the epitome of justice and mercy, the just critic of the rich and powerful, the forgiver of sins, lover of the unlovable, physician to spirits and bodies. His greatest compassion is for social outcasts, but his mercy knows no bounds. Jesus' first sermon (in the Gospel of Luke), based on a text from the prophet Isaiah, announces as part of his mission good news to the poor, release to captives, sight for the blind, and liberty for the oppressed (Luke 4:18).

The Fifth Beatitude recognizes the holiness of Christlike mercy alive in the attitudes and actions of believers. The Greek word for "merciful" here typically means "to render aid," and Matthew 5:7 is most often applied to those Christians who relieve human distress. This is appropriate (though not the whole of it, as will be discussed below). Matthew 25 points out the Christian responsibility to feed the hungry, care for strangers, clothe the naked, and tend the sick and imprisoned.

Christians great in mercy are great humanitarians, but their motives are not only humanitarian impulses. Their compassion and service imitate the God of mercy. They serve God by serving God's children, and sometimes they recognize Christ himself in the hungry, sick, oppressed people they serve. The awareness of Christ as synonymous with the sufferer is clearly stated by Mother Teresa of Calcutta in the opening lines of a prayer entitled "Jesus My Patient":

Dearest Lord, may I see you today and every day in the person of your sick, and, whilst nursing them, minister unto you.

Though you hide yourself behind the unattractive disguise of the irritable, the exacting, the unreasonable, may I still recognize you, and say: "Jesus, my patient, how sweet it is to serve you."[1]

Mercy, however, need not be limited to charitable deeds. Extending forgiveness and willingly assuming the physical or nonphysical cares of others are also merciful acts. As Mother Teresa states in a poem based on Matthew 25, service to Christ is more than feeding the hungry or nursing the sick. It is also teaching the young to read, smiling at the aged, carrying the cross for mocked races, listening to the restless, and sharing human joys.

Justice as a social goal can be required by law; mercy goes beyond any legal requirement. Human mercy modeled on Christ cannot be extracted by social pressure; it is beyond common expectations. None of the Christians discussed in this chapter *had* to be merciful in response to a legislature or court, or to maintain good reputations in their communities. The Gospel alone compelled them to go beyond justice to mercy.

The Holy Company includes many Christians for whom ministries of mercy are a calling, a vocation. Mercy is also an impulse not limited to professionals, and great mercy may emerge in a life in some specific situation without having appeared before or reappearing afterward. Flashes of mercy can occur in quite unexpected quarters. For example, Clement VI, a fourteenth-century pope remembered more for enlarging his palace than for spiritual prowess, came to the defense of European Jews accused by the Christian masses of causing an outbreak of Black Death in 1348. In opposition to the common notions of both divine and human justice in his day, this worldly churchman declared that any who believed Jews responsible for plague were "seduced by that liar, the Devil," and he welcomed persecuted Jews to Avignon (where the popes lived in the 1300s).[2] Even Oliver Cromwell, who turned England into a Puritan oligarchy in the 1650s, was occasionally kind to Anglicans, Roman Catholics, and Quakers. He once opposed a fine against a Quaker who processed into Bristol in imitation of Jesus' Palm Sunday entry into Jerusalem.

Mercy very much entails the protection of the innocent against injustice; it is not, however, primarily a matter of political programs. Christian mercy goes beyond simple justice, to love.

Callistus I (?–222)

A slave who became pope, Callistus had a great capacity to both accept and bestow mercy in the form of forgiveness; in fact, his forgiving spirit got him in trouble in early third-century Rome. Callistus took seriously the biblical evidence of God's constant forgiveness, and he thought the church should be generous in remitting sins. His enemies said he went too far.

The place and date of his birth are unknown. Most of the sketchy information on his early life comes from an unfavorable account written by Hippolytus, an adversary who wanted to be pope in Callistus' place. Although unfriendly, Hippolytus' account is probably correct in outline. When a slave, it seems that Callistus, possibly through bad investments, lost money entrusted to him by his master and other depositors. Seized and punished, he was released on request of the creditors. In an attempt to make good the investments, he engaged in a dispute with a group of businessmen in Rome (one story says he disrupted services at a synagogue). Denounced as a Christian —Christianity was then illegal—he was sent to the salt mines of Sardinia. Some sources say Callistus and other Christians in the mines were freed by the Emperor Commodus on the insistence of an imperial mistress.

Back in Rome, about A.D. 199, Callistus was put in charge of a Christian cemetery by Pope Zephyrinus. That cemetery, named for Callistus, is still found on the Via Appia. Zephyrinus liked the former slave, ordained him deacon, and made him an adviser.

Zephyrinus died in 217. The Christian clergy and laity of Rome, who then elected popes, chose Callistus as his successor. A rival party, led by Hippolytus, was furious. Hippolytus, an ambitious priest and an important Christian writer, was a vigorous opponent of anything he considered a departure from Christian orthodoxy, and to him Callistus was a heretic.

Callistus particularly scandalized Hippolytus by admitting to Holy Communion Christians who had done public penance for murder and adultery. Hippolytus said persons guilty of such mortal sins were forever excluded from the sacraments. Callistus believed the church should recognize second repentance. Hippolytus accused the pope of general laxity in discipline and of allowing heretical ideas to flourish. He said Callistus favored Patripassianism.

Patripassianism is easier to understand than to pronounce. It was a heresy that, in effect, denied the Holy Trinity. Also called Modalism, it claimed that no distinctions can be drawn among God the Father, God the Son, and God the Holy Spirit but that God only *seems* to be manifested in three modes. Modalism arose in part to counteract an earlier heresy that turned the Trinity into a triumvirate of separate gods.

Modalism was rather popular in Rome under Zephyrinus and his two predecessors. Callistus may have toyed with it, but if he embraced it he had a strange way of honoring his modalist colleagues. He condemned and excommunicated one Sabellius, the major modalist teacher of the day.

Hippolytus did everything he could to undercut Callistus, who evidently never took action against his adversary. Finally, Hippolytus set himself up as antipope (he was reconciled to the church later). With all his learning, Hippolytus never seemed to grasp something that the simpler Callistus understood about the early Roman church. Rome in the third century, before the first formal creed was issued by the Council of Nicaea in 325, did not represent a single stream of Christian doctrine. Some scholars think Rome gained power in the Church because it allowed diversity of thought within limits. As an ecclesiastical center, Rome listened to many schools of theology and took its time in deciding on acceptable doctrine. Orthodoxy was still taking shape, and to it Callistus contributed an understanding of the wideness of God's mercy.

Callistus died in 222. Ironically, he and his archenemy Hippolytus are both canonical saints. Sanctity is indeed diverse.

Olympias (360?–408)

A wealthy widow, strong-willed but finally betrayed, Olympias was a fourth-century pioneer in creating social institutions to extend Christian mercy. She stands near the start of a line of Eastern and Western women who insisted that followers of Christ must care for the sick, house orphans, and feed the poor. Her stage was imperial Constantinople, the great city on the Bosporus superseding Rome as capital of the late Roman Empire.

Herself an orphan, Olympias inherited a great fortune. Before her death (at about age forty) her money would be confiscated by scoundrel bishops and politicians, but not before she had spent much of it on hospitals, orphanages, programs for the poor, and in buying the freedom of slaves.

Olympias' generosity, her sense of mercy toward the needy, may have served as a model for a younger contemporary, the Empress Pulcheria (399–453), the first woman to rule the Roman Empire in her own name. Olympias' concern for the welfare of young women, often abused in the patriarchal society of her time, may also have inspired the Empress Theodora a century later. This is far from certain, since Theodora had more immediate motivation for an unrelenting campaign against fathers and businessmen who forced young girls into prostitution. The shrewd and sometimes pious Theodora was herself a prostitute before meeting her husband, a prince who became the powerful Emperor Justinian, the codifier of Roman law. Though basically dissimilar, Olympias and Theodora were alike in their use of wealth and position to force attention on glaring social ills in a supposedly Christian society.

Riches and influence were by no means all Olympias had. Her chief aim was to pattern her life on the model of Christ, and in this pursuit her money was a nagging problem.

The fortune brought many suitors to her door, and Olympias' marriage was a matter of political importance, especially to the Emperor Theodosius. She accepted the proposal of one Nebridius, an official of the royal court, but the groom died twenty months later, again making Olympias a target of the matchmakers. Theodosius wanted her to marry a Spanish relative of his. She refused, refused all offers, saying she would remain a widow. This decision so angered the emperor that he relieved her of the administration of her money and property until she reached the age of thirty. In response, Olympias wrote thanking Theodosius for lifting the "heavy burden" of her wealth and instructing him to divide the property between the church and the poor people of Constantinople. "I have long been seeking a fit opportunity to avoid the vanity of making the distribution myself, as well as of attaching my heart to perishable goods instead of keeping it fixed on true riches," she said.

Outwitted by Olympias, Theodosius returned the fortune to the widow, who proceeded to find fit opportunities to dispose of it herself. She became a deaconess—a lay woman pledged to care for human needs in Christ's name—and opened a house to shelter girls wishing to devote themselves to Christian worship and service. Her generosity to the poor was so great that John Chrysostom, bishop of Constantinople, advised her to moderate her giving lest she encourage the lazy not to work.

Olympias might have lived out her days and exhausted her means in Constantinople had it not been for her close friendship with John Chrysostom, not only a bishop but also one of the major Christian theologians of the fourth century. John Chrysostom offended the Empress Eudoxia, a woman of wayward inclinations. Eudoxia, the mother of the notably devout Pulcheria, had no appreciation of the moral opinions of the bishop and had him banished in 404.

When Olympias refused to recognize Chrysostom's replacement, she felt imperial wrath. She was exiled in 405, then brought back to the capital to stand trial. Found guilty of disrupting the life of the church, the rich widow was ordered to pay a large fine. The remains of her money were eventually seized and her charities closed by adversaries.

Olympias died poor in 408, less than a year after John Chrysostom died, or was murdered. The two friends stayed in touch by letter during their ordeals. He wrote to Olympias:

I cannot cease to call you blessed. The patience and dignity with which you have borne your sorrows, the prudence and wisdom with which you have managed delicate affairs, and the charity which has made you throw a veil over the malice of your persecutors have won a glory and reward which here-after will make all your suffering seem light and passing in the presence of eternal joy.

Elizabeth of Hungary (1207–1231)

Elizabeth is one of those medieval saints who seem too good, too merciful to have been real. She is, to be sure, the subject of tall, tall tales embellishing her character and charity, yet behind the legends is a real heroine, a woman of sensitivity and service in a brutal time and place—early thirteenth-century Germany.

She is called Elizabeth of Hungary, but lived most of her twenty-four years in Thuringia, a region of southern Germany that three centuries later produced Protestant Reformer Martin Luther. Many of the same sites figured in her life and Luther's, but the influences molding these two great Christians had little in common.

Elizabeth was the child of King Andrew II of Hungary. Born in 1207 in what is now Bratislava, she was engaged at age four to Ludwig, eldest son of the landgrave (prince) of Thuringia, and sent to grow up with her future husband. The couple married when she was fourteen and he twenty-one. Their six years together produced three or four children and a grand medieval love epic. Elizabeth and Ludwig loved one another with passion and childhearted glee, and they were ardent friends.

The teen-aged landgravine was given to intense Christian piety and extensive charity. She arose by night to pray. She devoted herself unsparingly to the poor and sick, especially to homeless children and lepers. Persons suffering leprosy in the thirteenth century were treated much as were lepers in Jesus' day. They were outcasts, forced to wander with no expectation of welcome or care. Elizabeth caused a leprosarium to be built near the Wartburg Castle, her husband's stronghold, and is said to have tended lepers with her own hands. One oft-told but possibly legendary story tells of her laying a leper on Ludwig's royal couch.

How much personal nursing of lepers Elizabeth did is a matter of speculation. There is more evidence of her generosity to the poor, giving from her own means and, when need arose, dispersing the public treasury. In 1225, Thuringia was struck by famine. Hungry people marched to the Wartburg demanding bread. Ludwig was away. Elizabeth, assuming she was in charge, baked up all the grain in the royal storehouses. When Ludwig returned, his advisers complained of his wife's benefactions. "Has she alienated any of my dominions?" the prince asked. "No," the complainers said. "We shall not want as long as we continue to let her relieve the poor," the ruler replied.

In 1227 Ludwig decided to accompany the Sixth Crusade to the Holy Land. This expedition, organized by the German emperor, was a modest military success; it was fatal for the landgrave of Thuringia. He died of plague along the way. News of his death was months reaching Germany. When it came, Elizabeth was undone: "The world is dead to me, and all that was joyous in the world."

Ludwig's brother was named regent, since the new landgrave, Elizabeth's son, was but a child. Elizabeth and the regent quarreled. Whether she left the Wartburg voluntarily or was forced out is not clear, but she left with her children, resettled in Marburg, and took the habit of a Franciscan nun. Her life was not joyous but she continued her ministries of mercy.

Great pain and distress came to her in the form of her spiritual counselor, one Conrad to whom she had taken a vow of spiritual obedience before her husband died. Conrad of Marburg was highly regarded as a professional religious adviser by some people in his day. He was also a harsh, cruel man. Wishing to make an official saint of his already holy spiritual ward, Elizabeth, he set grueling tasks for the young woman. Conrad deprived her of lifelong friends, and physically abused her.

The princess never submitted totally to Conrad. With clandestine friends she sometimes made a joke of him, and she had holy tasks to command her mind. She had established a hospice to care for the sick and dying. After her death in 1231 Conrad became a publicist for Elizabeth's canonization by the Roman Catholic Church. Justly, he did not live to witness her elevation to sainthood in 1235.

In her last years Elizabeth was a familiar but strange sight in Marburg. A royal princess of Hungary, landgravine of Thuringia, dressed in a grey robe, visiting the homes of the poor, and, when she had time, taking pole in hand to go fishing. The princess sold her catch to earn extra money to aid the suffering.

Margaret of Navarre (1492–1549)

Margaret, queen of Navarre from 1525 to 1549, is probably better called Margaret of Angouleme, the French province where she was born, to distinguish her from a later Margaret, her grandson's wife, the evil and licentious Margaret of Valois. The Margaret meant here, a woman of unchallenged piety, was one of the first European rulers to be merciful to religious dissenters. She contributed significantly, if indirectly, to the Edict of Nantes, a landmark in the struggle for religious liberty.

Margaret, born the year Christopher Columbus sailed west, was twenty-five years old when Martin Luther nailed his Ninety-Five Theses to a church door in Germany, touching off the Protestant Reformation. She saw the start of the wars and persecution that wrecked Europe in the name of religion. She disapproved of the use of force against persons raising questions about theology or suggesting church reform. Margaret became a protector of reformers, scholars, and artists. For that she is a great heroine to Protestants, although she never joined a Protestant church.

Margaret, sister of King Francis I of France, was twice married. After her first husband, a duke, died, she obliged her brother politically in 1525 by marrying Henry II of Navarre, lord of an independent kingdom along the French side of the Pyrenees mountains. She and Henry had one daughter, Jeanne d'Albret, but they did not get along well together and lived more or less separate lives.

As queen consort of Navarre and sister of the king of France, Margaret enjoyed latitude to do as she pleased, and she pleased to be religious and charitable and to befriend the persecuted. Henry cooperated with her in improving the schools, hospitals, and economy of the small kingdom, strategically located along the commercial route between France and Spain. Henry was not overjoyed when his merciful wife began housing fugitive Protestants in the palace at Nerac. Margaret found it helpful to remind her husband who her brother was. Francis I was no Protestant sympathizer, but he adored his sister. Responding to her critics he once said, "My sister Margaret is the only woman I ever knew who had every virtue and every grace without any vice mixed in."

She was also a woman of broad learning. Her court became an intellectual center as she patronized and protected artists, writers, and musicians, along with Reformers. Margaret's interest in theological and social questions probably sprang from pre-Reformation contacts with humanism. Late Renaissance humanism, best exemplified in Erasmus (see page 115), was engaged in the exploration of human values, of free will, and of the human relationship to God.

In a civilization dominated by the church, humanists were as suspect as Protestants. Margaret welcomed all, and never got into trouble with the Roman Catholic Church, most likely because no sixteenth-century pope was interested in offending the king of France by criticizing his sister. Margaret extended her protection of humanists and Reformers into France when she could. She was not always successful. Her brother was under pressure to oppose the Huguenots (French Protestants). Among those Margaret could not ultimately save was Clément Marot, a noted hymn writer she had managed to free on an earlier occasion.

Margaret acted in the political sphere, but behind her public stands was a deep, mystical faith reflected in her religious stories and poems.

The Mirror of the Sinful Soul, a collection of verse published in 1533 was based on lines from Psalm 51:

> Create in me a clean heart, O God,
>> and put a new and right spirit
>> within me.
> Cast me not away from thy presence,
>> and take not thy holy Spirit from me.
> Restore to me the joy of thy salvation,
>> and uphold me with a willing spirit.

> (Psalm 51:10–12, RSV)

Psalm 51 opens with an affirmation of the steadfast love and mercy of God. Margaret's poems ponder the meaning of sin and of spiritual purity. The author longed for a world remade by the love and mercy of Christ.

Before her death in 1549, Margaret's relationship with her daughter Jeanne was strained because the latter became a fiery Protestant—a Calvinist, and an intolerant one. As *de facto* ruler of Navarre once her parents died, Jeanne d'Albret tried to abolish Catholicism in the realm. She led troops in the Protestant cause, and was probably poisoned by Catherine de' Medici, ruler of France and widow of Jeanne's cousin Henry II.

Jeanne's son Henry of Navarre, raised a Huguenot, became the king of France in 1589. In order to claim the throne he had to declare himself Catholic. Eleven years later he issued the Edict of Nantes granting freedom of worship to French Protestants. That edict ended the sixteenth-century wars of religion in France, but Louis XIV revoked it in 1685. Its principles, however, would return in the eighteenth century to influence democratic thought.

Vincent de Paul (1580–1660)

As the queen of France attended her kingdom on a typical day in the late 1640s, an old priest moved about Paris attending the Kingdom.

Vincent de Paul on that typical day might visit a prison, encourage hospital-based Sisters of Charity, counsel missionary priests off to the countryside (or Africa), and personally collect a child or two abandoned on the street. If money for his work was running short, he might make a mental note to ask for a large donation when he saw the queen (Anne of Austria) in her palace the next morning. "A queen has no need of jewels," he once said to her, never imagining that she had done more than she should in handing over her necklace.

His last three decades (he lived to the age of eighty) were a study in contrasts. The son of peasants, "Monsieur Vincent," as he was known, gained entry into the hall of government and the quarters of royalty. All the rich and powerful people wanted to know him; his heart was with foundlings, galley-slaves, and the spiritually and physically hungry common people of seventeenth-century France. From the rich he gathered funds for his real patrons and masters, the poor and sick who, he said, "are taking the place of the Son of God who chose to be poor."

Few, if any, individuals in the history of the church have done more than Vincent de Paul to make mercy manifest in the world. He is the patron saint of all Roman Catholic charitable institutions, and he could well be the patron of middle-age creativity. His major work all came after he was forty years old. That work included founding (with Louise de Marillac) the Sisters of Charity; organizing a preaching order, the Congregation of the Mission (members are called Vincentians, for the founder, or Lazarists, from the order's headquarters at Saint-Lazare); and building numerous hospitals, orphanages, and homes for old people. However, his foundations were only part of Vincent's work. As important as these, and indeed the framework for them, were the mercy and piety he awakened by his own holiness. "It was not charity that made him a saint, but his saintliness that made him charitable," the historian Brémond said of Vincent.

Vincent de Paul is known as a major figure in the French Counter-Reformation; he was, but his role must be carefully defined. The Counter-Reformation, the shoring up of Catholicism after the Protestant advent, was both theological and political, and in France included efforts to check, or at least counteract, the Huguenots (Protestants). The French Counter-Reformation was at times bloody. It included the Saint Bartholomew's Day massacre of Huguenots in 1572 and periodic pressure against Protestants even while the Edict of Nantes, a declaration of toleration, was in effect, from 1598 to 1685.

Monsieur Vincent clearly wanted France Catholic. He wanted the monarchy to endorse the definitions of the Catholic faith set forth by the Council of Trent in 1549 (the crown steadfastly refused to comply and did not, right up to its abolition in 1789). But Vincent did not approve of hatred or violence in remaking Catholic France. His strategies were instruction, compassion, and service reflecting spiritual renewal within the church. He told the Vincentian preacher-priests to approach non-Catholics humbly and gently "so that it may be seen that what is said proceeds from a compassionate, charitable, and not a bitter heart." In this his attitude was similar to that of his older contemporary François de Sales, also a major French Catholic saint of the seventeenth century.

Despite vigorous political and social opposition, Protestantism flourished in France during the second half of the sixteenth century; its appeal was greatest among peasants and small business families of towns traditionally hostile to the nobility clustered in Paris. Some areas of southern France were almost totally Protestant by the 1570s. The popularity of Protestantism troubled but did not surprise Vincent as he assayed the French religious situation in the early 1600s. Catholic instruction to peasants and townspeople was haphazard, often a mere formality. The Catholic Church was not engaging the people; it was expecting people to be Christian simply because they were part of a society that called itself Christian. To Vincent, being Christian in name only was not enough; to be real, faith must be personal.

Vincent's major contribution to the Counter-Reformation was not political but spiritual, a combination of mysticism and practical love in the world. Both he and François de Sales were theologically influenced by Spanish mysticism given a French flavor. Post-Reformation Spanish mysticism as taught by persons such as Teresa of Avila (see page 26) and John of the Cross stressed individual awareness of God and deliberate adherence to Christ in love; it was extremely personal. French mystics, including Vincent de Paul, took this stress on a personal relationship with Christ and broke it out of the narrow confines of the monasteries and convents where it first developed. They said that ordinary believers as well as monks, priests, and nuns can know the mystical presence of Christ,[3] and this democratization of mysticism proved the best defense French Catholicism had against the appeal of Protestant personal piety. The message was quite simple: each person can know and experience God.

The Christian way to Vincent was the way of love. Love, he said, is "affective" and "effective." The first flows from a person into the beloved, like a parent's love of a child; the second, "effective," responds to the needs of the beloved. By dealing in both "affective" and "effective" Christian love, Vincent de Paul did more to missionize

France for Catholicism than the prelates, advisers to the crown, who led armies.

The seeds of greatness grew slowly in the farm boy born at Pouy (now Saint Vincent de Paul) in 1581, though he alone of eight children showed an interest in education. To send Vincent to school at Dax, his father is said to have sold a yoke of oxen. After Dax came theological studies at the University of Toulouse. Vincent was ordained in 1600, and immediately thereafter a gap of several years appears in his chronology. The popular story says he was captured by Barbary pirates, sold as a slave, and suffered abuse until he converted his master (variously said to be a French monk or an African Muslim). Some scholars reject the piracy story as total fiction; others defend it as truth, and in support cite his later ministry among galley slaves and his compassion in ransoming as many as twelve hundred Christians enslaved in Africa. Actually, his work among convicted criminals sent to the galleys as oarsmen says nothing about special compassion born of common experience. For a man of his day, Vincent treated galley slaves with unusual kindness. He demanded and got better dungeons for them onshore, looked to their medical needs, and ministered to their souls. But the abolition of slavery in general and of galley-slavery in particular was not on his agenda.

The silent period over, Vincent appeared in Paris, possibly as chaplain to Queen Margaret of Valois, she of notable impiety. His inclinations by all indications were toward worldly comforts until he came under the influence of Cardinal Pierre de Bérulle, a mystic. Bérulle sent him as tutor to the children of Count Philip de Gondi, master of the French fleet, and a large estate holder. Vincent became confessor and a great friend to Mme de Gondi who would later endow his first foundation, the Congregation of the Mission.

Vincent's first modest efforts at putting "effective love" into action among the masses came during a short pastorate in Chatillon-sur-Lombes, a poor village near Paris, about 1617. He had left the Gondis. In Chatillon he organized "ladies of charity" to assist the poor. Soon he was back to Mme de Gondi, who claimed the family could not function without him. He remained eight years (until the countess' death in 1625), and in that period organized ministries of spiritual and physical mercy for the peasants of the Gondi estates.

With an endowment from Mme de Gondi and a building from the archbishop of Paris, he opened his college for preachers at Saint-Lazare in 1625. From that point, Vincent's organizing on behalf of love never ceased. Vincentian houses operated throughout France and in several foreign countries by the time of his death.

Major credit for the Sisters of Charity is given to Vincent, but the story belongs also to Louise de Marillac (canonized by the Catholic church in 1934). Louise, a widow also known by her married name, Le Gras, was to Vincent what Mme de Chantal was to François de Sales and his Order of the Visitation, that is, she did much of the day-to-day work of organizing and running the order.

Vincent's original idea was to form a group, not an order, of faith-filled aristocratic women to serve "our lords the poor." He was an able recruiter. Titled ladies, who had to prepare themselves spiritually, donned grey frocks for visits of mercy to poorhouse and prison. Vincent set the movement's spiritual tone—he prayed hourly—and took part himself in the lowly labor. But the needs of the poor were too much for one priest and volunteer grey ladies. Many nurses and new institutions were needed. The poor themselves offered a source of workers—widows and peasant girls, but how would they be educated and assigned? Louise de Marillac provided the answer. She moved the Sisters of Charity from a lay movement into a religious order. Vincent was not totally happy about that. He thought the laity should assume more responsibility in "effective love." Not until 1642, nine years after Louise opened a training program in her home, did he permit the Sisters of Charity to take vows of poverty, obedience, and chastity. It was 1655 before the Vatican was asked to charter the foundation as a formal religious order of noncloistered nuns.

In the 1640s and 1650s Monsieur Vincent engaged in politics to the extent that it served his religious purposes. For example, he sat on a commission that proposed persons to be elevated in the church hierarchy (the French monarchs named bishops). He argued for men of high spiritual qualities, and was almost always vetoed by secular voices, some of which belonged to cardinals. Vincent was not fond of Cardinal Jules Mazarin, first minister of France from 1642 to 1661, and during a series of public protests against increased taxation attempted in vain to persuade Queen Anne to dismiss the prelate.

Vincent de Paul died in the fall of 1660 as he sat quietly in a chair. His life was a missive of mercy. The Christian churches do not always follow, but they can never escape, his words:

. . . we must care for the poor, console them, help them, support their cause. Since Christ willed to be born poor, he chose for himself disciples who were poor. He made himself the servant of the poor and shared their poverty. He went so far as to say that he would consider every deed which helps or harms the poor as done for or against himself.

Nicolaus Ludwig von Zinzendorf (1700–1760)

The idea of teenagers *voluntarily* getting together to discuss their service to Christ seems far-fetched, yet when children receive good religious instruction it sometimes happens; it happened at the Halle (Germany) boarding school where Nicolaus Ludwig von Zinzendorf studied from 1710 to 1716. Zinzendorf, in fact, started the small prayer and Christian planning group whose members stayed in touch after graduation and, as scattered college students, made covenant with God and one another in an informal fraternity, the Order of the Grain of Mustard Seed.

Zinzendorf and friends took the name of their order from Jesus' parable of the Kingdom of God growing from small beginnings. They hoped their youthful enthusiasm, nourished by God, would become leaven in the world. No public organization was formed. Members individually pledged to work for the conversion and salvation of all people, including the "heathens" across the seas, to improve human morals, to promote the unity of all Christians, and to protect persons persecuted for faith. In short, "knights" of the mustard seed were to "love the whole human family."

To Zinzendorf the greatest of all God's special blessings, God's mercy, was the Gospel of love, the good news of soul-saving forgiveness in Christ (always "the Lamb" to Zinzendorf). He believed that as recipients of saving mercy Christians had the responsibility to take the Gospel to Hottentots and Eskimos, American Indians and black slaves in the West Indies. He also thought Christians ought to love one another, to find in their faith a common ground above the divisions of eighteenth-century Christianity. Hottentot and Eskimo should not even be told of the denominational differences in Europe and America; they should hear only the story of Christ.

The purposes of the Order of the Grain of Mustard Seed shaped Zinzendorf's life, and across his sixty years he pursued them with a vigor that fathered the Protestant missionary enterprise and foreshadowed the modern movement for Christian unity. He first used the word "ecumenical" for Christian fellowship like that described in one of his many hymns:

Christian hearts, in love united,
 Seek alone in Jesus rest;
Has He not your love excited?
 Then let love inspire each breast;
Members—on our Head depending,
 Lights—reflecting Him our Sun,
Brethren—His commands attending,
 We in Him, our Lord, are one.

Zinzendorf had no specific plan for his Christian service when he entered the University of Wittenberg at age sixteen. The child of Lutheran nobility, he studied law, thinking he would follow his father, who had died when he was six months old, into a government career. His family—his mother, who had remarried, his paternal grandmother, and an aunt—considered the ministry beneath his social level; his heritage clearly indicated a position close to the Elector (prince) of Saxony (Germany in the eighteenth century was a nest of small states). The young student bowed to his family's wishes.

Zinzendorf, a graduate in law, set out in 1719 on a "grand tour" of Europe, spending most of his time discussing religion with Calvinists and Catholics. He found a kindred spirit in Cardinal Louis de Noailles of Paris and presented the insignia of the Order of the Grain of Mustard Seed to the Catholic friend. The tour over, he took an insignificant job with the Saxon state in Dresden, married Erdmuthe Dorothea of Reuss (she bore about a dozen children), and assumed a family estate at Berthelsdorf (Zinzendorf was by inheritance a German count).

The channel for his Christian service came to the count unexpectedly in 1722 in the person of Christian David, a young religious refugee from Moravia, a part of modern Czechoslovakia. David was a convert from Catholicism to the *Unitas Fratrum* (Unity of the Brethren), a small sect dating back to pre-Reformation reformer John Hus (see page 239), burned by the Roman Catholic Church in 1415. The Brethren taught human equality and unity before God, practiced strict moral and spiritual disciplines, and allowed the laity to receive both bread and wine at Holy Communion. Despite persecution, the movement survived in Catholic Moravia and welcomed and identified with the Protestant Reformation of the sixteenth century but remained distinct. Most Brethren left Moravia when they were outlawed anew in 1548; a few remained, and Christian David represented a cell of ten looking for asylum.

Did Count Zinzendorf have land to spare to a persecuted ban of believers? He did, and he was obligated by his Mustard Seed pledge to protect those harassed for religion. Moreover, the Brethren theology was not too different from his own. Zinzendorf was at that point Lutheran, but a particular sort of Lutheran. He and his family were pietists. Pietism, which can take many forms, was in origin a seventeenth-century reaction to what its advocates saw as the "dead orthodoxy" of official Lutheranism. As Europe settled down after the Reformation, most nations and the petty states of Germany decided whether they were Catholic or some variety of Protestant (and the different Protestant camps bickered constantly). Whatever the religion, all the people in a realm were expected to conform, and conformity in Lutheran Germany produced a cold formalism often called "Lutheran scholasticism." Early pietists, especially Philipp Jacob Spener, Zinzendorf's godfather, preached a warmer, heartfelt faith of personal devotion and positive effect on moral behavior. Opposed by the establishment, pietism spread rapidly, influencing the whole of Protestantism (about ninety percent of all American Protestants are basically pietists). The Brethren outlook had pietistic themes.

The refugees were allowed to build a village—Herrnhut, or "Watch of the Lord,"—on Zinzendorf land. Meanwhile, the count continued his job in Dresden and imagined the village becoming a refuge for any persecuted Christians. Others besides Brethren were encouraged to come, and soon the Lord's village was seething with dissension. Zinzendorf considered ending the experiment; instead he gave up his job, returned to Bertheldorf, and took over the new community himself in 1727. Building on Brethren fundamentals, and not hesitant to use his autocratic tendencies, he shaped Herrnhut into a model Christian commune and from it spread the Moravian movement.

Herrnhut flourished under Zinzendorf, and in 1732 the first missionaries were on their way to the West Indies. Lutheran officials in Saxony were alarmed: Count Zinzendorf was schismatic. Even though he professed his orthodoxy and had himself ordained to the Lutheran clergy, to no immediate avail, he was banished in 1736 and spent the next eleven years away from Herrnhut. His headquarters-in-exile was in the German principality of Wetteravia, near Frankfurt-am-Main, but he traveled most of the time—the Baltic states, Holland, England, the American colonies, and the West Indies—founding communities and visiting missionaries. Zinzendorf

had a personal hand in launching the still numerous Moravian settlements in eastern Pennsylvania (Nazareth and Bethlehem, for example). To expedite his work he was consecrated a Moravian bishop in
1737. (The Brethren episcopacy claims apostolic succession from a
fifteenth-century Catholic prelate friendly to their movement. Saxony recognized the validity of this claim in 1747, and in 1749 the
British Parliament did likewise, calling the Brethren "an ancient Protestant Episcopal Church.")

Sixty-eight missionaries had gone out to the "heathen" by 1740,
two hundred twenty-six by 1760 (many died in the tropics). Most
early missionaries were laymen. They preached, healed the sick (ru-
dimentary medical training was a requirement for mission service),
gave instruction, particularly in geography relevant to native peoples
and in indigenous languages (so people could read the Bible in their
own tongue), and helped converts learn trades. These missionaries
supported themselves; they had no material goods to distribute to
Africans or "Red Indians," as Zinzendorf called native Americans.
Moravians wanted no "rice Christians," that is, converts for a meal.
While they helped people learn to support themselves, their basic gift
was the love and mercy of the Lamb.

Zinzendorf was not a great builder of charitable institutions,
though the Moravians were pioneers in Protestant medical missions.
He was not a great social reformer, though the Moravian emphasis on
equality before God would influence liberal Protestant theology. Like
Vincent de Paul he had a benign view of slavery in a century in which
Christian distress over forced servitude was growing. Zinzendorf did
accept Africans as full participants in the fellowship of Christ—once
embracing a black bride in the West Indies to the consternation of
other Europeans present. His first concern was the freedom of the
spirit ransomed by the blood of the Lamb. That was mercy.

The count was allowed to return to Saxony in 1747, and the
Moravians were reconciled to the state Lutheran church; however,
Zinzendorf spent most of the years from 1749 to 1755 attending to
affairs in England. His last five years, most at Herrnhut, were troubled by personal and financial worries. His wife died in 1756, and he
remarried the next year. Of their twelve children, only four reached
maturity, and the talented son Zinzendorf expected to succeed him in
the movement died in 1752. He fretted over the Moravian future and
wondered how to pay his bills. Personal funds had been used up in his

travels; the estates were heavily mortgaged. Willed to the church, the estates had to be redeemed by the Brethren, who also settled pensions on three surviving daughters of the Zinzendorfs.

The Moravian church became a denomination among denominations, but Zinzendorf had sparked the Protestant missionary movement, an enterprise of as much mercy as self-interest. And his longing for Christian unity would return as an overarching Christian theme in the twentieth century.

Florence Nightingale (1820–1910)

On a bright Egyptian day in 1846 a fashionable twenty-six-year-old Englishwoman, pounds to spare in her purse, sat in a better section of Cairo pondering her future. She felt a calling, had felt it more than once, and formed it as a prayer, "O God, Thou puttest into my heart this great desire to devote myself to the sick and sorrowful." She saw herself a nurse. Could she muster the courage to enter medical training over the objections of a family quick to remind her that nurses were on a social par with charwomen? A few weeks later, on her way home to England, she knew her future. "Give me my work to do," she prayed to God.

Her name was Florence Nightingale.

A dozen years later Nurse Nightingale was second only to Queen Victoria among the women famous in the English-speaking (and, sometimes, non–English-speaking) world. She was "the Lady with the Lamp," the heroine of the Crimean war immortalized by Henry Wadsworth Longfellow as the nineteenth century's Saint Philomena (a saint of uncertain date to whose bones miracles of healing have been attributed). From the 1850s until her death in 1910, Florence Nightingale was a living symbol of a medical revolution bringing the nursing profession into the modern age.

Her name is today a household word, a synonym for any devoted nurse, and a byword for determined womanhood. But except that she was a pioneer of scientific nursing, relatively few people know exactly what she did or how her work mattered, and fewer still know why she did it. Florence Nightingale the person is almost mythical within the fame accumulated to her name, and one reality of her life obscured by the legend was a strong consciousness of the hand of God in making her a servant of mercy.

The Nightingale family was right about the low social station of nurses in early Victorian England. Medical attendants were poorly trained if at all. They commanded no respect, and, even if they were naturally skilled and conscientious, the public facilities for the sick were abysmal. Just when young Florence first contemplated taking the lowly rank of a nurse cannot be pinpointed. Some biographers trace her interest to childhood pity for a dog she and the parish priest (Anglican) treated. She may well have pitied and nursed the dog, but the story hardly explains her motivation. Besides, her correspondence and later writings indicate indecision about her life's work until she was a young adult.

Her canine-loving priest may have had more to do with her direction than the dog, because Florence Nightingale's understanding of her career was distinctly religious. Lytton Strachey implies in *Eminent Victorians* that she was compelled to a life of mercy by an overwhelming sense of sinfulness; not a bad motive for Christian service, though it was thought so in Strachey's circle, but not one supported by her mature faith. She was a religious child. Like Joan of Arc she heard voices, and she recalled a voice in her youth telling her an important work lay ahead. The nature of that work was not specified.

To the consternation of her mother she refused any consideration of marriage as she awaited her appointed mission. The Nightingale family inherited wealth, maintained homes in Derbyshire and London, and traveled widely. Florence was born in Italy, in Florence, where her parents were living temporarily in May 1820. Her father personally provided a broad education. Mrs. Nightingale and a sister could never imagine why Florence wanted anything other than social glitter and a husband.

Florence was hard pressed to justify her affluence during the economic depression and bouts with hunger England experienced in the early 1840s. "My mind is absorbed with the ideas of the suffering of men, it besets me behind and before," she wrote. Her work would relate to the poor and oppressed. She mentioned the possibility of nursing; the family flatly refused, so she turned to reading government reports on hospital care in Great Britain and on the continent. Three years of reading made her an expert on public medicine—its shortcomings and potentials.

On the way back from Egypt, her commitment to God made, the wealthy young woman visited the Institute of Protestant Deaconesses at Kaiserwerth, Germany, a school for training peasant girls in nursing. "Now I know what it is to live and love life," she wrote. Her family's hold on her was broken. She returned to Kaiserwerth for a four-year course.

Finally a nurse, Florence Nightingale was named superintendent of a London charity hospital in 1853. She did not last long at the Institution for the Care of Sick Gentlewomen in Distressed Circumstances. The place was, she said, "a molehill." Nurse Nightingale did not feel called to a small work. She left the distressed gentlewomen to direct the nurses engaged in battling an outbreak of cholera in England.

The prelude to her great work was an unblessed event: war. In late 1853 Russia and the Ottoman Empire (Turkey) went to war. One cause of the conflict was a Russian demand to act as protector of Eastern Orthodox Christians living under the Turkish Muslims. Early the next year England and France joined the battle on Turkey's side. The fighting came to focus on the Crimean peninsula jutting down from Russia into the Black Sea. Britain's major army hospital was at Scutari on the Turkish side of the water.

Except for Florence Nightingale the Crimean war produced nothing good. The whole sorry event was medieval. More soldiers died of disease than of wounds. When reports of the squalid conditions at the front and at Scutari reached England, a call for volunteer nurses was made by the government. Nurse Nightingale responded and was armed with authority to manage the hospital and other nurses at Scutari.

Her arrival provoked hostility from the military doctors, who initially refused to cooperate with her. But as the wounded filled the filthy barracks to overflowing, she was given charge. Her first request was for 200 scrub brushes.

Florence Nightingale and the other nurses in her care worked like possessed slaves, labors for which they are honored as angels of mercy. She did not allow the other women to go among the male patients past eight o'clock at night, but she went on a final round lighting her way with a small lamp. Those vigils made her world famous, because the soldiers and visiting journalists remembered the gentle night-visitor silhouetted against death. A reporter for *The Times* wrote: "When all the medical officers have retired for the night and silence and darkness have settled upon those miles of prostrate sick, she may be observed alone, with a little lamp in her hand, making the solitary rounds."

That and similar reports provided the nurse with the popular

following she needed to do the rest of her work. Florence Nightingale was by all reports a superb bedside nurse, but she had a larger plan. She would reform the entire British medical corps so that a Scutari could never again happen. In the East only eighteen months, her personal service at Scutari (where her fame was made) lasted a mere six months, then she was off to the Crimea itself, "interfering" the generals said, but active. She wanted full authority over all female nurses in the British army, and she got it, although officially not until the peace treaty ending the Crimean war was being signed.

She was no longer physically well. Nightingale caught a fever in the East and that may or may not account for the poor health she experienced thereafter. She took to her couch shortly after returning to England and remained an invalid (almost never getting up) for the next fifty-three years! No specific ailment was ever diagnosed. Was she sick? Thought she was sick? Wanted to be sick? No one knows, but she was not being lazy.

Even if the invalid "Lady with the Lamp" could not go out, her work could go on. From her couch she reorganized the medical services of the British military, and then took hold of the civilian sector. A fund raised to express public thanks for her war efforts she used to establish the world's first modern school of nursing. She generated programs for training midwives, for preparing special nurses for workhouses, and for improving public sanitation. Anyone engaged in upgrading nursing sought her advice, and she wrote a nursing textbook.

Florence Nightingale never accepted any public recognition for her work except the British Order of Merit, and that she did not accept so much as allowed it to be put into her hands when she was a senile, blind old woman of eighty-seven. Her comment was, "too kind, too kind." On her instructions, an offer to bury her body in Westminster Abbey was rejected. Mortal remains were laid to rest in a family plot in East Wellow. The marker reads: "F.N. Born 1820. Died 1910."

"Christ is the author of our profession," she once told a group of nurses. Believing her mercy was Christ's mercy, she looked for no reward. No voice ever told her to expect reward; it told her to work.

Walter Rauschenbusch (1861–1918)

The young pastor went to the Second German Baptist church, New York City, in 1886 expecting "to save souls in the ordinarily accepted religious sense." His job seen from his conservative, pietistic background was to convert individuals to Christ and instruct them in personal morality.

A pastor in the accepted pattern Walter Rauschenbusch would never be, though he was skilled at winning converts; his arrival in New York City was the first step in the making of America's most influential spokesman for the "social gospel," a movement affecting the future of Western Christianity, turning the churches toward unprecedented concern for social welfare.

Rauschenbusch's new parish—his first and only parish—was on Manhattan's West 45th Street, at the edge of "Hell's Kitchen" —tenement city, crime city, hot in summer, cold in winter, always crowded, peopled with hungry, sick, ignorant, unemployed social rejects. Looking at the backside of industrial prosperity, the twenty-five-year-old clergyman knew that more than pious sermons was required to answer his call to ministry.

He worked on the West Side for eleven years, pastoring a growing flock and engaging in countless personal acts of mercy. His concern for the people of Hell's Kitchen made him unconcerned for himself and resulted in the loss of his hearing. Seriously ill during the winter of 1888, the young pastor insisted on resuming errands of mercy during a blizzard, and this exposure closed the world of sound to him for the rest of his life. Rauschenbusch refused to let the handicap daunt his public service, and it did not, said a contemporary, "interfere with that gracious and sparkling humor of his which was so marked a characteristic of his thinking and of his word."

But Rauschenbusch could not be content with personal acts of mercy. His way to help the poor would not be Christian soup lines, food baskets, or even new charity hospitals. He looked to basic social reform, especially economic reform, as the only answer to all the Hell's Kitchens. After his first venture in a reform political campaign, friends told him he went beyond what was required of the ministry; he did not need to push himself so hard. Yes he did, he replied, "the work was Christ's work."

Rauschenbusch is not properly called an "activist" in the current sense of the word. While he agitated for political and economic reform by supporting such public causes as the labor movement, his greater contribution was as a theologian explaining why Christians and their churches have a social obligation. And behind his theological arguments were images of specific people. Especially in his years as pastor, Rauschenbusch did not hesitate to use bleak and often sentimental experiences from his ministry to tug at the heartstrings of the lords of capitalism; for example, his story of Minnie and her father, included in an 1887 newspaper article:

There, do you see that big clothing house on the corner there? Brilliantly lighted; show windows gorgeous; all hum and happiness. But somewhere in that big house there's a little bullet-headed tailor doubled up over the coat he is to alter, and . . . I know too that he is choking down the sobs and trying to keep the water out of his eyes. Why? Because his little girl is going to die tonight and he can't be there. Consumption, pulmonary. Been wasting away for months, can't sleep except her head on his breast. And then he can't sleep when her panting is in his ears. He has just been draining his life to sustain hers, and yet Minnie is all the world to him. She's the only drop of sweetness in his cup; all the rest is gall. Hard work; nothing to look forward to; wife grown bitter and snarling; and tonight the girl dies . . . Saturday night, you know; very busy; sorry, but can't spare him. O yes, you can say that: ought to go home, permission or none; But that means throwing up a job that he has been hanging to by his finger nails . . . And so he has to sew away and let his little girl die three blocks off.[4]

Rauschenbusch laid the responsibility of reforming the economic system on the doorstep of the Christian majority in America. Christianity, he said, must never be separated from social reality, but he also stressed personal faith as the motivation for social reform. Never rejecting the pietism learned from his father, a Lutheran immigrant who became a Baptist, he combined an emphasis on personal faith with a social consciousness. "The social gospel is the old message of salvation, but enlarged and intensified," he said.

The social gospel predated Rauschenbusch. This movement arose simultaneously on both sides of the Atlantic in response to a variety of nineteenth-century social and religious stimuli. Marxism in Europe challenged the churches to a new appraisal of Christian obligation to the masses. The antislavery cause followed by programs to assist freed blacks was a special impetus in the United States. And liberal theology was the foundation. Classical Protestant liberalism taught the sacredness of human life, deemphasized human sinfulness, and took an optimistic, progressive view of the future.

Far from being a secular movement, the social gospel based itself in Scripture, notably in its reading of the ethics of Jesus. Charles M.

Shelton's *In His Steps*, a novel in which people make decisions by asking "What would Jesus do?" was a great popularizer of the social gospel. The most important theological concept to social gospelers was the kingdom of God. Indeed, they affirmed, "at the very heart of his [Jesus'] gospel was the message of the kingdom, which they interpreted as a possibility within history. . . . The spokesmen for the social gospel expected that, through the efforts of men of good will, the Kingdom of God would soon become a reality, bringing with it social harmony and the elimination of the worst of social injustices."[5]

Of course, the social gospel was enormously controversial (and still is). Word battles raged among liberals and a range of conservatives and defenders of assorted orthodoxies. The movement did raise serious theological problems. Its definition of sin as selfishness to be eradicated by good will was questionable; its view of inevitable social progress was challenged by two world wars.

Rauschenbusch saw a rosy future, but he took a more sober view than some colleagues on issues that came to haunt the social gospel. He never said, for example, that people can create the Kingdom of God on earth. To him, the kingdom is always God's kingdom—no perfection on earth, but progress toward perfection. All material benefits, he believed, are outcomes of both the present and future kingdom, still coming but "pressing in on the present, always big with possibility, and always inviting immediate action."

His own immediate action in the late 1880s was private and public. Rauschenbusch and two other Baptist ministers formed a Society of Jesus (no connection with the Jesuits), a study circle to help them focus their own social thinking. This society grew into a larger Brotherhood of the Kingdom, a forum with an annual meeting, devoted to "the ethical and spiritual principles of Jesus, both in their individual and their social aspects."

Publicly, he launched a newspaper, *For the Right*, to champion his new cause. The first issue, in November, 1889, declared:

All unhappiness in private life and all wretchedness in human society is caused by wrong. Only *Right* can set things right. Therefore this paper is *For the Right*; for right cooking and dressing and living; for right thinking and speaking; for right relations between men and men; for right relations between men and God. We cannot set all things right. But as God gives us to see it, we can point out what would be right.[6]

Discontinued in 1891 when Rauschenbusch took a study leave from his parish, *For the Right* made its editor a hero to social gospelers and a villain to many capitalists. The economic world, he said, had never been converted to Christianity. Critics called him a socialist, and he was in a nonpolitical sense, but he was no Marxist. Rauschenbusch was actually very bullish on the American experiment, and had he drawn a design for the kingdom of God it would have looked like a purified United States.

Rauschenbusch married in 1893. He and his wife, Pauline, had five children. In 1897 he left Hell's Kitchen, going to teach at Rochester Theological Seminary, his alma mater, in Rochester, New York, where he was born in 1861 and died in 1918.

Rochester Seminary was in those days a major fountainhead of liberal theology, and within its walls Rauschenbusch wrote the books, beginning with *Christianity and the Social Crisis* in 1907, that made him the chief framer of a theology *for* the social gospel. To him, the social side of Christianity was a matter of leaving the world a better place than one found it. In a collection of "prayers of the social awakening," he wrote:

When our use of this world is over and we make room for others, may we not leave anything ravished by our greed or spoiled by our ignorance, but may we hand on our common heritage fairer and sweeter through our use of it, undiminished in fertility and joy, that so our bodies may return in peace to the great mother who nourished them and our spirit may round the circle of a perfect life in Thee.

Toward the end of his life, Rauschenbusch believed the social gospel had triumphed over individualism and conservatism in the major American Protestant churches. He was wrong about that, but the movement he fostered did have immeasurable and continuing impact on the whole of Christianity. While hardly endorsing Rauschenbuschian thought, Popes Leo XIII (1878–1903) and Pius XI (1922–1939) approved Christian activism for social reform. The Protestant denominations in the United States and Europe did turn in social directions during the first two decades of the present century, and many social gospel interests were institutionally embodied in the forerunners of what are today the U.S. National Council of Churches and the World Council of Churches.

In the 1980s even the most theologically conservative American

Christian is expected to have a social conscience, and Walter Rauschenbusch pioneered that expectation. Perhaps his greatest service of mercy was his forceful insistence that the social gospel is part of the "return to Christ."

CHAPTER VI

Washed in Love

"Holy are the pure in heart . . ."

THE TIN WOODSMAN in *The Wizard of Oz* wants a heart, and every child who reads Frank Baum's story or sees the play or movie based on it knows why. The reason has nothing to do with pumping life-giving blood; after all, the Tin Man can already talk and dance down the yellow brick road.

That the heart is the symbolic seat of feelings, of the emotions, needs no explanation—the understanding is bred in by the culture: heartfelt is sincere; heartache, pain; heartstrings, affection; heartless, cold; the passionate heart, love or lust; the true heart, loyalty, and on and on. This language of the heart is almost universal.

The heart as the symbolic center of feeling comes from religion, from ancient religion before science identified the emotive powers with the brain. Poetry and everyday language kept the heart as the source of sensation once its merely organic function was established. However, ancient religion assigned more than emotions to the heart. In biblical times both Judaism and Christianity used heart as their chief psychological term. *Heart* in the Bible means nothing less than the whole inner life—the seat of emotions, intellect, willpower, and morality (or immorality).[1] Of the psychological use of *heart* in Jewish and Christian Scripture, *The Interpreter's Dictionary of the Bible* states:

Since the term "heart" can mean the totality of the feelings, thoughts, and desires of a man, traced back to their deepest source in his inner life, it sometimes has almost the value of the modern psychological term "personality."[2]

"Holy are the pure in heart . . . ," the Sixth Beatitude, was written with these psychological and religious meanings in mind. The passage of time and the influence of science has not diminished their clarity: the heart represents the inner self, the "me."

Pure in this Beatitude could introduce a lengthy discussion of clean and unclean in religion, particularly in Judaism. That discussion is unnecessary. Ritual purification, laws on clean and unclean food, and guidelines on avoiding religious defilement are of marginal concern in the New Testament. Greater emphasis is on moral purity—a matter of the heart, the inner life. Jesus was apparently impatient with the numerous Jewish regulations on clean and unclean foods. Mark 7:15 has him saying, "Hear me, all of you, and understand: there is nothing outside a man which by going into him can defile him; but the things which come out of a man are what defile him." The early church, influenced by the Apostle Paul, decided that Christians need not observe the Jewish religious laws on clean and unclean.

The Greek word for pure in the Sixth Beatitude has approximately the same meanings as the English. Pure is cleansed, as in purified thoughts or a scrubbed shirt, also unalloyed, as purified silver or unmixed motives. Purity of heart in the Beatitudes clearly means a clean—spiritually and morally cleansed—inner self, the real person down where motivations are set and actions determined.

Purity of heart, like the other qualities of holiness in the Beatitudes, is found in its natural state only in Jesus Christ, who radiates God's purity. The Gospel writers stress Jesus' purity in the many passages in which evil spirits recognize him and flee: for example, the story of the madman of the Gerasenes. According to the thinking of the day, this possessed man was internally directed by an unclean spirit. He runs to Jesus, shouting, "What have you to do with me, Jesus, Son of the Most High God" (Mark 5:7). Rebuked by Jesus, the spirit departs.

The purity of Jesus' love is also shown in the Gospels by his forgiveness of sins, his refusal to be compromised by critics or the devil, and, supremely, in the Crucifixion. Paul had the unmixed, lovingly pure, motives of the man of the cross in mind when, writing to the Philippians, he told Christians to try to express among themselves the humble, unselfish, sacrificial mind of Christ (Philippians 2:1–4).

Christ in Christian theology is purity; any possibility of human purity comes through him, not in this case only by imitation, but *through* Christ, the source of God-given cleansing—salvation. Purity of heart accompanies redemption and, therefore, should be reflected in the inner life and outward behavior of all Christians.

The pure in heart are Christians who with "Everyman" in the medieval morality play have been to the "glorious fountain that all uncleanness doth clarify" and, in a word, have been washed —washed, but not perfectly cleansed compared with Christ. The pure in heart know their impurities, often to the point of agony. Any of the persons in this chapter would be comfortable saying the prayer of the fourth-century poet Aurelius Prudentius Clemens:

> Carefully inspect our feelings;
> see every moment of our lives.
> Many foul stains can be found there
> much in need of your cleansing light.[3]

Examples of great, albeit imperfect, purity of heart among the followers of Christ are as diverse as the human experience in faith. At the same time, the emphasis on the inner life in the Sixth Beatitude suggests two types of saints, heroes, and heroines as particularly good examples. One type is the mystic, who has a highly developed interior spirituality. The relevance of the mystics is even stronger when the whole of Matthew 5:8 is recalled: "Holy are the pure in heart; they shall see God." As stated in Chapter Two, Christian mystics are noted for their visionary experiences and the ability to reveal, or claim to reveal, the divine will.

Mystics who seek and demonstrate purity could fill many chapters. They are well-known figures, such as Francis of Assisi, or obscure ones, such as Juliana of Norwich. Juliana, a fourteenth-century Englishwoman, spent years in a small room built into the wall of a Norman church in Norwich. Voluntarily confined to her cell, she quested internally for purity of heart and union with divine love. Uneducated, she wrote a moving book on her *Sixteen Revelations of Divine Love;* partly paralyzed, she had the universe in her heart and of it learned three truths: "The first is that God made it; the second is that he loved it; the third is that God keeps it."

Or, an entirely different kind of mystic, Frank C. Laubach, a twentieth-century Protestant missionary and educator, who wrote of being taken internally by the "love hungry" God who requires that the love be given away if it shall be kept.

The second type of Christian suggested by the Sixth Beatitude is the pietist (who may also be a mystic), he or she of heartfelt faith, stressing internal conversion and personal morality. Fascinating pietists are also numerous—famous evangelists such as the American layman Dwight L. Moody, or almost forgotten figures such as Sundar Singh, a wandering Indian missionary in the early twentieth century. Born in the Sikh religion, Singh had an inner longing that was never satisfied until he opened his heart to Christ. He wrote: "In comparison with this big world, the human heart is only a small thing. Though the world is so large, it is utterly unable to satisfy this tiny heart. Man's ever-growing soul and its capacities can be satisfied only in the infinite God."

But to fill this chapter only with examples from classical mysticism or pietism would be inappropriate. Christians of other spiritual exercises also long for and mirror purity. Some mystics, some pietists appear, but the selections here are diverse, especially in manners of examining inner selves and of giving expression to the Christ-directed heart.

The saints, heroes, and heroines washed in love also have something in common. With Scottish theologian–hymn writer George Matheson, each sings to God: "I cannot close my heart to thee."

Origen (186–253)

The author of a best-selling book of the early 1960s argued that references to God "up there" or "out there" make no sense in the space age. No physical spot for God seems to remain in a universe explored by telescopes and rockets, said Anglican Bishop J. A. T. Robinson, and his book, *Honest to God*,[4] created a passing stir with its criticism of traditional images of the divine habitat. People lined up for or against the "new" idea that God may not live in the sky—new to many of the readers of the bishop's book; not really new.

Almost eighteen centuries before *Honest to God*, Origen, a great theologian, rejected spatial and physical God-language. Scriptural references to God in heaven, he said, are symbolic. When Christians pray, "Our Father who art in heaven" they are not to think God has "bodily fashion and dwells in heaven," he wrote. God, he said, does not occupy space or come and go between heaven and earth. Origen understood God as all-embracing love and intellect, the very power of creation—revealed, made real, in Jesus Christ; and he taught that people see and know God in the heart, which to Origen also meant the mind.

Origen lived constantly with and tried to follow the Beatitude on purity of heart since, to him, the inner, nonphysical self is the point of contact with God. "Dedication to God" was his definition of the Christian life. His way toward purity included prayer, mental concentration in his scholarship, and an ascetic lifestyle. "His manner of life was as his doctrine, and his doctrine as his life," said Eusebius, the early church historian. Origen's preoccupation with asceticism was so intense in one period that he committed an act of physical abuse later complicating his role in the church. Taking to heart Matthew 19:12 ("and there are eunuchs who have made themselves eunuchs for the sake of the kingdom"), he castrated himself.

The early church frowned on self-mutilation. Origen's precipitous act, when it became known, hurt his reputation. His reputation has also suffered over the course of the Christian centuries because his orthodoxy on some points of doctrine was questioned in his lifetime and is still debated; yet castrated and questioned, he remains the greatest Christian theologian between Paul of Tarsus in the mid–first century and Augustine of Hippo in the early fifth.

Born in Alexandria, Egypt, in A.D. 186, Origen was raised in the church in a day when Christians were periodically persecuted by the Roman state; his own father died a martyr when Origen was sixteen. Accounts say he wanted to join his father in the sacrifice for faith, but was prevented when his mother hid his clothes. Resigned to life, he turned himself entirely to God.

Origen was the church's first major Bible scholar, the first theologian to attempt to state Christian beliefs in a systematic way, and the first eighteen-year-old to head an established center of Christian instruction, the Catechetical School at Alexandria.

The Catechetical School was hardly a university, but it was more than a school of thought. Free classes, not all in religion, were offered to students who gathered around noted teachers. Origen studied there. The chief attraction in his student years was a theologian, Clement of Alexandria, who fled the persecution in which Origen's father died. When classes could resume, the local bishop, Demetrius, asked Origen, a layman, to become headmaster. Origen was literally eighteen years of age, but he soon became famous in Egypt and throughout the church for his scholarship and talent as a teacher.

As Origen taught he also studied, and wrote. He composed more than six thousand pieces of literature, few of which have survived. To help his study of the Old Testament, he devised the first comparative text by arranging the Hebrew original and six Greek versions side by side. He also travelled.

A trip to Palestine in 215 was a turning point in his life because it put him in conflict with his bishop in Egypt. The host bishop in Palestine asked Origen to preach, and he agreed. Demetrius, his bishop in Alexandria, was furious because, in his opinion, laymen should not enter the pulpit. (Rules on such matters differed from area to area in the third-century church.) He called Origen home, and the young theologian spent the next fifteen years doing more writing than teaching. A patron provided a staff of secretaries to take his dictation.

Origen revisited Palestine in 230 and got into even worse trouble with Demetrius. This time he agreed to be ordained. Demetrius was irritated because the bishop of Caesarea had ordained an Alexandrian teacher who was self-castrated. Self-mutilation is condemned in Jewish law, and was considered abhorrent in Roman culture. While the church did not officially condemn such acts until 325, castration was considered an impediment to priestly orders from an early date, at least in some places. Demetrius spread the news of Origen's incompleteness. Many local bishops agreed with his decision not to recognize the ordination, but not the prelates in Palestine, who continued to treat him as a priest.

Condemned in Alexandria, Origen could not go home. He established his new base of operations in Casearea, opening a school but also continuing his travels. During an outbreak of persecution in 249–250, he was jailed and tortured in a vain attempt to force him to renounce Christianity. The experience broke him physically. Origen died in the city of Tyre in 253 or 254.

The purity of heart toward which he aimed was profoundly illustrated in his reaction to Demetrius' anger and actions in 230. Exiled from home, emotionally hurt, repudiated by much of the church for an act he regretted but considered external, Origen was most concerned that his reaction not adversely affect his inner spiritual life and his scholarship. He did not want to hate Demetrius. The Logos (reason or the Word), he wrote, called him to "stand firm for the contest and to preserve the inner self, lest haply evil thoughts should have power to bring the storm against my soul also." He weathered the storm without hatred.

Origen has been both praised and blamed for using elements of Greek philosophy in his theology. He studied ancient thinkers, such as Plato, and borrowed some of their language. His purpose, howev-

er, was not to Hellenize the Gospel, but to bring all human knowledge into line with knowledge of God. Toward that same end he did
theological battle with Gnostics (sects claiming that special secret
knowledge was necessary to be Christian) and other heretics he felt
defiled the faith.

The theologian of Alexandria and Caesarea was not perfect, probably not correct in all his theology—few theologians are, but he offers
a worthy challenge to any Christian who would be pure in heart. His
aim was "to see life steadily, and see it whole."

Hildegard of Bingen (1098–1179)

Hildegard in old age was not the kind of local celebrity a Rhineland
prince would have automatically invited to meet a visiting archbishop. The abbess of the Benedictine convent at Bingen could not be
trusted not to accost the visitor, telling him how to conduct his affairs
and describing what would happen to him if he ignored her advice;
she knew, she would say, she had it in a vision.

The "Sibyl of the Rhine" enjoyed a mixed reputation among her
contemporaries. To some, her visions and prophecies were the very
voice of God; to others, she was more witch than nun, tiresome and
self-righteous. She considered herself nothing but "a poor earthen
vessel," saying what came to her from "the Living Light," the phrase
she used for God.

Abrasive Hildegard was—not the least reluctant to tell a bishop he
would die for failing to upgrade the spiritual and moral deportment of
the clergy in his charge. At the same time, her criticism was usually
right. The twelfth-century church was notoriously lax in moral and
spiritual discipline; bishops played politics instead of minding the
faithful. In the 1170s Hildegard pleaded unsuccessfully with her
superior, the archbishop of Mainz, to give up his intrigues in Italy and
resume his German pastorate.

Hildegard was not, however, primarily a reformer. She was first
and foremost a mystic, the first of the great medieval German mystics. *Know the Ways of the Lord*, the title of her most important work,
can be taken as her personal motto. To her God's ways were learned
by allowing divine love to conquer the boastful heart. Although said
to be gifted with foresight from childhood, she counted herself of no
significance until her forty-third year when, in her words, "a shaft of
light of dazzling brilliancy came from the heavens and pierced my

mind and heart like a flame that warms but does not burn, as the sun heats by its rays." That shaft of light, she said, opened to her the meaning of the Scripture despite her inability to read the texts.

A woman of almost no formal education, Hildegard was remarkably well informed on theology, philosophy, medicine, natural history, politics, and psychology. She understood the influence of dread and obsession on health; she argued on psychological grounds that sick people in a frenzy are not possessed by devils. The abbess of Bingen understood the rudiments of music and composed more than sixty hymns.

Hildegard claimed her knowledge came from God—that shaft of light—and her claim may be true, since she probably could not read.

She was born at Böckelheim (southwest Germany) in 1098. Her father was a petty feudal lord, and her mother dedicated the child to God (which means she may have been extremely pious or she may not have wanted to raise the girl). Hildegard was turned over to a Diessenberg recluse named Jutta who gradually gathered a community of nuns taking the Benedictine rule.

Receiving her nun's habit when she was fifteen years old, Hildegard lived an uneventful life for more than twenty years. At Jutta's death about 1136 she became head of the Diessenberg community, and around that same time reports of her visions began to circulate. The twelfth-century church maintained a cautious attitude toward visionaries and prophets. Written accounts of the revelations to Hildegard were submitted to the archbishop of Mainz and later came to the attention of Pope Eugenius III. Both men judged them favorably.

Hildegard and the authors of the biblical books of Ezekiel and Revelation have much in common. Their writings—Hildegard dictated hers—are filled with strange forms and patterns of movement, symbols, and secret meanings (unlike her predecessors, Hildegard usually explained her symbols). She spoke of iron-colored mountains with wings that to her represented the steadfast kingdom of God, and at the mountain's base "a shape covered over and over with eye upon eye, so that this multitude of eyes prevented me from seeing anything that resembled a human form." This shape represented a self looking only to the Kingdom. Radiance is everywhere in Hildegard's visions.

Sometime before 1150 Hildegard moved her nuns from Diessenberg to a new isolated but comfortable convent (it had plumbing) at Rupertsberg, near Bingen on the Rhine. There she became Sibyl and scourge, conducting an enormous correspondence with other mystics, secular rulers, and church leaders. She denounced avarice in the clergy, and on occasion took to the road with her message of purifying light.

The Living Light, she said, is what the individual heart needs to be flooded with love, and what the church needs to be holy. A voice from Hildegard's iron-colored mountain says: "He who governs all His creatures in goodness and might, He pervades all who fear Him and serve Him in love and delight and humility with the clarity of heaven, and guides the patient pilgrim on the right path to the joyful beholding of eternity."

Hildegard's last months were plagued by a dispute with church officials in Mainz over her decision to bury an excommunicated man in her convent cemetery. She said the deceased had received Holy Communion before breathing his last and, besides, she had a vision saying her action was right. The "Sibyl of the Rhine" won the dispute before dying in September, 1179.

Thomas Aquinas (1225–1274)

His fellow students at the University of Paris in 1245 called him "the dumb ox." The tall, robust son of the count of Aquino had little to say initially in class debates, but when the teacher examined his written work he exclaimed, "he will make his lowing heard to the uttermost parts of the earth."

"Lowing" was a good choice of words; Thomas affected the course of Christianity without a rampage or a show of his own importance. When a classmate offered to explain the daily lesson, "the dumb ox" listened. Thomas's writings fill sixty volumes, but near the end of his forty-eight years he called them "straw." He built a new theological silo feeding Christian thought for centuries; he was controversial, but no one ever accused Thomas of a boastful heart.

In a different way, in a very different time and place, Thomas was like Origen in his zeal to bring all knowledge to the service of God and the Gospel, and he pursued his goal with a purity of heart matched by few academic theologians. Theologians often seem tempted to develop inflated egos; not Thomas. Once asked if vainglory tugged at him, he replied in the negative, adding that common sense taught him that pride was unreasonable.

Thomas was born in 1225 into a changing church. Monasticism

was changing under the impact of the wandering friars of the new Franciscan and Dominican orders. Augustinian theology, the epitome of Western orthodoxy for six hundred years, was being tested and challenged in newly important universities. Beginning about 1200, the universities introduced a new dimension into theology with the rediscovery of the philosophy of Aristotle, the pre-Christian Greek who glorified human reason. Could reason be a pathway to God? The question alone clashed with Augustine's doctrine of the total depravity of humanity; reason, said Augustine, is hopelessly spoiled by sin, and only faith in response to grace leads to God. But was Augustine right? The great and continuing debate over faith and reason was in progress.

Thomas's pivotal role in the debate was to synthesize faith and reason. He adored Aristotle but did not want to jettison Augustine, so he combined them. Reason, he said, is damaged but not destroyed by sin. It can serve and point to the revealed truths of faith. Thomas was the innovator in harmonizing Aristotle with Christian doctrine, but he inherited his method from the profession he chose to enter. He was a "schoolman," a Scholastic.

The medieval Scholastics were not advocates of a single school of thought called "scholasticism." Scholasticism was a method more than it was a message. It tried to harmonize Christian doctrine with new knowledge emerging from the universities. Usually traced from the eleventh century, scholasticism established systems holding together science and reason, faith and revelation. Practitioners were called schoolmen because they were often lecturers in the universities.

Thomas almost did not become a schoolman. His feudal family intended him to become a cloistered monk. The family estate was near Aquino on the road from Rome to Naples. Nearby was the famous monastery of Monte Cassino, and there he was deposited at age five. Because of political squabbles Monte Cassino was temporarily evacuated in 1239. Thomas went home, and instead of returning to the monastery, enrolled at the new University of Naples. He encountered Dominicans whose still young order was committed to an educated clergy and was establishing houses at many universities. Thomas joined the order when he was nineteen years old, and his work must be interpreted in large part as evangelistic. His scholarship was always aimed at explaining faith.

A Benedictine, yes; a Dominican, no, said Thomas's strong-willed mother. The young monk was kidnapped by his brother and held in confinement for more than a year. Unable to budge Thomas's determination, the family relented in 1245, allowing him to pursue his friar's life as a student in Paris. The "dumb ox" became the star pupil of Albert Magnus, the teacher mainly responsible for introducing Aristotle into theology. Thomas studied with Albert in Paris for three or four years, then accompanied him to another teaching post in Cologne.

Back in Paris in 1252 as student, then teacher, Thomas quickly became a major theological attraction of Europe. Witty, fair-minded in listening to critics, and sure of his vocation, he saw himself not as an oracle of truth but as a pilgrim in quest of truth satisfying the inner struggle to know God. He admired the contemplative life because, he said, its chief interest is "the contemplation of truth." But, he added, genuine contemplation of God requires purity: "For it is written: *Blessed are the clean of heart, for they shall see God,* and, *Follow peace with all men, and holiness, without which no man shall see God.*"

So great was his reputation that in 1259 Thomas was called to Rome as lecturer and preacher to the papal court (curia). He began his monumental work, *Summa Theologica,* during his nine years in Rome. The *Summa* was designed to be precisely what its title implies—the summation of Christian theology. While the work was never finished, it was the most comprehensive statement on the Christian faith produced by the medieval world—the high point of scholasticism, with its harmony of faith and reason. Canonized in 1323, Thomas was named a "doctor" (highest teacher) of the Roman Catholic church in 1576, and in 1879 Pope Leo XIII declared the *Summa* the basic instrument of Catholic teachings. The Protestant Reformation argued with scholasticism and with Thomas over the relationship of faith and reason (and even more over his ideas of the papacy's importance), but Reformer Martin Luther called Thomas "that sainted man," and no serious theologian since the thirteenth century dares to proceed without reading him.

Thomas returned to Paris in 1268 to engage in a sharp debate over whether two truths—faith and reason—can be contradictory. He maintained that two truths cannot contradict, but his insistence that within faith reason can operate by its own laws brought down the wrath of the Augustinian party. Thomas was a remarkably compassionate adversary, as demonstrated in his debates with his friend, the Franciscan Bonaventura, who disapproved of Thomas's heavy reliance on the philosophy of Aristotle.

The arguments between Thomas and Bonaventura took place in Naples, where Thomas went in 1272 to establish a Dominican house at the new university. Thomas was at the height of his career, still working on the *Summa Theologica*, and consulted on every point of theology. His advice was needed in 1274 at the Council of Lyons, a meeting organized to heal the schism between Eastern and Western Christianity (the council failed). Pope Gregory X sent for the great schoolman, and Thomas set out, getting sick on the road and dying on March 7 at a Cistercian abbey at Fossanova.

In addition to scholarly theology, Thomas wrote liturgical material and hymns, many still used by churches of all denominations. His emphasis on inward purity is clearly seen in a verse of his eucharistic hymn "Thee We Adore, O Hidden Savior":

> Fountain of goodness,
>   Jesus, Lord and God:
> Cleanse us, unclean,
>   with thy most cleansing blood;
> Increase our faith and love,
>   that we may know
> The hope and peace
>   which from thy presence flow.[5]

Philip Melanchthon (1497–1560)

The human heart, the emotions, he said, are ruined by self-love; neither reason nor law, religious or civil, can control self-interest: the blight is sin blocking love for God and love for neighbor, and only the grace of God can forgive the sin and turn the heart to love and goodness.

So Philip Melanchthon believed—purity of heart by grace, accepted in faith, not by merit or bargaining with God. So he tried to live, as one with a sinful heart regenerated by God.

Theologies that teach sin as part of the human condition are not popular today, though self-love is, having been elevated to the psychological throne. Actually, theologians who take sin seriously are today not so unpopular as they are simply unknown, and among them was Philip Melanchthon. He and the Christian doctrine of sin are worth rediscovery in a world trying to find its way to goodness.

In 1518 Melanchthon accepted a job teaching Greek in a small German university in the process of revising its theological education program. The school in Wittenberg was replacing a curriculum fixed on medieval scholasticism with an approach centered on Bible study; it needed a professor to teach the original language of the New Testament to future clergy. This curriculum change went along with other reforms taking place at the university. Melanchthon was invited to Wittenberg by Martin Luther.

The Protestant Reformation had already begun when Melanchthon arrived in Wittenberg, Saxony, but no one really knew that, or was using that term (not for more than ten years). Luther, who taught at the university, had the year before issued a serious theological challenge in his Ninety-five Theses to a papal-approved practice he and others considered scandalous. That practice was the selling of indulgences supposed to guarantee the release of souls from purgatory. Proceeds from some indulgences went toward the building of Saint Peter's Basilica in Rome. Luther, in effect, accused church and pope of perpetrating a spiritual fraud, and the Lutheran Reformation emerged (to oversimplify the situation) from the debate started over indulgences.

Melanchthon in 1518 was a humanist, a particular kind of Renaissance scholar informed about religion but also committed to what today are the liberal arts—language, literature, and the classics (see Erasmus, p. 115). Only twenty-one years old when he accepted Luther's invitation, the son of an armor maker from Bretten (in Bravaria) was already an outstanding humanist, author of a Greek textbook, and a forceful lecturer. His education had been directed by a great uncle, John Reuchlin, one of the most famous humanists, who recommended Melanchthon to Luther. (Reuchlin also advised the young scholar to change his name, originally Schwartzerd, meaning "black earth"; Melanchthon is the Greek equivalent.)

Though not primarily a theologian in 1518, Melanchthon found himself in agreement with the reforming ideas of Luther. He lived the rest of his life in Wittenberg, marrying and having four children. Education was his special interest. He was instrumental in founding three universities (Marburg, Jena, and Königsberg) and in reforming ten others. Melanchthon wrote the Augsburg Confession, the major statement of Lutheran belief, and in a sense succeeded Luther as the chief figure in German Protestantism, outliving his friend by sixteen chaotic years. At his death in 1560 Melanchthon was buried beside Martin Luther.

Melanchthon is usually merely a footnote to Luther in history books or, especially among some Lutheran groups, is cast as a perverter of pure Lutheran doctrine because of controversies of interpretation befalling the movement after Luther's death. Actually, he was Luther's trusted partner in reformation, a man who happened not to function well as a theological arbiter, as was needed in the ideological and political confusion of mid–sixteenth-century Germany.

The first widely noticed indication of Melanchthon's important role in the Reformation came in 1521 with the publication of *Loci Communes*, the first systematic presentation of Luthern doctrine. (The title means "the cardinal points of theology".) This was written under the most adverse conditions. Luther was in hiding to escape arrest. Wittenberg was in turmoil, wracked not by disputes between Protestants and Catholics but among different reforming parties, some of which wanted to go faster and further than Luther. Melanchthon was substituting for Luther as lecturer on Scripture. His classes were huge. The *Loci* resulted from his study of Paul's Letter to the Romans, and was published despite an imperial ban on anything favorable to Luther and the reforming cause.

Luther said the *Loci* should be canonized as Scripture, and Elizabeth I of England is said to have memorized it so she could discuss theology. The book covered numerous topics, none more significant than Melanchthon's consideration of the inner self. "The first and chief affection of human nature," he said, "is self-love, by which it is drawn away to wish for and desire only what seems to its nature good, sweet, pleasant and glorious."

Melanchthon did not deny the role of reason in social organization and church affairs; his appreciation of reason in those realms increased with age as he saw the disruption of religious and social order. He allowed that in a spiritual, inward sense, reason may be able to nudge people toward goodness; not far, however, because he concluded that the emotions—the heart—rule the person, and people are a mass of self-love, or sin. In this, Melanchthon broke with the scholastic understanding, developed in part from Aquinas, that sin is human defect. He returned to a more Augustinian framework and reasserted the reality of original sin.

To Melanchthon original sin was not so much physically transmitted, as with Augustine, as it was the universal phenomenon of self-love. "All men according to their natural powers are truly sinners and do always sin," he said.

The self-love of the heart, Melanchthon taught, cannot be eradicated by obeying the law (religious or secular) or by good works; salvation does not result from buying an indulgence or obeying the pope. The only hope for inward purity, he said, is the grace of God that comes to people continuously, not making them instantly and forever pure but continuously regenerating the heart tuned in faith toward grace. The faithful Christian, he maintained, remains a sinner—a forgiven sinner justified (made right before God) by faith. "This reliance on the benevolence or mercy of God first pacifies the heart, and then incites us to give thanks to God for his mercy . . ." he wrote.

Furthermore, Melanchthon believed that the joy of the forgiven, purified heart expresses itself in compassion and service to neighbors without "self-seeking and with no malice."

Melanchthon from 1521 until his death lived at the center of the storm caused by Luther. He fought many theological battles, published books, lectured, taught Greek, negotiated with princes and non-Lutheran Protestants, and in his old age began to wish for the calmer days of youth. After Luther died he was criticized for almost everything he said or did; he had the misfortune to be Luther's close associate without being Luther, and no one who inherited Luther's theological shoes could possibly fill them.

Interestingly, Melanchthon was apparently not criticized for his devotion to astrology, which was a part of the early sixteenth century. Kings, queens, and Pope Paul III (1534–1549) had court astrologers. True astrology, Melanchthon said, depends on correct observation of divine order. He once commented that had he read his son-in-law's horoscope he would never have permitted the marriage.

But grace and forgiveness were always more important to him than the stars. In one of his many written prayers, Melanchthon left no doubt where his heart was: "O God of Wisdom and Goodness, Righteousness, Truth, Mercy, and Lovingkindness; with my heart full of thanks I remember thy favors and blessings which are so many and so great that I cannot count them or reflect upon them enough."[6]

Rose of Lima (1586–1617)

That Rose of Lima, patron saint of South America, wanted and worked for inner purity is certain. Her single desire was to banish self-love from her heart. That her methods are unattractive to most people is likewise certain. She was a recluse, an extreme ascetic who hid herself in a hut in a garden and wore a silver headband with thorns on the inner surface.

Christened Isabel (and called Rose for her beauty), she was born in Lima in 1586, about fifty years after the Spanish completed their conquest of Peru's Inca people. Her father was Spanish; some accounts say her mother was Inca, but she too may have been Spanish. The family fortune fluctuated.

Rose, according to the stories, objected as a child to mention of her physical beauty because she found praise an obstacle to humility. She is said to have rubbed her face with lime (a painful experience) to discourage compliments. As a young woman Rose wished to enter a convent; she was prevented by her family, but refused to marry. When her father suffered a financial loss in a mining venture, she took up needlework to help the family.

The young Catherine of Siena, who shut herself in a room for years to perfect her spirituality (see page 203), seems to have been Rose's model. Finally allowed to join a noncloistered Dominican order, Rose elected to live in a small enclosure in the garden. She did hand work, tended the flowers, prayed, and kept up her guard against the devil invading her heart.

Rose emerged from seclusion around 1614. She lived her remaining three years in the home of a government official. At her death in 1617 at the age of thirty-one, the city of Lima gave her a heroine's funeral.

Why bother with Rose of Lima? Details of her life are skimpy and undramatic, and the miracles attributed to her after death are outside the scope of this book. How does she exemplify purity of heart?

She is significant here as a type found in Roman Catholic, Eastern Orthodox, and occasionally Protestant spirituality. Rose has a considerable company of sisters (and some brothers) across the centuries who have believed, in her words, that "we cannot obtain grace unless we suffer affliction." With such persons, purity of heart becomes an obsession, almost a mania, tied up with the desire to "see" God—to know the Divine immediately.

It would be quite easy to argue that Rose of Lima and her kind are neurotics, even freaks. Rose may well have suffered from a warped personality, but she was conscious and articulate in her actions. She was no frenzied flagellant, and as said earlier, religious motivation is not amenable to the standards of the twentieth-century cult of psy-

chological sameness and well-adjustment. Holy people do not necessarily require either happiness or social approval.

Modern activist Christians sometimes ask of the Roses of the
church, "What good do they do?" A sort of answer, but not a very
interesting one, can be formed by turning the question around,
"What harm do they do?" Actually, neither question is interesting.
What is fascinating is a whole company of Roses—ancient, medieval,
and modern—seeking purity along a course where the tempo is set by
a drummer most people cannot hear, perhaps should not hear. Rose is
even hard to hear: "We must heap trouble upon trouble to attain a
deep participation in the divine nature."

That the interior theology of Rose of Lima conflicts with much
modern Catholic and Protestant thought is hardly troubling. Christian theology is a many-colored coat. What is troubling is her general-
ization that God's grace comes only after tribulation. This suggests
that grace is purchased by pain, a dubious assertion in any system of
doctrine.

At the same time, she struck important chords in realizing that
suffering can be "beautiful . . . noble . . . precious" when endured
for the love of Christ. She also pointed strongly toward the cross as
the source of purity.

Rose's spirituality, her obsession with purity of heart, seems bizarre in the 1980s, unless it is read in terms of Saint Paul's observation
in I Corinthians 1:28–29: "God chose what is low and despised in the
world . . . so that no human being might boast in the presence of
God."

Blaise Pascal (1623–1662)

A few days after Blaise Pascal, the father of integral calculus, died
in August, 1662, a servant arranging his personal effects found a piece
of parchment sewed inside the lining of the last coat he had worn. On
the parchment, neatly folded and with a paper copy, was Pascal's
account of a religious experience some eight years earlier, on November 23, 1654:

> From about half past ten in the evening
> until about half past twelve

FIRE

Fire inside burning away doubt and distress:

Certitude. Certitude. Feeling. Joy. Peace
God of Jesus Christ.

Fire in the mind:

Forgetfulness of the world and of everything,
except God.
He is to be found only by ways taught in the
Gospel.

Fire in the heart:

"Righteous Father, the world hath not known Thee,
but I have known Thee."
Joy, joy, joy, tears of joy.

Forgiving fire.

Jesus Christ.
Jesus Christ.
I have separated myself from Him: I have fled
from Him, denied Him, crucified Him.
Let me never be separated from Him.
We keep hold of Him only by the ways taught
in the Gospel.
Renunciation, total and sweet.[7]

For eight years Pascal kept the parchment about him to remind him
of the truth he could never find in science: Greatness is total submis-
sion to Jesus Christ. His two major literary works, *Les Provinciales*
("Letters to a Provincial") and *Pensées* ("Thoughts"), were defenses of
his faith.

Blaise Pascal was a scientific genius, one of the first and most
significant mathematicians and physicists of the modern world. The
Frenchman not only introduced calculus; he created the hydraulic
press and did pioneering work in atmospheric pressure and the principle of the vacuum. He also invented the computer, but more important was his work on probability—the bet on God's existence.

Pascal was a scientific genius in a religious age, and since in the
seventeenth century science was still closer to philosophy than to
technology, a scientist was not necessarily at odds with religion.
Pascal was formally and personally religious—a Roman Catholic
—before his "night of fire" in 1654. But that experience so touched
the core of his being and remained so immediate that subsequent inter-

preters have often viewed him as a renegade scientist elevating "heart" (faith) above "head" (reason). To read such a dichotomy into Pascal is unfortunate, because it misses the wholeness of Pascal's religious outlook.

Pascal had a biblical understanding of the inner life—mind and emotions unified in response to God. God, he wrote in *Pensées*, is *"felt* by the heart, not by reason" (italics added), but this does not make the heart antirational. For he said, "It is the way of God who does all things gently to put religion into the mind by reason, and into the heart by grace."

The idea that Pascal elevated heart over head comes from taking fragments of the *Pensées* out of context (an easy error since "Thoughts" is not a book but an outline and collection of ideas he intended to use in a never written apology for Christianity). On heart and reason in Pascal, T. S. Eliot put the matter right: "The heart, in Pascal's terminology, is itself truly rational if it is truly the heart."[8]

Pascal's "night of fire" was his baptism by God's grace, and grace is the key in his views on purity of heart and mind. Persons cannot establish a right relationship with God by what they do or think, he said; that comes only by faith in response to the fire of grace: "Comfort yourselves. It is not from yourselves that you should expect grace; but, on the contrary, it is in expecting nothing from yourselves, that you must hope for it."

Born in 1623 in Clermont-Ferrand, Pascal received a sound education in mathematics and religion from his father, a well-to-do government official. Around 1646 the entire Pascal family was introduced to the theology of a Dutch bishop, Cornelius Jansen. This bishop, who died in 1638, wrote a book (*Augustinus*) advocating a kind of evangelical Catholicism characterized by moral strictness. Jansen was no Protestant, but he was a fierce critic of the Jesuits, who exerted great influence in the post-Reformation Catholic church and who, Jansen believed, encouraged moral laxity by teaching that the yoke of Christ is light on believers. Rejecting much of the scholastic theology popular among the Jesuits, *Augustinus* proposed a revival of the teachings of Augustine of Hippo (see page 110), including emphasis on inherent human sinfulness and the cleansing grace of God.

Jansen's ideas took hold among a significant number of French Catholics and found its main center of support at Port Royal, a religious community, south of Versailles, associated with the prominent Arnauld family. Pascal's sister Jacqueline, two years his junior, became a nun at Port Royal, and he sometimes lived there though he never officially joined the community.

Pascal continued his interest in physics after his 1654 night of fire, but most of his subsequent writings were religious, and his experience and understanding of grace became factors in the storm that broke over Jansenism. Neither his later life nor his writings can be understood apart from the controversy centering on Port Royal.

Vigorously attacked by the Jesuits, Jansenism was condemned by the Roman Catholic church in 1653. Armed with Vatican approval, the French Jesuits and the theological faculty at the University of Paris set about to root out the heresy, and a prime target was the Jansenist leader Antoine Arnauld, a lawyer whose sisters Angelique and Agnes led the nuns of Port Royal. Arnauld persuaded Pascal to come to his defense.

Les Provinciales constituted that defense. The letters, originally published under a pseudonym, were a scathing denunciation of the Jesuits from the perspective of a moral puritan who believed only grace could cleanse the sinful heart and mind. Pascal was a skillful, careful polemicist hanging the Jesuits on their own words as he excoriated them for teaching "easy devotion." At the same time, his overall tone was probably unfair to the Society of Jesus, and Pascal was really uninterested in comprehending what the Jesuits, as agents of the Counter-Reformation, were attempting to do in "moving out to meet people who seemed to be abandoning their traditional faith."[9]

Les Provinciales both popularized Jansenism and intensified the attacks against it. Pascal himself became a target of the Jesuits and of philosophers who thought he had taken leave of his senses in discussing truth as a matter of loving God. *Pensées* was planned as a defense against Jesuits and skeptics. Pascal wanted to demonstrate the truth of Christianity in terms of grace. Faith, he said, is always a matter of a "wager." God either is or God is not, he said, and the wager must be made one way or the other. To skeptics who deny God, he said: "Let us weigh the gain and the loss in wagering that God is. . . . If you gain, you gain all; if you lose, you lose nothing."

Pascal advised against compromise as the church moved against Port Royal in 1660, but he was also apparently tired of the whole controversy and of the bickering within the Jansenist movement. "To Thy tribunal, Lord Jesus, I appeal," he said, and waited to die.

Never physically strong, Pascal suffered terrible headaches that made him irritable and hard to please. Yet he was also extremely generous, taking a destitute family into his home in Clermont shortly before his death, and leaving himself when a child in that family came down with smallpox, rather than ask the poor people to leave.

Pascal died in the village of Saint-Etienne-du-Mont. Afterwards controversy arose over whether the parish priest should have given deathbed Holy Communion to a Jansenist sympathizer, and a debate on his orthodoxy has since continued. Pascal never doubted his orthodoxy. His will began, "First, as a good Christian, Catholic, Apostolic, Roman . . ."

He was a complex man, embarrassed at times by his own greatness of mind, but wishing only to have Christ in his heart and his head. T. S. Eliot said of him:

I can think of no Christian writer . . . more to be commended than Pascal to those who doubt, but who have the mind to conceive, and the sensibility to feel, the disorder, the futility, the meaninglessness, the mystery of life and suffering, and who can only find peace through a satisfaction of the whole being.[10]

Susanna Wesley (1669–1742)
John Wesley (1703–1791)
Charles Wesley (1707–1788)

Once upon a time most every Protestant knew the story of John Wesley's "heart-warming" experience. Few preachers could get through a year without telling it at least once, but since accounts of conversions are rarely heard from typical pulpits today, this historically important episode may be entirely new to many people.

Wesley was a failed, dejected, and doubting Anglican missionary just returned to England from Georgia. His spirits had been lifted by Moravians (see Count Zinzendorf, page 154) met in homeward passage, and in London he encountered others of this pietistic movement. "Come to a Moravian meeting," one said. Wesley went on May 24, 1738, as he wrote in his *Journal*:

In the evening, I went very unwillingly to a society in Aldersgate Street, where one was reading Luther's preface to the *Epistle to the Romans*. About a quarter to nine, while he was describing the change which God works in the heart through faith in Christ, I felt my heart strangely warmed. I felt that I did trust in Christ, Christ alone, for salvation; and an assurance was given me that he had taken away *my* sins, even *mine*, and saved me from the law of sin and death.

The young priest's heart could not have been warmed at a better time. Philosophical rationalism dominated the Church of England, and, in the words of one historian, "the hearts of the multitudes were hungry."[11] Furthermore, the Hanoverian kings may have sat on the throne but the masses of people in the burgeoning industrial society were ruled by ignorance and poverty. Neither the church nor the aristocrats felt much warmth toward the thronging poor.

Within a year of his visit to Aldersgate Street, Wesley was preaching warm faith heated by divine forgiveness to some of the largest crowds ever gathered for sermons before the invention of the loudspeaker. (He is said to have addressed as many as twenty thousand people on occasion.) Most of his hearers at the outdoor services were poor; the rich were uninterested. "I submitted to be more vile and in the highway," he said.

Wesley preached faith, forgiveness, and the regeneration of the heart by divine love. He also preached spiritual discipline and moral purity. The poor found new dignity before God in the Wesleyan movement. They found fellowship, even leadership opportunities, in the local societies that sprang up everywhere Wesley preached. Though never a social reformer in the modern sense, Wesley believed God's love requires justice and charity among people, and he was a sharp critic of the slave trade.

The man with the warm heart was by the 1740s the symbol of a religious revival often credited with saving England from the likes of the French Revolution. Of course, he did not single-handedly launch the revival. In the field before him, for example, was evangelist George Whitefield. Wesley and Whitefield were colleagues until they disagreed on the issues of free will and predestination. Wesley taught free will and the possibility of salvation for all; Whitefield, a Calvinist, stressed the predetermining God, so they went separate ways. The "free grace" Wesley proclaimed was one reason he is the primary historical symbol of England's eighteenth-century revival. The poor loved the message. Another reason is that his work produced a new denomination. Without setting out to do it and never himself leaving the Anglican fold, Wesley created Methodism—once Protestantism's warmest, most zealous and most successful revival movement, the dominant religious force on the American frontier.

If John Wesley was neither the first nor the only prominent preacher in the highway, neither was he alone in starting the particular expression of the awakening he came to dominate. Beside him was his younger brother Charles, and behind them both was the towering spirit of their mother, Susanna.

Home for the Wesley family was the Anglican rectory at Epworth, north of London in Lincolnshire. Samuel Wesley, the husband and father, had a poetic, not always practical, mind. He knew the smell of debtors' prison. Susanna kept bodies and souls together in the large household. (She gave birth to nineteen children, only ten of whom lived beyond infancy.) Samuel said the liturgy at church; Susanna held worship in her kitchen on Sunday nights. She schooled the children, disciplined them sternly, and loved them gently. Susanna encouraged her sons to go to the university. She counseled John when he felt called to the ministry. And Susanna paid the bills when she could, and wrote a book on religious truth to edify her children. She also wrote moving prayers concerned with the way of holiness and purity in everyday life:

Be pleased, O God, to grant unto me that great freedom of mind that will enable me to follow and attend on Jesus with a pure heart; to be ever prepared and disposed to observe His example and obey His precepts. And do Thou further help me to achieve that consummate prudence, great purity, great separation from the world, much liberty and a firm steadfast faith in the Lord Jesus that will enable me to manage the common affairs of life in such wise as not to misemploy or neglect the improvement of my talents; to be industrious without covetousness; diligent without anxiety; as exact in each punctilio of action as if success were dependent upon it, and yet so resigned as to leave all events to Thee and still attributing to Thee the praise of every good work.

John studied at Charterhouse School in London and, at age seventeen, entered Oxford. Graduated and ordained, he helped his father in Epworth for two years, then in 1729 returned as a fellow to Oxford where brother Charles was enrolled. The Wesleys and a group of friends, including Whitefield, formed a "Holy Club" for self-discipline, worship, and social service, including visits to the local jail. So punctual at prayer and work were the club members that other students called them "methodists"—followers of a method.

Unsatisfied in their incipient methodism, the brothers Wesley in 1735 undertook missionary work in the new colony of Georgia. The conversion of Indians was their goal. Charles soon discovered his aversion to the American forests and returned to England. John stayed on until 1738, never preached to Indians, and found life as a

Savannah cleric bleak and frustrating. He was especially frustrated by the rejection of a young woman, Sophy Hopkey, whom he proceeded in his priestly power to exclude from Holy Communion when she married another man. (Wesley married at age forty-eight. The union was as ill-fated as his missionary efforts in Georgia. He and the bride, a widow with children, soon separated and rarely saw one another thereafter.)

Back in England, John learned that Charles and their friend Whitefield had experienced heart-warming conversions similar to his of May, 1738. They would go forth with a message of love to cleanse sinful hearts. These young preachers had no idea of separating from the Church of England. Their public preaching was to "call sinners to repentance." Without mentioning himself, Wesley wrote in his *Journal* that "two or three clergymen of the Church of England . . . sounded the alarm to the utmost borders of the land. Many thousands gathered to hear them; and in every place where they came, many began to show such a concern for religion as they never had done before."

Few preachers across the Christian centuries have matched John Wesley's pace. He was constantly on the move right up to his death in 1791 at age eighty-eight. His *Journal* reflects the compulsion he had to preach and to visit the Methodist societies and the homes of everyday people. An entry for 1746 reads:

"Monday, February 3, and the following day, I visited several of the county societies. Mon. 10—I preached at Paulton; on Thursday noon, at Shepton Mallet, and Oak Hill in the evening. The next morning I walked . . . to Coleford. Sun. 16—I took my leave of Bristol and Kingswood; and Mon. 17, set out for Newcastle. I preached near Thornbury about noon; and in the evening at Wall Bridge, near Stroud."

He was still at it in March, 1789:

"Fri. 13—I spent some time with poor Richard Henderson, deeply affected with the loss of his only son . . . Sat. 14—In the evening I preached in Temple church . . . Sun. 15—Having Mr. Baddiley to assist me in the morning, I preached at Kingswood in the afternoon . . . Mon. 16—We set out early, and dined at Stroud . . . and I suppose two hundred were present at five in the morning. Tues. 17—Many were present at Gloucester in the evening . . . Wed. 18—I preached at Tewkesbury at noon . . ."

John Wesley rode more than 250,000 miles on horseback in England and Scotland during his career, and he also visited Ireland.

Official Anglican reaction to his evangelism was mixed. Some bishops applauded the Wesleys; other condemned. The preachers encountered hecklers and closed doors and were also met by considerable support among the common people and the merchant class.

Charles is less prominent in church history than John, but he was no less important in the evangelical movement. His great contribution was as a writer of hymns. The revival grew on preaching and singing, and Charles Wesley was a master at getting people to sing. He wrote some sixty-five hundred hymn texts, many of which he set to easy music, often borrowed from folk traditions and the popular songs of his day. His hymns are sung today by all churches. Among his works are "Hark! the Herald Angels Sing" and "O For a Thousand Tongues to Sing." Charles was as much a mystic as a pietist. A stanza of "O For a Heart to Praise My God" asks the Almighty for

> A heart in every thought renewed
> And full of love divine,
> Perfect and right and pure and good,
> A copy, Lord, of thine.

Relations between the brothers cooled as the Methodist societies —given the same name used to ridicule the old Holy Club—showed inclinations toward separatism. An England-wide "United Society" was formed in 1740, and as time passed it took more and more steps away from the Church of England—and sometimes was pushed away. Charles had no intention of leaving the mother church. John shared his hope that the Methodists could remain Anglican, but he saw problems in trying to keep a reform movement within narrow confines.

The Methodist Society formally functioned under the Anglican umbrella until 1784. In that year it became independent, and a Methodist Church was also organized in the embryonic United States. The final break with the Church of England came when John Wesley decided to ordain clergy for the American branch. For several reasons, including opposition to rebellious colonists, the Anglican bishop of London refused Wesley's request to ordain ministers for the American Methodists, who were considered a group within the established church. Wesley opposed American independence but found it unconscionable that believers in the New World should be without access to clergy and the sacraments. By accepted practice, only bishops were allowed to ordain priests. Wesley respected church tradition but felt that the unusual situation justified unusual action, and he found precedent for his ordinations in the practices of the early Christians before the episcopal system developed. It was permissible, he said, for priests to ordain other priests. Such an idea was totally unacceptable to Anglican authorities, and the Methodist Church was chartered as an independent organization in 1785.

Charles disapproved of the steps toward independence and died in 1788 in the arms of the Anglican Church. Susanna was long dead before the movement reached maturity, but she had lived to take part in the early revival. Samuel Wesley died before his sons went to Georgia. Susanna lived with a daughter for several years, then made her home with John in London and frequently accompanied him on preaching trips. She died in July 1742 after requesting her children to sing a psalm of praise when she breathed her last.

Despite the break with the Church of England, Wesley was the grand old man of English religion in the late eighteenth century. Humble, he could be irascible; forgiving, he could be rigorous. He required strict moral and spiritual behavior within the Methodist societies, because he knew something many of his descendants have forgotten: only strict religions last; lax religions never flourish for long.

Wesley was remarkably open for a man of his age to the possibility of diverse paths to faith and purity of heart. For example, he denounced "popery," but his warmth extended to Roman Catholics without necessarily trying to convert them. He wrote to a Catholic friend in Ireland proposing that Protestants and Catholics resolve never to be unkind in act, word, temper, or thought to one another. He continued:

. . . let us examine all that rises in our heart, and suffer no disposition there which is contrary to tender affection. . . . Let us . . . endeavour to help each other on in whatever we are agreed leads to the Kingdom. So far as we can, let us always rejoice to strengthen each other's hands in God.

To all the Wesleys, the religion of love came first. John considered the whole world his parish, and said, "If your heart is as my heart, give me your hand."

Evelyn Underhill (1875–1941)

For Christian purity, she said, the senses and the mind—the whole self—must be "unselfed" by the cleansing Spirit. For what purpose?

For the "limp acquiescence of the quietist"? No, for truth and for "the undivided vigour of the abandoned but energetic will."

Evelyn Underhill herself was as energetic and as "unselfed" a saint as any given to the church by the Spirit in the twentieth century. Her vocation was not that of evangelist, organizer, or Christian social worker. She was a guide to the inner life through her writings and her work as spiritual counselor with individuals and groups. With utter self-abandon she wrote more than thirty books between 1904 and her death in 1941. She conducted spiritual retreats and carried on a voluminous correspondence on the interior life. Evelyn Underhill prayed an hour each day, practiced the presence of Christ taught by Brother Lawrence (see page 85), and three times a week visited London's poor, to help if she could, but also to give and receive Christ's love.

She knew what it meant to *learn* to be a Christian; knew the internal tug-of-war between skepticism and piety, intellect and emotion, and she knew that human spiritual needs vary with experience and expectations. Hers was the task of helping people from university professors to cleaning women explore their religious needs and relationship to God.

Evelyn Underhill had to learn to be a Christian because the British Tory family into which she was born in late 1875 was indifferent to all religion. Her father, a knighted lawyer, preferred to spend his Sundays yachting. Young Evelyn was baptized into the Church of England but learned to hoist a sail before she knew the catechism. Her family's broad interests in science and the humanities strongly influenced her. Throughout her life she was devoted to botany, archaeology, the study of languages, and the social sciences. She also loved cats. Her husband, Hubert Stuart Moore, shared these interests, as well as the passion for sailing she inherited from her father. (Evelyn Underhill retained her own name after her marriage.)

At age ten, Evelyn went to boarding school at Folkestone and there, five years later, was confirmed in the Church of England. If a passage in her diary for 1892 reflects her sentiments on confirmation, she was then an adolescent Christian humanist. She wrote:

As to religion, I don't quite know, except that I believe in a God, and think it better to love and help the poor people round me than to go on saying that I love an abstract Spirit whom I have never seen. If I can do both, all the better, but it is best to begin with the nearest. I do not think anything is gained by being orthodox, and a great deal of the beauty and sweetness of things is lost by being bigoted and dogmatic. If we are to see God at all it must be through nature and our fellow men."[12]

She would never lose her sense of obligation to the poor or become a dogmatic bigot. Underhill did move far beyond her teenaged humanism and pantheism, coming to find true beauty and sweetness in the God by no means limited to nature or other people. In her spiritual growth she was not bothered by having passed through stages of immature thinking. She later wrote, "Don't be ferocious with yourself because that is treating badly a precious (if imperfect) thing which God has made."

Before and after studying at Kings College for Women in London, Underhill traveled extensively in Europe, and at some point before her marriage in 1907 she began to study the Christian mystics. Just what turned her to an interest in mysticism is unknown. It may have been the influence of Catholic friends in London. Whatever, her personal inclinations and her concentration on the mystics combined to convince her she should convert to Catholicism. She probably would have save for two complications. First, her fiancé, Moore, objected to the projected move. He asked her to wait a year before leaving the Church of England. She agreed, and when the couple married in July, 1907, she was still intent on Catholicism. The second and more important stumbling block came three months later with Pope Pius X's encyclical *Pascendi gregis* condemning "Modernism" in virtually all theological forms. Among the persons covered by the blanket condemnation were Roman Catholic biblical scholars and mystics known and loved by Underhill. The young woman felt she could not join a church opposed to her own Modernist tendencies, and she was not willing to be untrue to herself.

Unhappy as an Anglican, shut out of the Catholic church, she was a spiritual wanderer for a time, continuing her study of mysticism and in 1911 publishing her first major theological work, entitled *Mysticism*. This book was her introduction to Baron Friedrich von Hügel, a Roman Catholic philosopher and mystic who strongly influenced her spiritual development. The baron, a naturalized British subject, was of particular value in helping Underhill establish her personal religious discipline and to come to terms with her tendency to neglect the person of Christ and the historical nature of the New Testament. "When I went to the baron he said I wasn't much better than a Unitarian," she wrote.

Von Hügel encouraged Underhill to find her way back into the

Church of England as an active communicant. She followed his advice, reembraced her church as a loyal critic; after all, she said, God put her in the Anglican communion, gave her enough tasks to do there, and never told her to move on.

Underhill was drawn toward pacifism but, nevertheless, served in British naval intelligence in Africa during World War I. (She would vigorously oppose World War II, insisting that the Christian church must never acquiesce to war.) Back in England, she lectured, wrote, and found a new calling as leader of spiritual retreats. Forty years before meditation became a fad in Europe and America, she was giving instruction in the art. Her methods, however, were not borrowed from the Orient, but came from the Christian mystics. And the goal she envisioned was not self-centered peace of mind, but rather spiritual union with Christ, the only source of inner peace for Christians.

The mysticism she taught and lived was not monastic. It was practical, applicable to Christians in ordinary life. For example, she advocated the historic Christian counsels of poverty, chastity, and obedience, though she did not think they required a special community withdrawn from the world or vows such as Catholic priests and nuns take. Poverty, she said, is the internal grace of being freed from possessions and possessiveness, chastity, a spirit of poverty applied to emotions, and obedience, total surrender of the will to God.

Her correspondence as a spiritual counselor was collected for publication by Charles Williams, a close friend, who along with Dorothy Sayers and others formed a remarkable group of British Christian authors in the early years of this century. Underhill's own last major book was on Christian worship.

She died in 1941 from complications arising from asthma. In her collected papers, issued in 1945, Underhill summed up the sentiments of her Christian heart: "Adoration is the unchanging heart of religion, and the only key to its mysterious truth. There is no dilemma for the adoring soul."

CHAPTER VII

Regiment of Shalom

"Holy are the peacemakers . . ."

ALFRED NOBEL must have had a lot of guilt about his contribution to the world's military arsenals. When the inventor of dynamite, the most lethal weapon of war since gunpowder, died in 1896, his will put his vast fortune in trust for prizes honoring people bringing great benefit to humanity. As is well known, he commanded a Peace Prize or, in his own words, an annual award "to the person who shall have done the most or best work for fraternity among nations, for the abolition or reduction of standing armies and for the holding and promotion of peace congresses."[1]

The Nobel prize in peace was first handed out in 1901. Since then sixty-five or so individuals and a handful of private organizations have received it. But before the prize was a half-century old two world wars engulfed the peoples of earth; standing armies of incredible size were permanent fixtures; and a weapon—atomic power—making dynamite seem like a firecracker was developed and used. Not a very good showing for persons working for fraternity among nations or promoting peace congresses.

If individuals have had pale success as emissaries of peace in this century, governments have no better record. The nations at the end of World War II declared themselves one in their determination "to save succeeding generations from the scourges of war," and through the United Nations agreed to take "effective collective measures for the prevention and removal of threats to the peace,"[2] etc., etc., etc. No "world war," of course, has happened since the United Nations was formed, but nations battled nations in Korea, Indochina, and the

Middle East; military invasions of neighboring states have taken place with medieval frequency, and a computer would be needed to recall all the civil wars.

Conflict, brutality, and armed struggle are old human habits, common to all centuries and races. Yet despite the apparent, ugly inevitability of the fight, humanity harbors, especially in its religions, the hope for a peaceable kingdom. Not by accident are the words of a religious genius, Isaiah of Jerusalem, the Hebrew prophet, chiseled deep into the wall above United Nations Plaza in New York City: "And they shall beat their swords into plowshares and their spears into pruning hooks" (Isaiah 2–4).

Men and women who would change human habit, individuals who, symbolically, nudge warriors to become farmers, take on the glow of holiness in part because they are different—people special, though not always popular, against the scenery of contention. While some Nobel peace laureates, especially an occasional military general, are strange choices inviting little respect, the peace prize has special public appeal. It touches the heart of human hope.

Peacemakers are special, but what of their effectiveness? Are they more than keepers of an impossible dream? This question nags at the Christian church as it reads the Seventh Beatitude. Just what did Jesus mean, the makers of peace are the children of God? Not wanting to say "peacemaker, peacemaker" when there is no peace, the church has usually handled this Beatitude in one of two oblique ways. First, peace and its making are seen as a blessing to be realized in a future, transformed world. Second, the Seventh Beatitude is spiritualized, turned into an inward condition, as in peace with oneself or personal peace with God. The early Christians, a minority in a world of conflict that they saw no possibility of pacifying, liked the second understanding, and given the continuing thirst for battle this spiritualized reading remains attractive.

The Beatitudes, as discussed in the Introduction, do have a future motif, and calming internal civil war is a noble, even holy, accomplishment. However, the Beatitudes and the God-centered qualities they specify also have objective and historical meaning. Peace in the here and now, peace as a practical condition, is an announced possibility in Jewish and Christian Scripture. How possible? Because God loves peace and would be the way to peace if people would follow. Isaiah of Jerusalem spoke in historical terms of the "prince of peace," of the day when nations shall no more learn war. The author of the

Gospel of Luke surely had passages from Isaiah in mind in writing his Christmas story. Luke's angelic chorus announces—not prophesies —peace on earth. And if Jesus in the Beatitudes meant only to bless the spiritually peaceful, or those awaiting the peace of a future world, why did he say peace*makers*. Making is creative, active; making is objective.

Jesus, according to the Gospels, is God's announcement of peace on earth, the creative, active Word making peace possible, and there is no reason to interpret Jesus the peacemaker only in spiritual or future terms. A clear expectation permeates the New Testament: peace can be on the strength of Christlike love, forgiveness, and mercy. Such a theology of peace on earth is sometimes challenged with a literal appeal to Matthew 10:34–36. In this passage Jesus says:

Do not think that I have come to bring peace on earth; I have not come to bring peace, but a sword. For I have come to set a man against his father, and a daughter against her mother, and a daughter-in-law against her mother-in-law, and a man's foes will be those of his own household (RSV).

The use to which these verses can be put is obvious. They can be, have been, cited as a divine blessing on war and conflict—Jesus himself brought a sword! This interpretation is off base. The paragraph, with its emphasis on division within a family, leaves no doubt that Jesus is speaking in symbolic language of reactions to him, of the split among those who accept and those who reject him as God's special one, the Messiah. What Jesus actually does is take a description of division from the Prophet Micah (7:6) and quote it in a new context. He is saying, "These things happen, people disagree, even in the same family, when the truth is at hand." Furthermore, the theme of division in families appears in rabbinical writings on the coming of the Messiah. In recognizing division over truth, over him, Jesus was hardly sanctioning the sword. Matthew 10:34–36 describes how things *are*, rather than how they *might be*. A difficult passage such as this must always be read in light of the biblical message as a whole, and peace is a central attribute of God, an attribute of holiness, in Scripture. Holy peace would have swords beaten into plows —something worthwhile for humanity.

The holiness of peacemakers is not alone a matter of eliminating warfare. To use a common saying, peace is more than the absence of war. The Greek word for "peace" in Matthew 5:9, the Seventh Beatitude, is a translation of the Hebrew *shalom,* a marvelous word of many meanings in Jewish sacred literature and in the New Testament.

Shalom means the reverse of political and social strife, the absence of war, the end of hostilities, the good and prosperous life, right relationship with God, and personal serenity. At base, it means completeness, wholeness, a matter of people, things, and conditions in healthy relationship. The breadth and depth of *shalom* comes into play in the Seventh Beatitude: "Holy are they who want completeness for themselves and their world before God."

But *shalom* does not imply human ability to create a perfect world. God alone is perfect *shalom*. For Christians Jesus Christ is the only perfect example of the *shalom*-maker, but disciples strive to follow the model, collectively to form a regiment of *shalom* raising high its banner in all political and personal relationships. Christian peacemaking takes many forms. Along with efforts to avert war, it involves work for social justice, political freedom, human welfare, and religious harmony. Some peacemakers are total pacifists rejecting all violence and even defensive combat. Others struggle mightily with the possibility of "just war," especially when oppression or aggression is the cause of unpeace. Peacemaking may be global or in the home.

Peacemakers take risks. They risk themselves in the belief that *shalom* is more worthwhile than chaos. They also run the risk of scorn and, most of all, of failure. Peacemakers often fail—fail to stop fighting, fail to win justice; fail too in convincing people that healthy human relationships depend on a wholeness found only in a healthy person-to-God relationship. Their failure, however, is not the failure of peace; the failure belongs to the belligerents, the lovers of incompleteness.

Peacemakers sometimes succeed, at least temporarily or in a situation, and even when they fail they have a kind of success in keeping open the option, the dream, of the better way. And since they embody peace, they are more than keepers of the dream; they are the building blocks of the truth of peace.

To define peace, *shalom*, as healthy people-to-people and people-to-God relationships means all of the Christian personalities in this book could be called peacemakers. At the same time, certain individuals, because of their time and place, have a keener awareness of the need to make for peace. The examples of peacemakers in this chapter had that keen awareness, working on different fronts for *shalom*. Some were active on behalf of national or international order, some stressed the peace-bringing aspects of justice, and others sought to lessen strife within the Christian family.

The persons discussed in this chapter are not as evenly distributed along the historical time line as the figures in other chapters. Concentration is deliberately on the more modern world for this reason: women and men great for peace against a contemporary background may be more inspiring than ancients whose worlds, while no less chaotic, were smaller in geography and simpler in the technology of violence. But the regiment of *shalom* in recent centuries has noble forbearers who must not be overlooked.

Leo I (?–461)

Leo lived in a fifth-century maze of conflict—political and religious. The Western Roman Empire was crashing around him. Bitter theological disputes gripped the Christian church. That Western Europe entered the Middle Ages with any social cohesion, that the church found a peaceful resolution in a moment of crisis, are testimonies to his greatness as a stabilizer of relationships. Leo was a born diplomat—not a negotiator but a man with a talent for making a case and convincing other people to accept it. He faced down Attila the Hun, and impressed his theological conclusions on bickering, sometimes violent, monks and scholars.

Bishop of Rome (pope) from 440 to 461, Leo was probably a native of Tuscany. Where and when he was born are neither known nor important. He considered himself Roman; Rome to him was a holy city, and he protected it with the only weapon he had or wanted: a nonviolent presence.

The Roman Empire in his day was divided East and West with two emperors, one in Constantinople (Istanbul) and one in Ravenna (in Italy). To the East, the empire was still relatively intact; the West was in shambles, ravaged on its frontiers by invading German tribes. Rome itself had been plundered in 410 by the Visigoths. Old social ways were breaking down as the invaders settled in the Roman provinces.

Leo had multiple reasons for concern. The political chaos threatened the church. Emperors since Constantine (in the early fourth century) had protected Christianity; the Western rulers at Ravenna a century later could not protect their palaces. Furthermore, many of the invading, settling Germans were Arians, members of a heretical

Christian movement denying the divinity of Christ. Pope Leo could do little directly about political instability. He could, he felt, take the matter of widespread heresy in hand.

Shortly after election as bishop of Rome, Leo began a campaign to bring heretics back to Christian orthodoxy and, at the same time, he also set about to extend the authority of the Roman church and the pope. In fact, he is sometimes called the first pope, in terms of the bishop of Rome as the highest authority in the church. Rome and its bishop before Leo enjoyed first honor throughout Christianity because the city was the original imperial capital and because of the traditional association of the Apostle Peter with the church there. But the bishop of Rome in no way ruled the whole church.

Leo claimed—and made the claim stick in the West—that Christ exercised power on earth through Rome's bishop, successor to Peter to whom, in Roman Catholic doctrine, Jesus entrusted the "keys to the Kingdom." Pope Leo consolidated church authority in the West (never in the East) into himself, and by doing this he established a social and political structure—the Roman Catholic Church—bringing a sense of unity and cohesion to Western Europe when the Roman Empire was gone.

This pope's force of personality and his skill in settling disputes between politicians and prelates were no small factors in his success in extending Rome's churchly power and the papacy's secular authority. His talent for diplomacy gave him a pivotal role in settling violent theological dispute within the church.

Christianity did not spring forth into the world fully defined or organized. Centuries were needed to spell out doctrines and set up structures; indeed, the defining and organizing still go on, though a core of orthodox teaching was determined (usually by church councils) across the first five centuries. This was not easy. Many ideas and interpretations competed for attention, disputes raged, blows were exchanged, and permanent divisions sometimes resulted.

A major theological argument broke out in the mid-400s over the teachings of a monk named Eutyches, head of a monastery near Constantinople. Eutyches denied, in effect, the humanity of Jesus (Christian orthodoxy says Jesus Christ was both fully divine and fully human—two natures together). The monk was put on trial for heresy, convicted, and excommunicated by the patriarch (bishop) of Constantinople.

Eutyches, an old man, might have been forgotten except for the fact he had powerful friends who agreed with his theology. In an attempt to win vindication, he wrote seeking Pope Leo's support. Leo thought Eutyches was out of his mind. In a letter to Constantinople, the pope took a pastoral, even charitable attitude toward the old monk, but firmly suggested that he reread the Scripture. The heart of the letter said: In Jesus Christ two fully complete natures, human and divine, come together in one person, but the union of these natures in no way decreases the integrity of either nature.

Leo's letter was withheld at a council in 449 controlled by Eutyches' friends who ruled the monk orthodox and physically forced the bishops to agree. Nothing was solved. The dispute continued and got worse. Another council was held in 451, this one at Chalcedon (in Asia Minor) under the protection of the Eastern Empress Pulcheria. The letter from Leo formed the basis of the Creed of Chalcedon, recognized by Roman Catholics, Eastern Orthodox, and Protestants as a true statement of the universal Christian faith.

If Leo had won a theological peace, he had pressing political disorders to face in Italy. A year after Chalcedon, Attila the Hun marched toward Rome, having already seized much of what was still called the Western Empire. Though he had no formal political office, Leo was not about to let his city be sacked. Dressed in priest's robes rather than armor, and accompanied by a small band of Romans, the pope went forth to meet the conqueror. Leo asked Attila to turn back, to spare the city. Surprisingly, the Hun agreed. Some historians say Attila's army was too weakened by fever to move against the defenders of Rome. A better story was told by Paul the Deacon, an eighth-century writer. Attila, according to this story, was asked by his own people why he stopped at the request of an old man. Was he afraid of the bishop? No, Attila replied, but he was afraid of another "venerable personage" no one else seemed to see, a "stately figure with hoary head" standing next to Leo.[3]

The pope would not be as successful in turning back the next German invader at the gates of Rome. The Vandals arrived in 455 looking for spoils. Unable to persuade this horde to retire, Leo convinced its leader to pillage without burning the city. After two weeks of plundering, the Vandals departed for North Africa, taking with them numerous Roman hostages and, according to one source, the treasure the Emperor Titus stole from the Jewish Temple in Jerusalem in A.D. 70.

Leo with characteristic speed dispatched priests to minister to the captives in Africa, and to restore Rome's churches and public order. He died in late 461. Leo is one of only three popes officially accorded the title "the Great" by the Roman Catholic Church, but not until the eighteenth century was he declared a "doctor," a designation for the greatest theologians.

Catherine of Siena (1347–1380)

"You must go forth from your own city for the welfare of souls," the heavenly voice upon which she relied for guidance told the twenty-three-year-old Dominican nun.

Catherine went forth in 1370 from Siena, the Tuscan city of her birth, to devote her last ten years to the tasks of building peace among the warring city states of Italy and unifying and purifying the church in western Europe. She accomplished neither, but she gained heroic stature in the efforts and was her century's brightest and best example of a life committed to Christ.

Mystic and healer as well as politician, Catherine compares in several respects with Francis of Assisi (see page 21), with whom she is co-patron saint of Italy. Both Francis and Catherine were children of urban tradesmen, though her leather-dyer father was less prosperous than Francis' father, a cloth merchant. Both loved Christ, the church, nature, and people, untiringly serving the poor and downtrodden, and each in their time was called to redirect Christianity to its foundations. And like Francis, Catherine experienced the stigmata, the signs of Christ's crucifixion on her body.

Catherine's call to public service in 1370 directed her to go before popes and princes to preach political peace and religious unity so that "the weak may confound the pride of the mighty." She entered the international arena with years of spiritual preparation molding her will to the will of God. The divine voice had told her: "In self-knowledge humble yourself; see that in yourself you do not even exist, for your very being, as you will learn, comes from Me, since I have loved both you and others before you existed."

She was born almost halfway through one of Europe's worst centuries. The Black Death swept through in 1348 devastating the continent and killing one-third of the people of Siena. The economy was in shambles. Social and religious structures were changing without having changed. The church was at every point enmeshed in worldly pursuits to the neglect of human souls. Large and small wars were common as raindrops. Italy especially was a political tangle. Central Italy technically belonged to the pope, but these Papal States were up for grabs because in 1309 a French king decided to clip the papacy's secular wings by forcibly moving the Holy See to Avignon, on the Rhone River. There a succession of pontiffs sat in "captivity" for the better part of the fourteenth century.

Government and everyday life across Europe was plagued by roving mercenary armies that sacked cities and towns when no prince or pope had them on a payroll. The restraints of the old feudal society, including its ideals of knighthood and chivalry, were gone, and the new nationalism was in many places too weak to keep public order.

The twenty-third of the twenty-five children born to Giacomo and Lapa Benincasa, Catherine had a childhood religious zeal surpassing that usually attributed to medieval saints. At the age of twelve she took a vow of virginity. Visions and voices summoned her to prayer and physical austerity as means of spiritual discipline. To prepare for membership in an order of Dominican sisters, she confined herself for three years to a cavelike room under her father's leather and dye shop.

She emerged from isolation in 1366 in response to an urge to serve the sick and imprisoned in Christ's name. Catherine became a familiar sight in Siena, she in her white robe and black cape ministering to the poor and visiting the jails. She also raised her voice in protest against acts of injustice, such as the execution of a young man accused of criticizing the city governor.

Catherine also taught, urging "fortitude" and "manly behavior" on any who would listen to her explanations of the courage needed to follow Christ in the world. Her accounts of spiritual visions and her acts of charity attracted a band of friend–followers who called the young woman "mamma." Catherine's mystical experiences inspired the *Book of Divine Doctrine*, the greatest writings on Christian mysticism of the fourteenth century. All of her writings soar with an awareness of the love and forgiveness of Christ; she conversed with God, who told her such things as why Christians must love neighbors: ". . . the soul that knows Me immediately expands to the love of her neighbor, because she sees that I love that neighbor ineffably, and so, herself, loves the object which she sees Me to have loved still more. She further knows that she can be of no use to Me and can in no way repay Me that pure love with which she feels herself to be loved by Me, and therefore endeavours to repay it through the medium which I have given her, namely, her neighbor, who is the medium through which you can all serve Me."

In the early 1370s, Catherine turned increasingly to public and church affairs beyond Siena. She particularly wanted to end the political conflict in Italy and for that to happen, she believed, the papacy had to return to Rome and direct the work of purifying the church.

One plank in her platform for peace and Christian unity is bothersome to modern people. While Catherine worked for peace in blood-soaked, war-intoxicated Europe, she promoted a Christian crusade against the Turks. Is it not inconsistent for a peacemaker to advocate war? Yes, in retrospect, by modern standards, and the fact that her crusade never happened only partly absolves Catherine from what can today be regarded as anti-*shalom* in a global sense.

But modern standards cannot be applied to a fourteenth-century Italian saint. As a woman of her own day, Catherine was not inconsistent. She wanted the crusade for the same reason she worked for European peace. To her, human spiritual and political welfare meant the security of the church and of the Christian commonwealth. Her crusade was to have accomplished two interrelated goals: crushing the Muslim "infidels" worrying Christendom's eastern frontier and delivering Europe from the roving mercenaries. She wanted to round up the hired swords and send them off to bother the Turks.

Catherine's initial efforts to persuade the reigning pope, Gregory XI, to return from Avignon to Rome were by letter. Addressing the pontiff as *dolce babbo* ("sweetest father") she begged him to come home and clean up the church. She denounced the material interests of cardinals and bishops and said the monasteries were "stables of swine."

Letters also poured forth to bishops, kings, and queens urging them to keep the true faith. Three secretaries kept busy taking her dictation; Catherine could never have been a nun under a vow of silence.

She took to the road, scurrying hither and thither talking peace to the belligerent Italian city states. The political situation was critical in the 1370s. In his absence, the pope had named a legate to rule the Papal States in his name and at that moment the legate was one Robert of Geneva, a man so loathsome that the cities of Italy banded together to drive him out. Robert persuaded Gregory XI to hire the most notorious mercenaries to put down the revolt, and though the military campaign was not a total success it produced atrocities worthy of the Nazis.

Catherine was in despair. She decided in 1376 that if the pope would not return to Italy voluntarily she would personally fetch him. Off to Avignon she went, becoming a thorn in the flesh of the easy-living French cardinals around Gregory. The pope himself rather liked the little Italian woman, and she evidently convinced him he belonged in Rome because in 1377 he set sail for the city on the Tiber. Catherine was jubilant, but her joy was short lived. She believed Gregory would launch church reforms, but he died in 1378 and the papacy fell to Urban VI, a most arrogant man, who also offended the French. A rump session of French cardinals elected a counter-pope, none other than bloody Robert of Geneva, and set him up in Avignon.

In the tug-of-war between the two popes, Catherine sided with Urban. She liked him little but thought his election valid and, therefore, judged him the best hope of unifying the church. Catherine wrote a round of letters supporting Urban, though her enthusiasm for institutions, even the papacy, as agents of peace or religious reform ran low. She asked to be left alone to write, pray, and devote herself to simple people.

Catherine of Siena could be classed as a failed peacemaker, a naive mystic trying to translate ideas of union with God into the body politic. To be sure, she did not stop the fourteenth-century political turmoil or effect a cleansed, unifying papacy. Her program failed; her ideas lived on. Catherine made a strong argument for the church to model peace by being peaceful. Centuries would lapse before the sense of her argument would be recognized.

She died at the age of thirty-three. Some say Catherine of Siena starved herself to death, a penitent mourning over a world of sin and conflict.

Emeric Crucé (1590–1648)

Catherine of Siena's concept of political peace, of kingdoms and cities living in harmony, was based on appeal to a common religion governed on earth by a single head, the pope. She was no internationalist in terms of independent nations cooperating to assure peace. Nationalism itself was just emerging as the most potent force in political life, and as unified, independence-minded nations, still monarchies, arose in Europe, so did the need for an overarching approach to peaceful relations. Dante, author of *The Divine Comedy*, in the early 1300s put forth a comprehensive peace plan based on universal recognition of the God-ordained authority of emperor and pope.

Neither Dante nor the many designers of peace proposals who followed him in the next century went far beyond Catherine's notion that political stability is bound up with recognition of a single ruler, though few of them looked to the pope. The ideal, as Peter Mayer shows in a documentary history of pacifism, was a great Christian king able to enforce peace.[4] For example, Cardinal Thomas Wolsey, adviser to England's Henry VIII in the early sixteenth century, hoped to bring peace between France and the German empire by increasing the authority of his king on the continent. Not even Marsilius of Padua (1280–1343), whose theories on the role of the people in choosing their rulers influenced modern thought, had much idea of nations in concert.

Proposals edging toward international cooperation as a peace strategy were confined in the era of the Renaissance and the Reformation to a few marginal thinkers, persons rarely mentioned in secular or religious history books. One of these little-known individuals was Emeric Crucé, born about 1590 in France, and possibly a monk.

Crucé wrote a book appealing to rulers to establish a permanent forum for dealing with conflicts and disputes. He set his book in pre-Christian times, presenting the author as one Cyneas, a peacemaker in the reign of Pyrrhus, a Hellenistic king. Crucé called his book *The New Cyneas*, and its implications for the seventeenth century were clear when it appeared in 1632.

The New Cyneas not only advocated a permanent peace assembly of princes or their delegates, it asked for open national borders, free international communication and trade, and a reduction, or elimination, of armaments. Furthermore, Crucé wanted the nations of Africa and Asia included in his plan.

"Why," he asked, "should I, a Frenchman, bear ill will against an Englishman or an Indian? I cannot, when I contemplate that they are men even as I, that I am like them subject to error and sin and that all nations are associated by a natural and, in consequence, indissoluble tie."[5]

The only sure thing about warfare, Crucé said, is its injustice. Soldiers and civilians are butchered, women raped, and houses of worship profaned. Fighting, he continued, is followed by famine and pestilence because crops are neglected or destroyed, resulting in malnourishment which produces disease. To end war and its accompanying evils would be a greater victory than even the conquests of Alexander the Great, Crucé told rulers. Princes who make peace, he said, will go down in history as men true to the image of God.

End the sins of arrogance and cruelty, Crucé declared, and the sword can be sheathed forever. And rulers should remember that God punishes sins, he said.

Crucé is usually called naive or simple-minded in his appeal to secular rulers to make a "holy resolve" for peace. True, his proposals were not accepted by the princes of Europe, Africa, or Asia. But *The New Cyneas* would influence the peace advocates of the eighteenth century and peace movements of the nineteenth.

Crucé died in 1648, the year the Peace of Westphalia ended eighty years of war between the Spanish and the Dutch and thirty years of fighting between France and the German emperor. The European wars of religion and the early nationalist conflicts were winding down. Some even thought the great era of peace on earth had arrived.

David Low Dodge (1774–1852)

Violence and war, he said, are un-Christian. All violence and all war—any war—are wrong, declared the New York merchant.

David Low Dodge was an original, an American pacifist pioneer, founder of one of the first, if not the very first, society in the world devoted to the total elimination of warfare. War, he said, is inhuman, unwise, and criminal; nothing good comes of it, Dodge insisted, sounding like Emeric Crucé, and he included the American Revolution in his condemnation. The Women's Strike for Peace of the 1960s would have liked Dodge. In the 1850s he asked his descendants never to give their children war toys.

When and why David Dodge became such a total, uncompromising pacifist are matters of argument. The cynical view finds his motivation in anger that the War of 1812 ruined his import-export business; the romantic traces his stand to a peace pledge taken while suffering from "spotted fever." Dodge in an autobiography admittedly written late in life said he was a pacifist before the business failed, and his peacemaking activities began before or at least simultaneously with the outbreak of U.S.-British hostilities known as the War of 1812 (ended in 1815).

Dodge himself probably gives the best explanation of how a Presbyterian cloth merchant turned to adamant pacifism. It was, he wrote, a process begun in the early 1800s. Dodge, a native of Connecticut, was then a store owner in Hartford, traveling occasionally to Boston for goods. He carried large sums of cash and to protect himself and the money, bought a brace of pistols, weapons that figured in an incident of singular importance to Dodge. One night at a Providence, Rhode Island, inn, the storekeeper was asleep when the host opened the door looking for space for new arrivals. Dodge recalled:

The noise aroused me. While half asleep, I seized the pistols, and by a kind providence I so far awoke as to recognize him by the light of the candle; by which means I just escaped taking his life.[6]

This incident preyed on Dodge's mind. He resolved to examine the issue of Christians arming themselves with deadly weapons. In proper Presbyterian fashion, his examination proceeded slowly; meanwhile, he was a busy merchant, becoming a partner in the expanding mercantile firm of S. & H. Higginson and relocating as its agent in New York.

Sometime in 1808 Dodge was confined with "spotted fever." His mind kept returning to the near-shooting of the Providence innkeeper. He decided that as a Christian he must lay his pistols aside. "From this period, my war spirit appears to be crucified and slain," he later wrote.

In 1798 Dodge had married Sarah Cleveland, daughter of a sometime Congregational preacher and ardent foe of slavery. Aaron Cleveland's social interpretation of Christianity evidently influenced his son-in-law. His war spirit slain in 1808, Dodge became an active opponent of guns, war, violence, and human cruelty. His anonymous 1809 antiwar tract, *The Mediator's Kingdom Not of This World*, was a public success. Dodge took heart and put his name on two essays, *War Inconsistent with the Religion of Jesus* in 1812 and *Kingdom of Peace under the Benign Reign of Messiah* in 1815.

The shipping embargo imposed during the War of 1812 destroyed S. & H. Higginson and Dodge's partnership in the company. He thoroughly disliked "Mr. Madison's war," but then David Low Dodge was never one to stay with a job too long. Raised around Pomfret, Connecticut, he had farmed and taught school before opening his store in Hartford. After Higginson failed, a series of mercantile and manufacturing interests kept him and his family moving between New York and New England, until he finally settled in New York in 1825. David Low Dodge retired in 1827 at age fifty-three to devote himself to peace and other good causes. He was apparently prosperous without being successful in business. His son, William E., established the family fortune and the Dodge name in American philanthropy (these are the copper Dodges, not the car Dodges). While pacifism did not become a family hallmark, descendants of David L. Dodge continue to assist some of his causes, including the YMCA.

When Dodge and a group of friends organized the New York Peace Society in 1815, he was elected president. This society is honored as the first flowering of a nineteenth-century peace movement that saw the formation of many organizations in America and Europe. It initially condemned all war, offensive and defensive, but as time passed some members grew uneasy with a blanket rejection of all defensive combat. What about the American Revolution? That too, said Dodge, who in explaining his role in the tension within the society wrote:

If it was morally wrong for individuals to quarrel and fight instead of returning good for evil, it was much more criminal for communities and nations to return evil for evil, and not strive to overcome evil with good. In fact, the great barrier to our progress was the example of our fathers in the American Revolution. That they were generally true patriots in the political sense of the term, and many hopefully pious, I would not call in question, while I consider them as ill directed by education as St. Paul when on his way to Damascus.[7]

Surprisingly, there seems to have been no significant public outcry against Dodge for saying the American Founding Fathers were as wrong in what they did in the Revolution as was Paul on his way to persecute Christians. Perhaps one reason he provoked little hostility is this: the American experiment in 1815 had barely started; many people were doubtful of its future, and some still thought it a bad idea to separate from England.

Dodge's major book, *War Inconsistent with the Religion of Jesus Christ*, presented a cogent theological argument against violence and warfare. The causes of conflict, he said, are human pride, avarice, and revenge, qualities directly opposite to the Christian Gospel, which "teaches humility, it inculcates love, it breathes pity and forgiveness, even to enemies, and forbids rendering evil for evil to any man."

The author explored at some length the inhuman, unwise, and

criminal aspects of war. Some of his arguments sound amazingly modern, for example, his conclusion that being prepared for defensive war is no strategy for peace: "The history of nations abundantly shows that few nations ever make great preparations for war and remain long in peace."

Along with his broadside against war, Dodge let go against slavery. War and slavery, he said, produce the same evils. They oppress the poor, spread terror, cause fatigue and famine, mutilate bodies, destroy youth, multiply widows and orphans, and clothe the lands in mourning.

War, David Low Dodge concluded, is always put forth as a prelude to peace. That to him was dumb reasoning: "War is no more adapted to preserve liberty and produce a lasting peace than midnight darkness is to produce noonday light."

Jane Addams (1860–1935)

Jane Addams is primarily remembered neither as a stalwart for peace nor as a notable Christian. When remembered at all today, she is thought of as a pioneering social worker, a humanitarian, and perhaps as a Victorian matron patronizing the poor and stirring the children of immigrants into the mythical American melting pot. Memory can be such a faulty device.

She was a Victorian lady, a social worker, and a humanitarian. Jane Addams also won the Nobel Peace Prize, though not for her labors among the poor, such social service only recently having been established as grounds for the prize (for example, to Mother Teresa of Calcutta in 1979). Furthermore, the founder of Chicago's Hull House, a model urban settlement house eight decades ago, was motivated by strong, if individual, Christian impulses in her humanitarian pursuits. And far from being a patronizing philanthropist trying to make America a common porridge, she had great respect for the religious and ethnic distinctions of immigrants.

Jane Addams was a pacifist, expelled from the Daughters of the American Revolution for opposing U.S. entry into World War I. In the political debate over that war, she chaired the Women's Peace Party in 1915, and that same year presided over a congress that gave birth to the Women's International League for Peace and Freedom. She was president of the league from 1919 to 1935. Behind her years of organized effort for world peace was a deep commitment to protect

life and improve its quality. That commitment arose from a simple
reading of the Gospels. Christianity to the adult Jane Addams was not
a matter of complicated doctrines, but rather a religion telling persons
who they are and ought to be. War and conflict had no place in her
view of what ought to be for humanity.

She grew up in Illinois, in the village of Cedarville. An early
detected curvature of the spine would cause her severe problems later
in life. Abraham Lincoln was one of her heroes, but Jane Addams
doted most on her father, a man of recognized integrity who sat for a
time in the Illinois state legislature. Her father considered himself a
Quaker of sorts. He belonged to no church and his noninstitutional
approach to Christianity strongly influenced his daughter, although
young Jane was instructed in the contents of the Bible and recalled a
compulsion to confess her sins.

Bright and inquisitive, she enrolled in Rockford College, graduating in 1881. In college she encountered and stoutly resisted pressure
to become a regular church member, maybe a missionary. In *Twenty
Years at Hull House*, she recalled, ". . . it was inevitable that the pressure toward religious profession should increase as graduation day
approached. So curious, however, are the paths of moral development
that several times during subsequent experiences have I felt that this
passive resistance of mine, this clinging to an individual conviction,
was the best moral training I received at Rockford College."[8]

Jane Addams knew she wanted to work among the poor so to
prepare herself she went to the Woman's Medical College of Philadelphia. Her career in medicine was cut short by her own physical
problem—the curved spine; for two years she was an invalid. On her
feet again, she travelled in Europe, first in 1883–1885, and on a
shorter trip in 1887–88. Rome was one of her favorite places, and
when her back permitted, she explored the catacombs, those ancient
caves providing shelter and places of worship to the harassed Christians of the second and third centuries. She liked to ponder the poetic
justice of slaves—as many early Christians were—spreading the Gospel of Christ among free Romans.

Between the trips, back in Cedarville, Jane Addams took an important step. Her words tell it best:

One Sunday morning I received the rite of baptism and became a member of
the Presbyterian church in the village. At this time there was certainly no
outside pressure pushing me towards such a decision, and at twenty-five one
does not ordinarily take such a step from a mere desire to conform. While I

was not conscious of any emotional "conversion," I took upon myself the outward expression of the religious life with all humility and sincerity . . . I was conscious of no change from my childish acceptance of the teachings of the Gospels, but at this moment something persuasive within made me long for an outward symbol of fellowhsip, some bond of peace, some blessed spot where unity of spirit might claim right of way over all differences. . . . Who was I, with my dreams of universal fellowship, that I did not identify myself with the institutional statement of this belief, as it stood in the little village in which I was born, and without which testimony in each remote hamlet of Christendom it would be so easy for the world to slip back into the doctrines of selection and aristocracy?[9]

Jane Addams' Christianity inspired and undergirded a fierce sense of democracy, and she knew what she must do. On her first trip to Europe she and her traveling companion, Ellen Gates Starr, had been introduced to Toynbee Hall, a center serving poor and working-class people in London's Whitechapel district, an industrial area. She would establish such a facility—a settlement house—in Chicago. Hull House, named for an old mansion where she set up shop, was the result. The settlement house, as it developed, offered a broad range of programs in education, nutrition, child care, industrial skills, and health. Most of its participants were slum dwellers, many of them black or first and second generation immigrants—Italian, Polish, Russian, Slovakian. Jane Addams worried mightily that the children of immigrants were too quick to abandon the language and customs of their parents, cutting themselves off from their roots for the sake of what looked like, but might not be, success in a new culture.

Asked why she, a proper young lady with options, had moved into a slum, the founder of Hull House answered in part with words of Jesus. Is it not natural, she said, to feed the hungry and care for the sick? "It is certainly natural to give pleasure to the young, comfort to the aged, and to minister to the deep-seated craving for social intercourse that all men feel."[10]

Volunteers and private financing solicited by Jane Addams made Hull House possible. The settlement grew to thirteen buildings before the site was taken over by a university in 1963. Hull House programs were relocated in various sections of the Chicago area.

Hull House was only one of her activities. Jane Addams also took up public causes: reform of the juvenile court system, an eight-hour working day for women, workmen's compensation laws, economic justice for immigrants and blacks, safe working conditions, women's suffrage, and world peace. Her reputation suffered a setback when she opposed U.S. entry into World War I but it had recovered substantially by 1931 when she shared the Nobel Peace Prize with Nicholas Murray Butler, president of Columbia University in New York.

Jane Addams knew a profound truth about peace, about the nature of peace, namely, that peace is more than the absence of war; peace is people living together in companionship. In her early days at Hull House she made a discovery: "the things which make men alike are finer and better than the things which keep them apart, and . . . these basic likenesses, if they are properly accentuated, easily transcend the less essential differences."[11]

Nathan Söderblom (1866–1931)

When Alfred Nobel died, leaving his money for prizes, his relatives summoned a Swedish Lutheran pastor to conduct a memorial service at the San Remo (Italy) villa of the dynamite king. That was 1896. Thirty-four years later the Nobel peace laureate was for the first time a clergyman. The pastor by the bier and the clergyman with the prize were the same Nathan Söderblom.

Söderblom's liturgical role in dispatching Alfred Nobel to his reward had nothing to do with his getting the 1930 Peace Prize, but a link exists between *why* he was called to San Remo and *who* he was thirty years later. He was sent for in 1896 because he was pastor of the Swedish Church in Paris where Nobel had sometimes worshipped. The prize winner was not only archbishop of Sweden but also the world's foremost champion of peace through Christian cooperation, and his career in the modern movement for practical unity among churches developed in large part from commitments made while in France.

Newly ordained and married, Söderblom arrived in Paris with an already expanded vision of Christian interaction across the dividing lines of history, doctrine, and geography. He was active at the University of Uppsala in the Christian Student Movement that produced most of the modern pioneers, and in 1890 he crossed the Atlantic to attend a Christian student conference in Massachusetts sponsored by American evangelist Dwight L. Moody.

His six years in Paris turned Söderblom's vision into a program. He returned to Sweden in 1901 with two interlocking goals: for Christians to do a better job putting faith to work in love for the practical benefit of humanity, and for the churches to act together in that work. He developed these goals as he labored among Swedish emigrants and sailors (his parish included the port of Calais) and through studies and contacts at the Sorbonne.

In addition to pastoral duties, Söderblom was a doctoral candidate in Paris (and was the first non-Frenchman to receive a doctorate in theology from the Sorbonne's Protestant faculty). A brilliant student of history and comparative religion, he understood the differences and similarities among systems of belief. His perception of the uniqueness of Christianity and of the core of faith shared by divided churches was also clear. Söderblom believed God was calling the churches to cooperation in life and work, and he considered this possible without treading upon valued doctrinal distinctions.

"Doctrine divides, but service unites," was a phrase he used, meaning not that differences are trivial, but that even before, or without, theological consensus churches can cooperate in practical ways benefiting humanity. Indeed, he thought such cooperation essential if war was ever to be eliminated, especially among Christian nations.

Söderblom looked for practical signs of the possibility for peace and mutual forgiveness within the universal church. Any typical hymnal was to him a sign that division and controversy can find resolve:

In the hymnbook Jewish and Christian, the ancient, medieval, and modern Church, Greeks, Roman Catholics and Evangelicals, mystics, orthodox and pietists, monks and patriarchs, troublesome witnesses to the truth, burnt heretics and solid Churchmen, outcasts and ornaments of society, praise and pray in one single harmonious choir, specimens as it were of the host who sing a new song before the throne. Forgetting their disputes in life, our hearts find expression during the same service in the hymns of those who once stood against each other.[12]

He also wondered why, if so many different, often bickering, Christians could lie together in death in a place like Westminster Abbey, live Christians could not stand up in spiritual fellowship.

Born in 1866 into a Swedish parsonage, Söderblom was himself spiritually raised by pietist parents, and pietism permeated his ap-

proach to inter-church cooperation. (Pietism stresses personal faith
and holiness, opposes the secularization of society, and takes a dim
view of rigid doctrinal codes; for a discussion of an earlier form see the
entry on Count Zinzendorf, page 154.) Söderblom, however, was not
a typical late nineteenth-century Swedish pietist. He was more willing than most to enter into dialogue with the secularizing forces of
theological liberalism, and he was not afraid of contact with Roman
Catholicism. One of his great diappointments was the lack of positive
response to ecumenical dialogue from the Vatican.

Back home in Sweden in 1901, Söderblom taught at the University
of Uppsala and in 1912–14 also held a professorship at the University
of Leipzig in Germany. The professor brought international breezes
into Swedish theology. He explored recent Protestant–Roman Catholic relations, began contacts leading to intercommunion in 1922 between the churches of Sweden and England, and worked for the
expansion of the international Christian student movement, especially the inclusion of the Eastern Orthodox.

No one was more surprised than Söderblom in 1914 when he was
chosen archbishop of Uppsala, primate of the Church of Sweden.
The choice was all the more surprising since he had never been a
bishop.

Hardly were the Söderbloms moved into the archbishop's palace
when World War I broke out; it was a sharp blow—Christians again
slaughtering one another and destroying Europe. Could nothing finally stop such madness? Sweden remained neutral during the war,
providing Söderblom with the opportunity to be a voice for peace.
One of his first acts as archbishop was to issue "an appeal for peace
and Christian fellowship" to all churches, urging them to "make
manifest the supra-national unity of Christians against the disruptive
forces of war."

Söderblom was determined to push for more than informal Christian fellowship. He wanted an organization of churches—a council
where representatives would come together to grapple with world
problems and plan Christian response to them. His organizing efforts
up to 1920 were primarily through a now forgotten International
Committee for the World Alliance for Promoting International
Friendship through the Churches. But this was a collection of individuals. The Swedish primate wanted the church institutions committed. He wanted cooperation on the official agendas of the German and
French churches, the English and Scandinavian churches, the Ameri-

can churches, the Orthodox churches, and the Roman Catholic Church.

Representatives of churches in fourteen countries convened in Geneva in 1920 and there formally launched the Life and Work movement, one of two streams of ecumenism later coming together to form the World Council of Churches. An international conference was planned. Söderblom, of course, was chairman. The meeting's purpose, according to a planning committee, was "to concentrate the thoughts of Christendom on the mind of Christ as revealed in the Gospels towards those great social questions, industrial and international, which are so acutely urgent in every country. Believing that only in Christ's way of life can the world find healing and rest, we desire to discover how best this can be confronted."

The Universal Christian Conference on Life and Work met in Stockholm in August, 1925. Hosted by the royal family of Sweden, it drew approximately six hundred delegates from ninety denominations in thirty-seven countries; not quite "universal." Eastern Orthodoxy was present but not the Roman Church, which would not unfold its ecumenical wings until the Second Vatican Council in the 1960s. The program at Stockholm ranged over dozens of specific and general subjects involving social and political issues. One outcome was a commitment to and the beginnings of a platform for "Christian internationalism" aimed at fulfillment of words from Psalm 85: "Mercy and truth shall meet together, righteousness and peace shall kiss each other."

Söderblom remained the major spokesman for the Life and Work movement until his death in 1931, the year after he was awarded the Nobel Peace Prize for his efforts at peace through Christian unity. His passing at age sixty-five seemed untimely; perhaps it was grace. World War II loomed. His movement survived that horror and survives still, saying to the world, as he said in his Nobel address, the church must never stop preaching that "all nations and communities, like individuals, must act according to ethical principles, basing their hopes for coexistence on the principles of truth, justice, and love."

The emblem on Söderblom's tomb in Uppsala Cathedral bears an inscription from the Gospel of Luke that can be taken as his motto as a peacemaker:

When you have done all that is commanded you, say, "We are unworthy servants; we have only done what was our duty." (Luke 17:10)

Albert Luthuli (1898–1967)

His ambitions, he once said, were modest—"they scarcely go beyond the desire to serve God and my neighbor, both at full stretch."

The full stretch of those ambitions, straight from Jesus' great commandment, can create a peacemaker or a revolutionary, and Chief Albert Luthuli was both. He was in peace-seeking revolt against white supremacist oppression of his people—the black majority—in what is today the Republic of South Africa. Luthuli understood the paradox of this. "Peace and revolution make uneasy bedfellows," he said in receving the 1960 Nobel Peace Prize. "There can be no peace until the forces of oppression are overthrown." His strategy for the overthrow was never armed conflict. Luthuli's way was nonviolence, his goal, *shalom*—justice, dignity, and wholeness—for all persons.

Luthuli, a member of the Zulu tribe, was in the 1950s president of the African National Congress in South Africa. From its founding in the second decade of the twentieth century until it was outlawed in 1960, the congress was the major organization trying to block the steady development of *apartheid* across the southern tip of Africa. Conceived and enforced by descendants of the British and Dutch settlers who colonized South Africa, *apartheid* is a policy of strict racial separation based on the notion of white superiority. It assigns the best land, the fabulous gold and diamond mines of South Africa, and all effective political power to the whites; the native peoples and other nonwhites are outcasts, restricted at every point. *Apartheid* rules South Africa today.

While *apartheid* did not become official policy until 1948, movement toward it began in 1910 when two British and two Dutch colonies joined in the old Union of South Africa. Restriction of Africans to reserves gave rise to the African National Congress, which for years tried to win the rights of blacks by making appeals to the government. Tactics in the 1950s turned to nonviolent protests and demonstrations like those used in the United States by Martin Luther King, Jr. (see page 134). In the thick of the resistance, when he was not under (a kind of house arrest), was Albert Luthuli.

Luthuli came into his own in the struggle rather late in life. He came not from a university or radical movement, but from a village in Natal (the region around Durban) where he was the elected chief, a former school teacher, and a prominent Christian (Congregationalist).

He was born on Rhodesian soil in 1898, though his father was from Groutville in Natal. His father died when he was six years old, and he and his mother eventually returned to Groutville, a village in a mission reserve established by American missionaries in the mid-1800s. Several of Luthuli's ancestors had been elected village chiefs.

Raised a Christian, he was educated in mission boarding schools and around 1920 entered Adams College, a school for training African teachers, run by the American Board of Commissioners for Foreign Missions, an agency of the American Congregational Church. Luthuli was at Adams fifteen years, staying on to teach after he graduated. He married there (the Luthulis had seven children), and during those years actively pursued greater opportunities for black athletes, teachers, and other professionals in South African society. Also, at Adams he learned that Christian faith is not only a private matter. He came to see it, as he wrote in his autobiography, as "a belief which equipped us in a unique way to meet the challenges of our society."[13]

Albert Luthuli was absolutely convinced of the truth of Christianity. Worship was his sustenance, but he believed the Faith was also relevant to road-building and to winning the freedom of his people. Later in life, when he was famous, he would be questioned by less devout, or nonreligious, colleagues: how could he defend Christianity when the architects of *apartheid* called themselves Christians, even appealed to the Bible for support of their policies? Were not missionaries a part of the forces of colonization?

The use of Christianity to justify racism pained Luthuli deeply. He was not, however, willing to let the misuse of the Faith destroy his belief. Christianity, he said, was not invented by white men; was not just Western. "I claim with no hesitation that it belongs to Africa as much as to Europe or America or India," he wrote. As far as the Faith coming to South Africa with missionaries, that did not bother him. He considered Africans smart enough to grasp the truth no matter who was the bearer.

Groutville called Luthuli as its chief. Reluctantly, he left Adams College in 1936 and for the next decade devoted himself to the five thousand land-poor, often hungry people of his hometown. He continued some of the larger interests from Adams days, but he was no political activist. His involvement in the African National Congress started in the late 1940s because he had friends in the Natal division.

At first Luthuli was just another member. His role as a leader unfolded during a power vacuum that lifted him to the presidency of the
congress in Natal. The year was 1951.

The congress was in process of changing from a policy of appeals to
one of open, nonviolent resistance—civil disobedience. Africans by
the thousands refused to abide by the segregation laws. For his
behind-the-scenes role in this campaign, Luthuli was dismissed as
Groutville's chief by the government, and in 1953 he was "banned"
for the first time. The restriction lasted about a year and presented
him with a spiritual as well as political dilemma. Prohibited by the
ban from attending public meetings, he was advised to get special
permission to go to church. Luthuli did not want to get into more
trouble by risking a violation of the ban, but he refused to seek
permission to worship. His solution was to limit his attendance to
Holy Communion, which he reasoned was private since only members participate. He later wrote: "I do not ever intend to ask permission to worship God with my fellow Christians—I do not concede
that any man has the right either to grant or to withhold this
'privilege'."[14]

African resistance to *apartheid* mounted across the decade of the
1950s. In July, 1955, a congress-inspired Freedom Charter (sounding
much like the United States Declaration of Independence) was issued
at a massive rally in Johannesburg. Luthuli was unable to attend; he
had suffered a mild stroke. The government responded to the charter
by rounding up one hundred fifty-five opponents of *apartheid* for trial
on charges of high treason. Luthuli was among them. No treason, of
course, could be proven, and none was.

Free of the treason trial in 1957, Luthuli was a major personality in
South Africa. Large crowds of blacks turned out for his speeches and
heeded his calls for work stoppages to protest oppression. When
whites began going to hear him, the government put him under a
strict five-year ban. Only with difficulty did he get a travel permit to
go to Norway to receive his Nobel prize.

Luthuli's last major involvement in the resistance was in 1960 in a
campaign against the hated passes all Africans were required to carry
at all times. The pass books were (and are) the constant symbol of
apartheid. After police fired on peaceful pass book protesters in Sharpes-
ville, killing seventy persons, Luthuli urged Africans to destroy their
passes, and publicly burned his.

The last ban expired in 1964, but the African National Congress

was gone. Luthuli continued living at Groutville, working his small farm. He was struck and killed by a train as he crossed a railroad bridge near his home in July, 1967.

South Africa maintains order and enforces *apartheid* with a strong police force and army; real peace has not come to the land, because oppression continues. Albert Luthuli had a better plan: peace through freedom.

Dag Hammarskjöld (1905–1961)

The General Assembly of the United Nations held a marathon meeting on the first day of its fall session opening on September 20, 1961. Delegates were not dealing with a new armed conflict threatening international peace, but they did face a grim reality. Dag Hammarskjöld, the U.N. secretary general, had died two days earlier in a plane crash in central Africa.

Ambassadors rose in turn to extol the Swedish diplomat. Praise heaped upon praise, even from individuals and nations that had quarreled with the secretary general. Poland's delegate, representing the Eastern European communist bloc, honored the sincerity of Hammarskjöld's persuasion for peace. The spokesman from India called him a "great world statesman." Tributes from the small, mostly poor countries emerging from colonial rule were especially moving. They recalled Hammarskjöld's defense of their rights, his concern for the "disinherited." Adlai Stevenson of the United States summed up the sentiments. No man of his day, he said of Hammarskjöld, did more "to further the search for a world in which men solve their problems by peaceful means and not by force."

The admiration expressed that autumn day was for a humanitarian, a person of unusually strong commitment to world peace and justice, and, again in Stevenson's words, a model "international civil servant." The United Nations during Hammarskjöld's eight and a half years as secretary general was its most effective to date as a force for peace. His flair for personal diplomacy lent credibility to the U.N.'s role in world affairs. "Give it to Dag," the staff would say when a tough problem came up at the General Secretariat. He travelled tirelessly in quest of peace. People could believe his word.

Dag Hammarskjöld was a great international civil servant, and he was more, much more. Unknown as he was mourned in September, 1961, was Hammarskjöld the peacemaker for God. The world's chief diplomat was first of all God's man, wanting no praise, bending himself to further peace and justice because he had given himself, not without difficulty, to the will of God. The words of the Lord's Prayer were embedded in his soul: "Hallowed be thy name, thy kingdom come, thy will be done . . ."

The private man of faith came to light in 1963 with the publication (first in Swedish) of a surprising book, Hammarskjöld's spiritual diary, an unusual record of the interior life motivating and supporting the public servant of peace. No one, not even close friends, knew that from the mid-1920s until a few weeks before his death (with the exception of the whole decade of the 1930s), Hammarskjöld had recorded his innermost thoughts—on God, life, duty, loneliness, hope and anxiety, humility; in short, to quote him, "my negotiations with myself—and with God." The diary was found in Hammarskjöld's apartment in New York. Attached was a letter telling a friend to use his judgment about whether it should be published.

Markings, the English title of the diary, is quite unlike most spiritual autobiographies, or "confessions." It is a collection of poems and short prose entries by the author blended with quotations from the Bible and religious writings. The quotations are sometimes with, sometimes without, commentary. Though it was a best-seller, *Markings* was probably read in full by relatively few people. Its style and extremely personal tone make the book hard to follow; however, it was clear enough to put Hammarskjöld in an entirely new perspective. His public service was his divine calling, his offering of himself to God.

The U.N. official had given clues to his deep Christian sentiments in a statement for Edward R. Murrow's *This I Believe* radio series in 1953. That statement made little public impact. But *Markings* could not be ignored. Here was a self-portrait of the inside of a man, struggling, often unsure of the way, on a peace pilgrimage touching heaven and earth. Influenced by the mystic's longing for union with God and by the example of service he saw in Albert Schweitzer, who gave up careers in music and theology to become a jungle doctor, Hammarskjöld found the grace to surrender himself to a cause he knew was God's cause: peacemaking. He wrote four months before his death:

I don't know Who—or what—put the question, I don't know when it was put. I don't even remember answering. But at some moment I did answer *Yes* to Someone—or something—and from that hour I was certain that existence is meaningful and that, therefore, my life, in self-surrender, had a goal.[15]

Hammarskjöld's pilgrimage began in Jonkoping, Sweden, in 1905. He was born to the good life in terms of social station and opportunity. His family, Lutheran like almost all Swedes, was old and distinguished, a long line of government officials on his father's side and of scholars and clergy on his mother's. Hjalmar Hammarskjöld, his father, was prime minister of neutral Sweden during World War I, leaving that post in a political shakeup to resume duties as governor of Uppland, the province including Uppsala and its famed university. The elder Hammarskjöld was also chairman of the Nobel Prize Foundation from 1929 to 1947.

In Uppsala the Hammarskjölds were close to Archbishop Nathan Söderblom (see page 214), and young Dag, just completing a degree at the university, was a page at the historic ecumenical conference on Life and Work held there in 1925 under the archbishop's initiation. Hammarskjöld took three degrees in Uppsala, in the humanities, economics, and law. A doctorate in economics was earned at the University of Stockholm.

His career choice was with his father's heritage: public service. Joining the Swedish government in the finance ministry he worked his way up to chairman of the Bank of Sweden, and in 1947 took on trade relations in the foreign affairs ministry. Hammarskjöld was vice chairman of the Swedish delegation to the United Nations in 1951 and chairman the next year.

Markings reveals a "dark night of the soul" for the scholarly, solitary young diplomat in the early 1950s. Married to his work, Hammarskjöld was often lonely. A spirit of desperation permeates his diary entries for three years. He could not see the way ahead, personally or in his profession. In 1952 he wrote: "Pray that your loneliness may spur you into finding something to live for, great enough to die for."[16] His prayer was answered.

Hammarskjöld was tapped in 1953 to succeed Trygve Lie of Norway as secretary general of the United Nations. He had no illusions about the U.N.—a struggling, weak human creation, but, as he wrote in *Markings*, "the greatest creation of mankind—the dream of mankind."[17] With a sense of humility and gratitude he accepted the challenge of helping move the dream of a just, peaceful world toward reality. "The way chose you—and you must be thankful,"[18] he wrote. The United Nations and its dream would be his "something to live for, great enough to die for." As theologian Gustaf Aulèn said in an analysis of *Markings*, Hammarskjöld "considered all good work as a work of God himself; man was only an instrumentality."[19]

Hammarskjöld could not, did not, persuade all the lions to lie down with the lambs. He understood the pull and tug, the give and take, of international diplomacy. The new secretary general expected no miracles as he walked into his office, but he went about his job with a contagious enthusiasm, boosting the morale of the U.N. staff with personal visits and taking on the hardest tasks. Hammarskjöld experienced significant failures in his years as secretary general. He and the U.N. failed to do anything constructive in response to the Soviet invasion of Hungary in 1956. His policy of using neutral U.N. forces to hold the peace in volatile situations was on shaky ground in the Belgian Congo (now Zaire) in 1961. A clash between U.N. soldiers and troops of the secessionist Katanga province took Hammarskjöld on his fatal plane ride.

Failures he knew, and at least partial successes. He made the first diplomatic breakthrough with China in 1954 by personally negotiating the release of a dozen U.S. airmen, prisoners from the Korean War, whom Peking had planned to try as spies. Along with Lester Pearson of Canada, he resolved the conflict following Egypt's seizure of the Suez Canal from England and France in 1957. He calmed the tensions between Lebanon and Jordan the next year, and was unrelenting in efforts to avoid war between Israel and its Arab neighbors. And Hammarskjöld wrote: "Your own efforts 'did not bring it to pass,' only God . . ."

He was on yet another mission of personal diplomacy, hoping to be God's instrument for peace, when for some cause never known, the plane went down. Charles Malik, the Lebanese statesman, said of Hammarskjöld in 1965:

Here is the knight of peace, the selfless servant of the peoples of the world, the tragic hero who dared all, in absolute courage and utter self-disregard . . . [20]

The only book Hammarskjöld took with him to the Congo was Thomas à Kempis' *The Imitation of Christ*.

CHAPTER VIII

Loyal All the Way

"Holy are those who are persecuted for the sake of righteousness . . ."

Around a.d. 200 a man came to Tertullian, a theologian in Carthage, with a question still asked today. He wanted to know how he could be both a faithful Christian and successful in business. Tertullian let the man talk. The questioner knew he was supposed to be completely loyal to Christ, yet he wondered if compromises in principle and practice might be possible to improve his dealings with his pagan neighbors. Christianity at that time lacked a firm foothold in the Roman Empire; it was ridiculed by popular writers, scorned by proper Romans, and sporadically persecuted by the government. Tertullian's visitor felt socially battered and, what was worse, he feared his church membership would ruin him financially.

"What can I do; I must live!" cried the distraught man.

"Must you?" Tertullian replied.

Belief that loyalty to Christ is more precious than prosperity, freedom, or life itself is deeply rooted in Christianity. Jesus anticipated his crucifixion, and in the four Gospels he minces no words in telling his followers they too may face abuse, pain, and death if they are true to him. The Eighth Beatitude announces the sanctity of all disciples who, like Jesus, suffer for the sake of righteousness, that is, for God's cause. Then, departing from the pattern of the other Beatitudes, Matthew 5:11 is a personal application of the point: "Holy are *you* when people revile you and persecute you and say all manner of evil against you falsely on my account."

Jesus in Beatitude Eight and the following verse is not saying that all suffering is blessed or that Christians should encourage persecutors. In the Garden of Gethsemane before his arrest, Jesus prayed for deliverance from the ordeal ahead of him. He anticipated but never went looking for crucifixion, never said it is holy to hurt. In his agony in the garden, Jesus embraced suffering to be loyal to the cause of righteousness he had accepted as his own, and by being loyal all the way he gave meaning to suffering. So with believers who endure persecution: their virtue is fidelity, and faith in Christ makes their suffering holy.

The last Beatitude can be taken as a historical prediction as well as a description of a quality of holiness. An uncountable host of women and men across the centuries have been reviled, imprisoned, tortured, burned, butchered, and falsely accused on account of that originally inauspicious Nazarene the faithful know as God in spirit and flesh. These are the martyrs.

Martyrs are witnesses—witnesses unshakably loyal to their stories, their truths, no matter the personal cost. Since Stephen, the first Christian martyr, was stoned to death in Jerusalem about A.D. 50, Christianity has honored the example of believers willing to suffer and die for faith. Among all churches and in most Christian theologies, martyrdom is a supreme expression of the "imitation of Christ."

But though the holiness of life-sacrificing loyalty is deeply rooted in Christianity, and examples honored by churches, modern people have a hard time making sense of martyrdom. Modern Christians, according to Gordon Zahn, are embarrassed by martyrs, and Zahn traces the embarrassment to a lack of respect for "extremists" or "fanatics" insistent on total commitment to virtue or total rejection of evil.[1] There is some truth in Zahn's explanation, but a modern lack of regard for "extremists" and "fanatics" is probably not caused by overexposure to zealots for virtue and foes of evil; it is the opposite. Fanaticism and extremism in the twentieth century have so seldom served virtue and so regularly accompanied evil that people have an understandable suspicion of anyone veering from what Zahn calls the "golden mean."

Christian martyrs are, of course, extremists in that they go as far as they can to be loyal to Christ. However, the modern problem with Christian martyrdom is not so much embarrassment over extreme virtue as it is a quandary over who among the persecuted are martyrs to the virtue and righteousness of Christ, and by whose decision. These are matters forced upon the modern Christian by history.

Christianity has always been a religion diverse in theology and ethnic composition, never monolithic even in administration or liturgy. This diversity has at times turned belligerent, so that Christians have persecuted one another, as happened, for example, among Roman Catholics and Protestants in sixteenth-century England. Furthermore, dominant churches have persecuted dissenters —"heretics"—as happened in the Catholic Inquisition of medieval times and in Puritan New England. Imposition of the death penalty on "heretics" is a particularly complicating historical reality when attempting to discuss the righteousness of the persecuted. It becomes even more complicating when joined with a Christian tendency in some times and places to deal harshly with non-Christians, as in Christianity's sorry history of intolerance toward the Jews. Christian persecution within the family and persecution of non-Christians is such a snag that a word must be said about it.

Harassed for its first three hundred years, Christianity was legalized by the Roman Empire in the early 300s, and soon became the only permissible religion. Out of a series of serious theological squabbles there arose the idea, never fully implemented, that the one church should observe common theology and practices. Standards of orthodoxy were set, and individuals and groups dissenting were subject to retribution as heretics. In the Western, or Latin, church, to take only one branch of Christianity as an example, for several centuries the penalties against heretics were normally expulsion, or involved loss of property. Stronger measures were introduced in the eleventh and twelfth centuries, notably in response to a movement of rather puritanical-minded folk called Cathari (the "pure") who by every standard of orthodoxy were heretics, though that hardly justifies what happened to them. Inspired in part by the crusades against the "infidels" (Muslims) who had overrun the Holy Land, the Latin church tried to crush the Cathari with force and bloodshed, and was relatively successful.

The campaign against the Cathari was a forerunner of the Inquisition, an instrument of the papacy set up in the thirteenth century to ferret out and punish heretics. More efficient and more often used in some countries of Christian Europe than in others, the Inquisition dispatched to the next world or imprisoned a great many persons over a period of several hundred years. It was turned against Protestants in some places in the late sixteenth century, although fairness demands the recognition that many Protestants had an inquisitorial disposition of their own to employ against Catholics and others departing from their own orthodoxy.

In the Middle Ages, the idea of religious toleration was embryonic, conceived at all. Error in the church, the body of Christ, was thought to be a mortal danger to be corrected at all costs. The absence of a sense of toleration and the desire to protect the church from heresy do not justify the Inquisition or any other religiously motivated butchery of people. But they do help to explain what happened. Moreover, Christian churches (Catholic or Protestant) at their worst as persecutors never came close to equaling the horrors and inhumanness of a Hitler or a Stalin. This observation does not justify church-led brutality, but it may put it into perspective.

Persecution within the Christian family makes it difficult to survey the past and come up with universally accepted examples of believers martyred for righteousness' sake—for Christ. The whole family generally recognizes the sanctity of martyrs made by the Romans during the first four centuries of Christianity and of others who suffered at the hands of later "pagans" and "infidels." Beyond this, formal and informal canons of martyrs differ from church to church, and sometimes compete. The Roman Catholic Church, for instance, has canonized as martyrs Jesuit missionaries and others who met torture and death in Elizabeth I's Protestant England, while Protestants in their less formal ways honor as heroes compatriots martyred in the Catholic reign of Mary I. Protestants remember John Hus, burned in 1415, as a hero; Catholicism considered him a heretic. A group of Catholic martyrs killed in Uganda in 1886 has its Protestant counterpart, although Protestants did not slay Catholics or vice versa, both groups being victims of an African chief out to eradicate Christianity in his domain. Within Protestantism, the Anglicans have their martyrs, the Baptists theirs, the Lutherans theirs, and so on through the alphabet of denominations.

While the multiplicity of martyrs hinders formation of a universally accepted list, it does not rule out appreciation of supreme loyalty to Christ wherever it is found. Christian holiness in all its manifestations has little correspondence to denomination, nationality, or race. Christian martyrs have historical and spiritual significance on the basis of the quality of their life, suffering, and sacrifice, not on the basis of ecclesiastical sponsorship. What is important is to allow each supremely loyal witness his or her own integrity before Christ in his or her own time and situation, letting them be real human beings willing to trust God all the way.

Unfortunately, some martyrs are not easy to approach as real human beings, the details of their lives and deaths having been lost or never recorded. This is especially true of the martyrs of the early centuries—those persecuted by pagan Rome. Names are remembered, but the real humanity of these noble persons is often clouded by legends or by stylized accounts hard to accept as fact. Early Christianity saw martyrdom as a reenactment of the passion of Christ, and written or oral reports on martyrs tended to repeat a literary formula based on a New Testament precedent, the stoning of Stephen, already mentioned as the first Christian martyr.

Stephen was a member of the very earliest Christian community in Jerusalem. His story is found in the book of the Acts of the Apostles and only there. Stephen's name is Greek, suggesting he was a Gentile, but that is not as important as its meaning: Stephen means "crown," and appropriately he was the first to be "crowned" with martyrdom. Acts says that Stephen was one in a group of seven men selected as deacons of the first church in Jerusalem. What a deacon did at that stage in the development of Christianity is not clear, but the assignment was one of service, likely helping to settle disputes among the members, and seeing that the needy were looked after (Acts 6). Stephen was also a preacher and a doer of "great wonders and signs," and it was such public activities that got him in trouble.

For his proclamations about Jesus Christ, Stephen was accused of violating the religious law in effect in Jerusalem, and brought up for a hearing. The accused, according to Acts 7, delivered a lengthy sermon that further enraged his critics and a city mob. Acts' story concludes:

Then they cast him out of the city and stoned him; . . . And as they were stoning Stephen, he prayed, "Lord Jesus, receive my spirit." And he knelt down and cried with a loud voice, "Lord do not hold this sin against them." And when he had said this, he fell asleep. (Acts 7:58–60, RSV)

Parallels between the martyrdom of Stephen and the trial and crucifixion of Jesus are numerous, and Stephen's story in Acts was to become a model for the accounts of many martyrs in Christianity's first four hundred years. Recurring elements in the stories include the seizure by authorities of persons guilty of nothing but proclaiming Christ, a hasty or unjust trial, insistence by the accused of loyalty to faith, and execution, usually accompanied by a prayer of forgiveness for the executioners.

While the pattern of persecution and steadfast Christian loyalty seen in Stephen's story no doubt has been replayed again and again, its constant repetition makes early Christian literature on martyrdom highly stylized, and stylized stories have a way of robbing their heroes and heroines of individual qualities. So much alike are so many of the early accounts that the martyrs seem two-dimensional, almost cardboard figures relatively unappealing as real human beings. This is not to say that saints Agnes, Cecilia, Eustace, Julian, and Lucy never existed as persons; it is only to say that little, if anything historical, is known of them. They have inspired interesting legends often filled with religious insights, but legends say more about the spirituality of their authors than about their subjects. Most of the loyal witnesses of the stylized early "acts of martyrs" can be honored as little more than symbols.

Fortunately, a great number of Christian martyrs of the far and recent past can be known as real people in real situations. Some left diaries or other writings of their experiences. Some were the subjects of reliable biographers and chroniclers in their own times. Others emerge as real human beings through the painstaking research of modern historians.

"Holy are those who are persecuted for the sake of righteousness:" members of the final phalanx in the Holy Company—martyrs, Christians loyal all the way.

Justin the Martyr (100?–165)

He was a seeker, a man looking for truth. Justin—history records no other proper name—was born about A.D. 100 in Palestine and there grew up in a Roman city on the site of modern Nablus. His parents were non-Christian, probably Greek, although Justin seems to have learned something of Judaism in his youth. Gifted with an alert, inquisitive mind sharpened by a good education, he set out to discover a philosophy, a doctrine, possessing the truth.

Justin studied ancient and newer Greek philosophies, discarding one after another because they did not provide what he wanted—a knowledge of God. He traveled great distances in search of teachers.

Most impressed by the thought of Plato, the young inquirer apparently attached himself to a prominent Platonist in Ephesus, a once great center of learning in what is today Turkey. The Platonist promised to guide him to God and truth, but Justin was still dissatisfied.

Whether by accident or deliberate decision, Justin encountered Christianity when he was about thirty years old. While the New Testament was not a set collection of books in the early second century, the Gospels and the letters of Paul were in circulation. Justin delved into these writings, and was especially moved by the Christian interpretation of the Hebrew prophets. He was also inspired by the fidelity of Christian martyrs, already numerous. In Christianity, Justin found the truth, the understanding of God he wanted.

Always a layman, Justin turned his considerable knowledge to the defense and explanation of the new religion centered in Jesus Christ. For reasons not altogether clear from historical evidence, the Roman government was sporadically vicious toward the church for more than three hundred years. Although the persecution waxed and waned, and was usually spotty even in the worst of times, a fair number of believers were burned, beheaded, or fed to beasts; enough died to inspire Tertullian to say, "the blood of martyrs is the seed of the church." Intellectuals devoted to Greek philosophy or Roman religion also attacked Christianity, which grew steadily despite state hostility. Christians were accused of heinous acts such as cannibalism (probably their critics' misconception of Holy Communion) and preoccupation with sex (a confused reading of the emphasis on love).

Justin had the credentials of a philosopher. Ancient philosophers served a role not unlike that of the newspaper columnist today who tries to explain what's what and why, usually in abstract terms, in order to influence both public opinion and the people in power. To challenge the charges levelled at Christianity, he wrote, lectured, and debated, offering an *apology* for the faith he had embraced. *Apology* here does not mean saying "I'm sorry"; rather, it means to speak in defense of some idea or person.

Three "apologetic" writings by Justin have been preserved. In them he argued that instead of persecuting the church the Roman authorities should join forces with Christianity in order to overcome the lies of pagan mythology, which he lampooned as superstition. Justin said that Christianity is God's plan to bring Jewish religion and Greek philosophy into a single stream of salvation. His First Apology, addressed to Emperor Antoninus Pius, appealed to all lovers of truth to consider the possibility that Christian truths are "not the products of human wisdom, but are spoken by the power of God."

The First Apology asked Caesar to stop the harassment of Christians, but betrayed no willingness to strike deals or make compromises to assure more favorable treatment. Justin invited the emperor and other Romans to accept the Christian truth; if they declined, the Christians would continue to endure persecution.

Justin himself met martyrdom in Rome, which he visited at least twice, and where he was living around 165 as one of several Christian teachers. He held no official position in the church. Christian institutions were few then. Teachers such as Justin gave instruction in their homes, which also served as centers of worship and Christian community life in the imperial capital. Perhaps because he was a major teacher, the accounts of Justin's trial are among the most genuine of the "acts of the martyrs" preserved from the early church.

Although considered authentic, the accounts do not supply all the details about the circumstances of his arrest or the charges brought against him and five other men and one woman condemned at the same time. Questions and answers from the trial suggest that the Christians may have been seized for holding allegedly illegal meetings in Justin's quarters, or because they refused to sacrifice a pinch of incense to the gods of Rome, or simply because they were Christian. Whatever the charge, Justin seems to have been a victim of a grudge. In his defense of Christianity on the previous visit to Italy, he had publicly disputed one Crescens the Cynic, an anti-Christian philosopher whom Justin found intolerably ignorant. Crescens was offended and denounced his adversary to the police when Justin returned to Rome.

Justin and his companions were tried before a judge named Rusticus, another philosopher, a teacher of the reigning emperor, Marcus Aurelius. In what is thought to be the earliest of three similar accounts of the trial, the proceedings opened with Rusticus questioning Justin:

Rusticus: What kind of life do you lead?
Justin: A blameless one, and without condemnation in the eyes of everyone.
Rusticus: What are the doctrines that you practice?
Justin: I have tried to become acquainted with all doctrines. But I have

committed myself to the true doctrines of the Christians, even though they may not please those who hold false beliefs.

Rusticus: Are these then the doctrines that you prefer?

Justin: Yes, for I adhere to them on the basis of belief.

Rusticus: What belief do you mean?

Justin: The belief that we piously hold regarding the God of the Christians, whom alone we hold to be the craftsman of the whole world from the beginning, and also regarding Jesus Christ, the child of God, who was also foretold by the prophets as one who was to come down to mankind as a herald of salvation and a teacher of good doctrines. What I say is insignificant when measured against his godhead; but I acknowledge the power of prophecy, for proclamation has been made about him whom I have just now said to be the Son of God. For know you that in earlier times the prophets foretold his coming among men.

Rusticus: Where do you meet?

Justin: Wherever it is each one's preference or opportunity. In any case, do you suppose we can all meet in the same place?

Rusticus: Tell me, where do you meet, in what place?

Justin: I have been living above the baths of Myrtinus for the entire period of my sojourn at Rome, and this is my second; and I have known no other meeting-place but here. Anyone who wished could come to my abode and I would impart to him the words of truth.

Rusticus: You do admit, then, that you are a Christian?

Justin: Yes, I am.[2]

The others in the dock answered the question, "Are you a Christian?" in the affirmative. All of them refused to consider making sacrifice to Roman gods. Rusticus pronounced the death sentence. Justin and his companions were beheaded on June 21, according to one account of the trial. Years earlier, in his First Apology, the quester for truth wrote his own epitaph, and that of all martyrs for Christ: "You can kill us, but cannot do us any real harm."[3]

Perpetua (180–202) and Felicitas (?–202)

The first widespread, coordinated move against Christians in the Roman Empire came in the early third century.[4] Emperor Septimius Severus in 202 issued an edict against conversion to either Judaism or Christianity. What immediately provoked his action is uncertain. A few years earlier the Jews had angered the emperor by opposing him in a civil war, and some historians speculate that Roman officials may

have looked upon Christians and Jews as all part of the same troublesome minority culture. Another explanation says the Romans did not
want the social order or the army upset by an emotional, visionary
movement predicting the end of the world that broke out in Christianity around 200. Also, Caesar Severus was a follower of Serapis, an
Egyptian god of the dead, and may not have liked the competition the
Christians presented to his cult, recently imported to Rome.

Coordinated and intense but confined primarily to urban areas, the
Severan persecution cast a shadow over the church at Carthage, a
great Roman city near what is now Tunis on the North African coast.
There, as a group, five Christian catechumens (adults receiving instruction in faith) were arrested, confined to a house, and given every
reason to believe they would be matched with wild beasts in the arena
for the enjoyment of the local population. The five increased to six
when Saturus, a deacon who had been instructing the catechumens,
refused to abandon his pupils.

Two women were in the group. Vibia Perpetua (the name means
"constant") was a young matron of twenty-two, a daughter of a good
family and the mother of an infant son. Felicitas (meaning "fortunate"
or "fruitful") was Perpetua's personal slave, and she was eight months
pregnant. Yes, some early Christians, as well as a great many later
ones, owned slaves. Almost anyone in the ancient world who could
afford them bought servants, a social reality even the Apostle Paul
accepted so long as Christian owners treated their slaves as brothers
and sisters. Slavery was probably more human in the ancient days
than it was in pre–Civil War America, but it was still slavery, and
century upon century would pass before the Christian nations would
rid themselves of the practice of owning other people. Many of the
first Christians were slaves, and they often converted their masters
and mistresses, although there is no indication that Felicitas evangelized Perpetua.

The account of the martyrdom of Perpetua, Felicitas, and their
companions (Saturus, Secundulus, Saturninus, and Revocatus, also a
slave) is well preserved and explicit. Except for an introduction and
the description of the final scene in the arena, the text is in the form of
a diary kept by Perpetua. Some part of the story may be legendary,
but compared with most hagiography of third-century martyrs the
account is filled with convincing human touches: Perpetua's concern
for her child, her father's embarrassment and distress over her predic-

ament, and the act of two unimprisoned Christians in getting better jail quarters for the women.

Perpetua's father was horrified that his only daughter—she had two living brothers, one also Christian—had been hauled to prison like a common criminal. A non-Christian, he could not understand what possessed her, and when he visited her he got so angry she thought he might tear out her eyes. Perpetua was more anxious about her child than about her father. The baby was not yet weaned, and he was finally brought to her:

I nursed my baby, who was faint from hunger. In my anxiety I spoke to my mother about the child, I tried to comfort my brother, and I gave the child in their charge. I was in pain because I saw them suffering out of pity for me. These were the trials I had to endure for many days. Then I got permission for my baby to stay with me in prison. At once I recovered my health, relieved as I was of my worry and anxiety over the child.[5]

Carthage was one of the places where an enthusiastic, visionary brand of Christianity flowered in the early third century. Traces of this movement, later condemned by the church, appear in the account of Perpetua and friends. The young woman had the gift of foresight, and in her diary recorded visions of physical defeat and spiritual triumph.

The imprisoned Christians had some mobility. Perpetua, and perhaps the others, was baptized in jail. The converts could receive visitors and associate with one another, a freedom permitting Perpetua to share her visions with her comrades.

Meanwhile, Felicitas was worried that she would be unable to ascend the ladder to heaven with her companions because pregnant women were excluded from the bloody games of the arena:

Her comrades in martyrdom were also saddened; for they were afraid that they would have to leave behind so fine a companion to travel alone on the same road to hope. And so, two days before the contest, they poured forth a prayer to the Lord in one torrent of common grief. And immediately after their prayer the birth pains came upon her. She suffered a good deal in her labour because of the natural difficulty of an eight months' delivery.[6]

A sort of trial, a hearing before the Roman governor of the region, had already been held. Perpetua's father was present, again begging her to at least go through the formality of sacrificing to the dieties of Rome to save her life for her baby's sake. The governor urged her to offer a sacrifice for the emperor's welfare and thus take pity on her father. She refused.

For their few remaining days, the Christians were more concerned about their worthiness, their loyalty to Christ, than about the suffering ahead of them. They prayed, spoke to the crowd outside about their faith, and celebrated their last meal together as an *agape*, a love feast. "The day of their victory dawned, and they marched from the prison to the amphitheatre joyful as though they were going to heaven, with calm faces, trembling, if at all, with joy rather than fear."[7]

The male Christians were pitted against a series of animals; none was killed immediately. Naked, tied in nets, Perpetua and Felicitas were exposed to a "mad heifer," but when the crowd saw the mother's milk dripping from Felicitas' breasts it demanded tunics on the women. Both were attacked by the cow, and Perpetua was quicker to cover her nakedness than to inspect her wounds. The spectators roared and allowed the two to live momentarily.

Prisoners thrown to the beasts in the Roman arena were often not slain but only mangled by the leopards, bears, and boars. Once the animals tired, or dined, the spectators grew weary of the game, and the victims were finished off by the gladiator's sword, and so it was with Perpetua, Felicitas, and their friends:

. . . the mob asked that their bodies be brought out into the open that their eyes might be the guilty witnesses of the sword that pierced their flesh. And so the martyrs got up and went to the spot of their own accord . . . and kissing one another they sealed their martyrdom with the ritual kiss of peace.[8]

The young gladiator assigned to cut Perpetua's throat missed the first time, inflicting a weak blow. She took the trembling hand of her executioner and guided it to her neck.

Between the ordeal in the ring and the sword, Perpetua had spoken briefly to her brother and other catechumens. "You must all stand fast in the faith and love one another," she said, "and do not be weakened by what we have gone through."[9]

Boniface (680?–754)

Boniface is remembered less for dying than for his productive life. He neither experienced organized suppression of Christianity, nor suffered extended personal duress for the faith, nor fell afoul of church authorities, who, after the gods of Rome were trounced, developed the bad habit of sometimes persecuting people who disagreed with official teaching. Boniface nevertheless belongs among the Holy Company of those who maintain supreme loyalty to Christ despite physical threat. This saint was murdered by a band of ruffians because he could not stop preaching the Gospel of Jesus Christ.

Emperors can legalize religions; laws and armies can enforce the formal observance of a new religion, as happened along the way in the expansion of Christianity, but the really important work, the grassroot work, of making the faith meaningful to people in their everyday lives belongs to missionaries. For a millenium they labored to cover Europe with a Christian mantle, a mantle often badly ripped over the years by intrareligious wars and theological squabbles.

The eighth century was one of aggressive mission effort in northern Europe, notably beyond the Danube, where "barbarian" tribes had resisted both the church and the Roman legions. The legions withdrew, but missionaries increased among the Germanic tribes after the empire fell apart in the fifth century. British Benedictines were especially active in this mission work, and among them none was more effective than Boniface, the great apostle to Germany. Boniface also revitalized the church of the Franks, a Germanic tribe from whose ranks came Charlemagne, founder of the Holy Roman Empire. Voltaire was probably right in saying the Holy Roman Empire was "neither holy, nor Roman, nor an empire," but for several centuries after the year 900 it afforded western Europe a sense of unity missing since Caesar's eagle died.

Baptized Winfred, Boniface was born in Wessex, a kingdom in the south of England, around A.D. 680, was educated in Benedictine monasteries, and became the headmaster of his own alma mater, an abbey school near Winchester. Boniface excelled as a scholar, writing one of the first Latin grammars prepared in England, and not until he was thirty years old did he enter the Benedictine Order. Once a priest, he grew restless with academic life and followed an inner urging into missions. His initial venture was in the Low Countries to a tribe of Saxons called Fresians. Radbod, king of these people, wanted no part of a Christian interloper, so Boniface, still Winfred, went home, where his brothers in the monastery at Nursling tried without success to make him their abbot.

Winfred traveled to Rome in 718 with a group of pilgrims and there received his new name and a missionary commission from Pope

Gregory II. He was to work east of the Rhine, and the pontiff was specific in telling him to establish churches in keeping with *Roman* Catholic practice and administration. The popes in those days had not extended their authority over all expressions of Christianity in western Europe. For example, in the north Rome was seriously challenged by Celtic Christianity, which assigned more authority to abbots than to bishops and used a different liturgy of baptism. Boniface was sympathetic to Rome and until his death in 754 was one of the papacy's main men in the mission field.

Radbod's death allowed Boniface to return to Friesland, where he labored with modest success for three years. In 722 he was summoned to Rome for consecration as regional bishop for Germany. Significantly, Pope Gregory gave him a letter of introduction to Charles Martel, the ruler of the Franks, a great hero after 732 for checking the advance of Islam in Europe, and the grandfather of Charlemagne, the first holy Roman emperor. Martel liked Boniface and agreed to be his protector.

The missionary went into Germany, to Hesse, with a determination reminiscent of the Prophet Elijah going against the priests of Baal on Mount Carmel in Old Testament times. To undercut belief in the Teutonic gods, he assailed an oak tree sacred to Thor, roughly equivalent to the Greek god Zeus or the Roman Jupiter. This god is no god, he declared, and proceeded to strike the old tree with an ax, an impropriety the Germans probably allowed only because Boniface was a friend of Martel. Thor's oak, according to the tale, split into four parts, crashing to the ground as a sign to pagans that their gods were powerless to protect even their own shrines.

An efficient organizer as well as a good tree cutter, Boniface had unexpected success in Germany. Opposition to Christianity steadily crumbled, permitting him to found churches, dioceses, and monasteries throughout Hesse, Thuringia, and Bavaria. Three times in his missionary career in Germany, he was called to Rome, each time given more episcopal authority and more territories to evangelize. Late in life, in 747, he was made archbishop of Mainz and primate of Germany.

Meanwhile, the church in Martel's Frankish kingdom was in sorry condition. The ruler seized church land and money at will; church offices were auctioned to the highest bidders, and there were no set standards of Christian behavior. Boniface wanted to reform the situation but could do little until Martel died in 741, leaving his power to his sons Carloman and Pepin. These successors, especially Carloman, who later entered a monastery, were more cooperative. They sponsored a series of regional councils that succeeded in shoring up church discipline and in correcting administrative abuses.

By the early 750s Boniface was anxious to hand over his episcopal duties to his successor, Bishop Lull (also a Catholic saint), one of scores of English Benedictines who assisted him. The primate of Germany had the heart of a missionary, and there was an unfinished job back in Friesland. Over 70, an advanced age in his century, Boniface boarded a boat going northwest down the Rhine.

Able to reclaim a fair number of previously converted Friesians who had lapsed into paganism, the missionary and a party of helpers turned to unevangelized country. Initial efforts were encouraging. Boniface scheduled an open-air service of preaching and confirmation near the Borne River on Pentecost Sunday, June 5, 754. While he was awaiting the appointed time, as he read Scripture either to himself or to a group of converts, a band of Friesian hoodlums swept down on the camp, killing Boniface and many of his companions. "In terms of medieval hagiography his life of service to the church thus had a perfect ending," medievalist Norman Cantor has said.[10] He was buried in the monastery he had established at Fulda in Hesse.

Boniface was untractably stubborn; he could be rash and disagreeable. Once he asked Pope Zachery (who declined) to excommunicate and imprison two Celtic missionaries he particularly disliked, but he was not notably harsh in a harsh age. Christianity in eighth-century Europe was still testing itself, defining its course in relation to emerging political and social forces. Boniface believed the church must first trust God, and then consistently follow its truth. In one of his letters he wrote:

In her voyage across the ocean of this world, the Church is like a great ship being pounded by the waves of life's different stresses. Our duty is not to abandon ship but to keep her on her course. Let us stand fast in what is right and prepare our souls for trial. Let us wait upon God's strengthening aid and say to him: "O Lord, you have been our refuge in all generations."[11]

John Hus (1374?–1415)

Hus is officially a heretic in the eyes of the Roman Catholic Church. He was burned at the stake in 1415 at the church's insistence, and there are some people today, not all Catholic, who wonder if he did not get what he deserved for helping stir up the religious and political chaos that battered the Christian ship in the fifteenth and sixteenth centuries. The Czech priest was certainly a lusty, if land-locked, sailor, a zealous nationalist in his native Bohemia, but he was also a man of genuine Christian piety, a reforming spirit in a time when the church desperately needed reform. Hus, long honored as a hero by Protestants, merits consideration as a universal Christian martyr because he was probably more righteous, more concerned for Christ's truth, than his ecclesiastical persecutors.

Christian Europe in the fourteenth and fifteenth centuries was a swirl of intrigue and competition; it was an age in which disputing Christians habitually treated one another with bold disrespect. Feu-dalism, the medieval social and political system based on a pyramid of loyalty, was breaking apart. Nationalism was on the rise in France, England, Spain, and the various German and Slavic states. A middle class was developing to challenge the hereditary aristocracy; peasants were restless. Kings and popes feuded. The papacy was in disarray throughout the fourteenth century. For seventy years beginning in 1305 the popes were "captives" in Avignon, a city that belonged to the king of Naples but was strongly influenced by France. Then for an-other fifty years there were two popes, one each in Rome and Avignon, and finally three popes, all demanding obedience and revenues.

Looming over this change and confusion was the horror of the black death, bubonic plague, that wiped out perhaps twenty million people—a third of the European population—in the late 1340s, and twenty years later reappeared in France and England. Some called it the wrath of God on a sinful world. Others, according to historian Barbara Tuchman, "could discover no Divine purpose" in the human suffering. Tuchman says the black death caused people to ques-tion the fixed order of things, including the seemingly everlasting order of medieval religion, and to begin to turn toward individual conscience.[12]

John Hus was not afraid to question the established order of the church or to rest his case on individual apprehension of God's will. In this he was influenced by the writings of John Wycliffe, a fiery Englishman who died in 1384, about a decade before Hus's birth. Wycliffe considered himself a disciple of Augustine and Francis of Assisi in stressing the simplicity of Christian life and the value of personal Christian initiative. He found the papacy decadent and considered loyalty to it inferior to loyalty to Christ. Wycliffe also denied the real presence of Christ in the bread and wine of Holy Communion, a point with which Hus disagreed. The Czech did believe that laity should be allowed to have the Eucharist in both kinds, bread and wine, as had been the custom in the early church, while the medieval Roman church restricted the laity to the bread. (Eastern Orthodoxy never withdrew the wine from the laity.)

Born of poor parents in southern Bohemia, Hus made his way to Prague, worked as a choirboy while attending the university, took a master's degree, and became a teacher. He was an arrogant dandy of a young man who abandoned his "foolish mind" by studying the Bible. Since the university paid him no salary, he was ordained and became the preacher at Prague's Bethlehem Chapel where he delivered rousing sermons heavy with the ideas of Wycliffe. His troubles with the church started in the early 1400s because of his Wycliffite leanings, but the conflict was complicated by Bohemian nationalism—exerted against German and Hungarian control—and already existing squabbles within the church.

Hus's enemies in Prague denounced him to the Roman curia in 1407. While that matter was pending, the king of Bohemia and the king of France decided to try to end the papal schism by convening a church council in Pisa. This action split the university of Prague, putting Hus on the side of the king, against the local archbishop who supported Pope Gregory XII in Rome. The schism in the papacy had given impetus to a movement called conciliarism, asserting the authority of church councils over the pope. The higher clergy tended to oppose the movement.

The Council of Pisa in 1409 said it needed no head but Jesus Christ, and proceeded to depose both sitting popes and elect an old Greek, the archbishop of Milan, as pontiff. But neither deposed pope would budge, so there were three supreme heads of the church. Hus and the Bohemian king, Wenceslas, supported the council's man, Alexander V, while the archbishop of Prague favored Gregory. Furthermore, the archbishop bribed Alexander to prohibit Hus from preaching in Bethlehem Chapel. Hus refused to obey and was excommunicated by the pope he helped make. Shortly thereafter he was called to Rome to answer the old charges against him. He sent regrets and was excommunicated a second time by a second pope.

The confusion got worse in 1411 when Pope John, the successor to Alexander, preached a crusade against the king of Naples and prom-

ised remission of sins for contributions to his cause. Hus was aghast
and led protests against the sale of indulgences (promises of forgiveness). This angered King Wenceslas, who would have shared the
profits with the pope. To bring order to Prague, Hus went into exile
for two years, during which he wrote his most important work, "On
the Church." In the book he disagreed with both those who said the
pope is supreme in the church and those who favored councils. The
church, he said, is "holy, Catholic, and universal" but is headed by
Christ alone. Hus also asserted that no reprobate is truly a member of
the church, although he did not say, as was later charged, that the
validity of sacraments depends on the moral virtue of the priest
administering them. He wanted it understood that he thought the
universal church was the Roman Catholic church, but said the church
was not constituted by the pope and his court.

In the wider world, something had to be done about the papal
schism. King Sigismund of Hungary, also the Holy Roman emperor
and unpopular in Bohemia, persuaded Pope John to call another
council in 1415 at Constance, Switzerland. It was decided to try Hus
at the same time. Hus agreed to appear in person after Sigismund
promised two-way safe conduct; once in Constance he was jailed,
eventually sharing the prison with Pope John, who was arrested by
the emperor for fleeing the meeting in an attempt to end it.

The Council of Constance was the largest gathering of the Middle
Ages and one of the most controversial church parleys of all time.
Conciliarism had a field day, though it took some strange twists. The
laity, which had expected to have a voice, was excluded. Votes were
assigned to power blocs, one each to England, France, Italy, Germany, Spain, and the cardinals as a group. Constance did end the papal
schism. The meeting adjourned with one new pope, Martin V, who
reluctantly sanctioned the council's declarations on the supremacy of
conciliarism. Renaissance popes, however, were not of a mind to be
ruled by councils. Pius II in 1460 condemned conciliarism in his
famous document *Execrabilis*. Ironically, he used the same argument,
an appeal to Christ, advanced by Hus against the conciliarists.[13]

Hus in Constance did not stand a chance. The charges against him
varied from week to week. Hearings were started, cancelled, and
started again. Finally asked to recant (repudiate) thirty alleged here-
sies, he asked how he could recant since the list did not reflect his
ideas; how could he renounce things he never believed? "I shall die
with joy today in the faith of the Gospel I have preached," he said.

Condemned, Hus was stripped of ordination, his soul abandoned to the devil, and his body handed over to the secular authorities for execution. He burned at the stake appealing to Christ.

Bohemian reaction to the travesty at Constance was severe. Civil war involving several groups of Hussites and the church–state forces dragged on for years. More immediately, Hus's close friend Jerome of Prague was burned for giving Holy Communion in both kinds to the laity. This practice was sanctioned by the Council of Basel in the 1430s but later revoked. Communion in both kinds for laity became a cardinal principle of the Protestant Reformation, and is today permissible for Catholic laity in special situations.

Anne Askew (1521?–1546)

She was twenty-five years old and the mother of two children when she was burned in 1546 as a dangerous criminal, a heretic threatening English life and religion. The bishop of London was sure of her crime: Anne preached false doctrine on the Eucharist—ironic in Tudor England, where accepted Christian doctrine seesawed between conflicting parties.

England never experienced anything like the Spanish Inquisition. In fact, the general inquisition started by Rome against heretics in the eleventh century was not popular there, but the island nation had its own blood-letting religious history, especially in the sixteenth and seventeenth centuries. That history is complex. Catholics, Anglicans, and Puritans (Presbyterians of a sort) were all on occasion the persecuted and on occasion the persecutors.

Anne Askew is regarded as a Protestant martyr; however, it does not necessarily follow that she was a victim of Roman Catholic intolerance. Officially, *Roman* Catholicism did not exist in England in 1546; there was only a state church trying to decide whether it would be Protestant or Catholic, and the state was the primary actor, the king demanding obedience to him before obedience to conscience. The heavy hand of King Henry VIII in the English Reformation produced several notable martyrs, including Thomas More, who refused to help the monarch establish a church separated from the rest of Christendom.

Protestant thought from Germany filtered into England in the 1520s to join ideological forces with the remnant of the Wycliffe movement. King Henry vigorously attacked Martin Luther. He defended the papacy, but Henry was not a man hesitant to change his mind. The king wanted Pope Clement VII to grant him permission to divorce his wife Catherine so he could marry a woman, Anne Boleyn, who he thought might bear him a male heir. Henry saw nothing wrong with the request, since many of his royal relatives and friends had gotten papal approval for divorce and remarriage. But Clement had problems with Henry's request. First, Rome's special permission had been required for Henry to marry Catherine, who had been his older brother's widow. Second, Catherine was not just any queen. She was the daughter of Ferdinand and Isabella of Spain and the aunt of the German emperor Charles V, who happened to be holding Pope Clement prisoner in Rome. Henry decided to act on his own. Supported by Parliament, English Protestants, and an independent-minded group of Catholics, he maneuvered so that papal authority in England was nullified. The king became the head of the church in his realm, and Henry married Anne Boleyn, whom he later beheaded.

The Church of England under Henry was neither Roman Catholic nor Protestant. It was an English version of something John Hus might have liked—"Catholicism without the papacy."[14] The king wanted most Catholic beliefs and practices kept. He certainly was not willing to abandon the Mass with its stress on the physical presence of Christ in favor of the Swiss Protestant teaching of symbolic presence. Anne Askew held the latter view.

Just why an example was made of Anne remains a mystery. Henry's government in his final years (he died in 1547) often let subjects dissent on doctrine, so convoluted was the whole religious scene. The king's chief adviser, the archbishop of Canterbury, was a convinced Protestant; Anne was a militant, noisy Protestant, though she led no massive public movement, wrote no pamphlets attacking the crown, and exercised little public influence.

Anne was the second daughter of William Askew, a minor nobleman in Lincolnshire. She married one Thomas Kyme—though history uses her maiden name—and had two children. The woman was evidently a Protestant nag at home because her husband, a Catholic, sent her packing. Anne went to London where she found a Protestant community to her liking. Somehow her beliefs on Holy Communion came to the attention of Bishop Edmund Bonner of London and city officials. She was called in for questioning. What is known of her ordeal comes from an account published shortly after her death. One session reportedly went as follows:

Questioner: Thou foolish woman, sayest thou, that the priests cannot make the body of Christ?

Anne: I say so, my Lord; for I have read that God made man; but that man can make God, I never yet read, nor, I suppose, ever shall read.

Questioner: After the words of consecration, is it not the Lord's body?

Anne: No, but it is consecrated bread.

Questioner: What if a mouse eat it after the consecration? What shall become of the mouse?

Anne: Alack poor mouse!

Impertinent and avowedly Protestant, Anne was sent to Newgate prison to reconsider her views. She stood firm, and after torture in the Tower of London, Bishop Bonner, the chancellor of Cambridge University, and other notables sent messages trying to persuade her to recant. She refused, and on June 18, 1546, was tried before a panel that called no witnesses for the defense. Burned a month later in Smithfield, Anne was too weak from torture to stand at the stake. The executioners put her in a chair and lit the kindling.

In prison Anne recorded her thoughts and prayers, including a petition for her persecutors:

. . . Lord, I heartily desire of Thee, that Thou wilt of Thy merciful goodness forgive them that violence which they do, and have done unto me. Open also their blind hearts, that they may hereafter do that thing in Thy sight which is only acceptable before Thee, and so set forth Thy verity aright, without all vain fantasies of sinful men. So be it, Lord.

An account of Anne Askew's life and martyrdom published shortly after her death is credited with a major role in turning English popular sentiment toward Protestantism.

Robert Southwell (1561–1595)

Religious toleration was an idea slow to unfold. Everyone in medieval Europe was expected to be Christian and dire trouble could befall anyone who was not. In the Reformation period different kinds of Christians competed, but there was little notion of religious pluralism within a country. Most nations or principalities wanted one and only one church—Catholic, Lutheran, Reformed, Anglican, or whatever, usually determined by the ruler.

So it was that England under Henry's son Edward VI suppressed Catholicism, and England under Mary I persecuted Protestants, and England under Elizabeth I made Catholic martyrs and harassed non-Anglican Protestants. And so it was that Robert Southwell died in 1595.

Southwell was a Jesuit priest, a missionary, and a poet still read today. He was born in 1561, four years after Elizabeth I ascended the throne. Since the England of his childhood in Norfolk was being shaped into a Protestant state, the Catholic Southwells sent their son to school in Douai, the city in northern France where English Catholics had an important center. In France, the youth encountered Jesuits and decided at an early age to join a religious order. The Society of Jesus at first turned him down, possibly because of his age, but in 1578, when he was seventeen years old, he was admitted to the novitiate in Rome. Ordained to the priesthood in 1584 or 1585, he became prefect at the English College in Rome. In 1586 he returned to his homeland as a missionary.

The Jesuit mission to Protestant England dated from 1580. Organized by a strong-willed man named William Allen, later a cardinal, the plan approved by the pope was to use Douai as the fountainhead for a continuous flow of priests into England. Most of these missionary priests were English Jesuits despite the Elizabethan ban on the order. The initial group to cross the Channel included Edmund Campion, canonized in 1970, the first of 120 martyred missionary priests in England.[15] To the English Protestants these missionaries were spreaders of sedition, agents of a foreign power. Of course, the pope and the Catholic states on the continent did want to bring England back into their fold, a feat impossible by military force after Elizabeth's navy crushed the Spanish Armada in 1588. The Jesuit missionaries wanted to convert Protestants, but they were not primarily public evangelizers. One of Allen's aims was to use the missionaries to "train Catholics to be plainly and openly Catholics."[16] That in itself was treason in sixteenth-century England.

Robert Southwell worked in England for six years. From 1587 until his arrest in 1592 he was chaplain to Anne Howard, the countess of Arundel, and an adviser to her husband Philip, the first earl of Arundel, confined to the Tower of London for his Catholic beliefs. The young Jesuit lived in hiding most of the time at the countess's London home, saying Mass for the household, writing letters of encouragement to Catholics, and preparing reports for his superiors in Rome. He also made occasional pastoral visits to other Catholic families, and does not seem to have practiced the kind of public preaching that got Campion in trouble.

As he said Mass in a house in Harrow, the priest was arrested by Richard Topcliffe, a noted Anglican inquisitor. Tortured in a vain attempt to extract information on the activities of other Catholics, he was sent to the Tower of London where he was held in solitary confinement for three years. Restless in his cell, Southwell appealed to the government to either try him or permit him a degree of liberty. He was tried and condemned, and on February 21, 1595, was hanged, drawn, and quartered at Tyburn. Robert Southwell was thirty-three years old.

While in prison Southwell wrote most of his best known poems, compositions of deep religious feeling but filled with paradox and lively imagery. Ben Johnson is supposed to have said that had he written Southwell's "The Burning Babe," he could have gladly destroyed many of his own poems. "The Burning Babe" was to become a favorite Christmas poem of Catholics and Protestants alike, and it and other Southwell pieces are commonly included in anthologies of great English literature. The poem, written near the time of his execution, is ample testimony to the author's loyalty to Christ:

As I in hoary winter's night stood shivering in the snow,
Surprised I was with sudden heat, which made my heart to glow;
And lifting up a fearful eye to view what fire was near,
A pretty Babe all burning bright, did in the air appear,
Who scorchéd with excessive heat, such floods of tears did shed,
As though His floods should quench His flames which with His tears
    were fed;
"Alas!" quoth He, "but newly born, in fiery heats I fry,
Yet none approach to warm their hearts or feel my fire but I!
My faultless breast the furnace is, the fuel wounding thorns,
Love is the fire, and sighs the smoke, the ashes shame and scorns;
The fuel Justice layeth on, and Mercy blows the coals,
The metal in this furnace wrought are men's defiled souls,
For which, as now on fire I am to work them to their good,
So will I melt into a bath to wash them in My blood."
With this He vanished out of sight, and swiftly shrunk away,
And straight I calléd unto mind that it was Christmas-day.

Mary Dyer (?–1660)

Boston's city fathers told her to leave and never return. Mary Dyer left that day in the 1650s, but she returned, not once but twice, and was twice sentenced to hang. Reprieved the first time with the rope around her neck, Mary could no more stay out of Boston than the Jesuits a century earlier could respect England's ban on them. She paid with her life on June 1, 1660.

Mary Dyer's crime? She was a Quaker.

The Society of Friends—Quakers—experienced intense persecution in both England and New England in the mid-seventeenth century. Few Quakers, however, were killed, Mary Dyer being one of only four known to have died for the faith. This movement was started in England by George Fox and others during the Commonwealth, the period from 1649 to 1660 when the monarchy was abolished and the government conducted first by Parliament and then by the Puritan dictator Oliver Cromwell.

Neither the Anglicans nor the Puritans (English Protestant dissenters from the state church) liked the Quakers.

The Friends movement challenged the theology and organization of all the existing churches in England and the American colonies. They taught that people can have an immediate, inward sense of God's presence without the mediation of church or sacraments and in this sense Quakerism is unorthodox. Quakers to this day trust the "inner light." They have no ordained clergy, and their worship consists of reverent group silence until someone is moved by the Holy Spirit to speak. Also, Quakers in the seventeenth century would not take oaths.

Mary Dyer and her husband William came from England to the Massachusetts Bay Colony in 1635, before Quakerism was born. They were Puritans, members of Boston's First Church. Only Puritans were welcome in the Bay Colony, a policy that drove Roger Williams to establish Rhode Island as a haven of religious liberty. The couple had six children, one of whom, a son, was named "Maher-shalal-hashbaz," a symbolic name given by the Hebrew prophet Isaiah to his second son and meaning "the spoil speeds, the prey hastes."

Mrs. Dyer did not like the restrictive religious atmosphere of Boston. She befriended and defended Anne Hutchinson, the liberal-minded Puritan who for her criticism of the clergy was tried, excommunicated, and banished. The Dyers followed the Hutchinsons to Rhode Island, where they became champions of religious toleration. When Roger Williams went to England in 1652 to obtain a charter for the new colony, Mary and William Dyer went along, Mr. Dyer returning to New England the next year, but Mary staying abroad four years. She became a Quaker in England.

Other Quakers who preceded Mary Dyer to Boston provoked the ire of the Puritan clergy. The colony's General Court on October 14, 1556, enacted strict laws against the "cursed sect of heretics . . . commonly called Quakers." Any Friend entering Massachusetts was to be "forthwith committed to the House of Correction; and, at their entrance, to be severely whipped." Mary had planned only to pass through Boston on the way to Rhode Island, but when she and a second Quaker woman arrived they were forthwith jailed and, as the law required, denied permission to speak with anyone. For a time William Dyer did not know his wife was in the Boston House of Corrections. Hearing the news, he secured her release by promising she would leave Massachusetts forever and talk to no one on the journey south.

Mary had not given her own word she would not return, and in 1659 went to Boston with Quakers intent on seeing Friends who were jailed there. She was arrested, and this time her release proved more difficult. The Quakers were tried before the General Court. Governor John Endicott assigned three, including Mary, to the gallows, a tree on Boston Common. On October 27 she was bound and ready for hoisting when she was remanded to prison, saved by a last minute appeal for clemency from her husband and a son. Mary was alive, but she boldly informed the court she would never agree to silence: "My life is not accepted, neither availeth me, in comparison with the lives and liberty of the Truth and servants of the living God, for which in the bowels of Love and Meekness I sought you."

Banished to Rhode Island, Mary went instead to Long Island, where she spent the winter contemplating her future. She knew what she must and would do. Back to Boston to preach she went in the spring. There would be no more legal reprieves. The court again tried her and delivered the death sentence. As she approached the gallows, Mary Dyer was given a last chance to live if she would admit her errors. "Nay," she said, "I cannot, for in obedience to the will of the Lord God I came, and in His will I abide faithful to the death."

Franz Jägerstätter[17] (1907–1943)

He is one of the lesser known martyrs of the Nazi rampage. Franz Jägerstätter was a farmer, an Austrian Catholic peasant, never a man of politics or movements. He was tending his family, his fields, and his faith in the village of Saint Radegund when a fateful choice crashed upon him: serve Christ or a ruthless caesar. The peasant farmer chose Christ.

The Nazis had been active in Austria for several years, subverting the political process when they could, and provoking debate on the pros and cons of National Socialism. Hitler marched into Austria on March 12, 1938, set up a puppet regime in Vienna, and within a short time absorbed the country into Nazi Germany. The German *Anschluss* (annexation) ended the public debate; most Austrians acquiesced, and many cooperated. Franz Jägerstätter wanted no part of Nazism, not even if Adolf Hitler had been born in nearby Braunau. From the start the farmer understood the evil befallen his homeland. He prayed harder and increased his personal penance. Jägerstätter's resistance, it could be said, began in prayer.

Born in 1907 in a small town near the Salzach River, the border between northwestern Austria and Bavaria, Jägerstätter's only unusual quality in the first three decades of his life seems to have been a strong religious devotion. One biographer says he considered a religious vocation but was dissuaded by a priest who judged him a "lively," somewhat rebellious young blade. The intensity of his early religious sentiments is really unknown. What seems more certain is that after a retreat made at a Bavarian shrine in 1934, Mass became a part of his daily life. Married in 1936, the farmer and his wife formed the practice of reading together from the Bible and the lives of saints.

The first public indication of Jägerstätter's feeling about Nazism surfaced with his opposition to the plebiscite in which Hitler wanted the Austrians to approve the annexation. Hitler won, but Jägerstätter stood his personal ground. He refused to make voluntary contributions to anything benefitting the Nazi cause. He never collected the state-provided family bonus that was his with the births of three daughters. And his soul would not let him serve in the Nazi army, although he reported twice when ordered up for training.

Jägerstätter's first military episode lasted only a few days, according to biographer Gordon Zahn. The second was not much longer, Msgr. Jakob Fried states in a book on Nazism and the Catholic church in Austria. Jägerstätter felt "tainted" when he went to church dressed as a soldier. Somehow he persuaded his superiors to let him go home, and he promised then he would make no third appearance in uniform. His friends said his attitude was suicidal, would leave his family destitute. "I may never cooperate in an unjust war," he said. "God will provide for my wife and family."[18]

To Jägerstätter conscientious objection was neither a principle derived from human rights nor a constitutional guarantee. Refusing to taint himself with Nazism's military maneuvering was a profoundly religious matter—a matter of fidelity to the love of God in Christ. In a few sparse writings, the defiant peasant made his case for Christian "struggle and striving toward the eternal kingdom," a striving not done with guns but with spiritual weapons such as prayer and love —love for neighbor and for the enemy.[19]

The third call to military training came in February, 1943. Jägerstätter discussed his dilemma with the bishop of the area. The prelate argued that he owed it to his family to comply, and told him he was not answerable for the actions of the government he was supposed to obey. Jägerstätter thought otherwise.

Rather than be arrested at home, he decided to show up at the training center, six days late. No argument could persuade him to serve. He was arrested, taken to Berlin, and on June 6, 1943 court-martialed for "undermining the military power." His sentence: death.

Renewed efforts were made to change his mind or save his life. Would he accept noncombatant service in the military? No. Dean Heinrich Kreuzberg, chaplain of the Berlin prison, tried to talk him out of his decision. The chaplain also told Jägerstätter about Franz Reinisch, a Palatine priest, executed earlier for refusing the military oath of allegiance to Hitler. Dean Kreuzberg later recalled: "Even as I told him this, his eyes lighted up and, heaving a deep sigh as if a heavy load had been lifted from his soul, he said joyously: 'I have always been sure that I could not be on the false path. If, therefore, a priest came to this same decision and died for it, I can, too.' "[20]

Franz Jägerstätter was beheaded in Berlin on August 9, 1943. His ashes are buried beside the church in Saint Radegund.

Some non-pacifists within the Catholic church have felt Jägerstätter should not be memorialized because he did not do his "duty." Little do they know. The farmer did his duty to God, and he knew why. He wrote:

For love will emerge victorious and will last for all eternity—and happy are they who live and die in God's love.[21]

Simon Kimbangu (1889–1951)

When Simon Kimbangu died in 1951, Belgian colonial officials in the Congo (now Zaire) did not bother to inform his family. After all, the man had been in prison for thirty years and, more important, the white overlords of the vast black-populated land probably thought the less said about Kimbangu the better. He had caused them enough trouble already: launching a "prophetic movement" that refused to die despite legal harassment and the combined opposition of the Roman Catholic Church and the Protestant missionaries in the crown colony.

Simon Kimbangu had one of the shortest careers of any major Christian evangelist since Stephen's sermon before he was stoned. His public ministry lasted about six months, three of them in hiding. He preached in no football stadiums, made no missionary journeys, and organized no parishes, although an indigenous African church, one of the largest on the continent today, was to spring from his brief labors. All Kimbangu wanted was to bear witness to Christ among his people in western Zaire. For that he spent the rest of his life in prison.

North Americans and Europeans sometimes find it hard to fit Kimbangu and the church he founded into the Christian family. The more than four-million-member Kimbanguist Church (officially, the Church of Jesus Christ on Earth by the Prophet Simon Kimbangu) did not celebrate the sacrament of Holy Communion until 1971. Some view him as an African nationalist rather than a religious prophet. They are bothered by erroneous reports that Kimbangu considered himself the Messiah. (The Kimbanguist Church makes no messianic claims for its founders, although members do venerate Kimbangu much as Roman Catholic and Eastern Orthodox Christians venerate the saints.[22])

Western skepticism about the Kimbanguist movement and the legitimacy of Kimbangu as a Christian martyr is understandable. The Church of Jesus Christ on Earth is not a western church; its instigator not an American or Italian or British pastor. The movement and the man are African—Christian, but African, which is exactly what upset the Belgian colonial authorities in the 1920s. Kimbangu announced Pentecost, the outpouring of the Holy Spirit, in Africa.

While many legends have collected around the early life of Kimbangu, as happens with almost all significant religious figures, information about his childhood is sketchy. Born in 1889, raised by an aunt after his parents died, Kimbangu and his wife Mivilu Marie became Christians—Protestants—in 1915. As a Belgian possession, the Congo was primarily Catholic country, but Protestant missionaries were permitted to function in certain regions. British Baptists were active in the vicinity of N'Kamba, Kimbangu's hometown in far western Zaire, south of Kinshasa. The young Christian seems to have taught in a mission school for a time and then to have done traditional evangelistic work in N'Kamba.

One of Kimbangu's three sons places his father's special calling in 1918 during the worldwide flu epidemic. Like the Hebrew prophets and like Joan of Arc and other saints, Kimbangu heard a voice. It said, "I am Christ, My servants are unfaithful. I have chosen you to bear witness before your brethren and convert them. Tend My flock."[23] Kimbangu resisted; he was no minister. But the voice insisted. To escape he found work in Kinshasa. The voice was there too. His job did not work out. Kimbangu went home to farm, and to do as the voice directed.

The Kimbanguist Church dates its founding from April 6, 1921, the day of Kimbangu's first miracle of healing. According to the accounts, Kimbangu was passing through a village near N'Kamba on his way to market; he felt compelled to enter a house where he found a critically sick woman. Like the early Apostles, he healed her in Jesus' name. Outside the house he met the woman's husband who asked if Kimbangu knew of any medicine that might cure his wife. "I told him that he didn't need to look further for medicines," Kimbangu replied, "seeing his wife had received more than these."[24]

By mid-April missionaries and colonial officials began to receive reports of miraculous healing attributed to one Simon Kimbangu of N'Kamba. They immediately investigated. Colonial administrations in central and southern Africa were constantly on the alert for would-be messiahs or witch doctors who might upset the status quo, even foment insurrection. Zealous "prophetic movements," usually blends of Christianity and African religion, were not unusual in the lower Congo River basin.

Investigators found the roads to N'Kamba crowded with Africans seeking the new healer. They found Kimbangu and a band of followers praying and singing hymns. (Singing is a major feature of the Kimbanguist Church.) They found the makings of what they saw as another dangerous "prophetic movement."

Kimbangu no doubt thought of himself as filling a prophetic role, that is, speaking for God. (In Judaism and Christianity, prophets are not fortune-tellers; they are speakers for God.) There was, however, a difference between him and most of the other African prophets of his time, and some who later used his name. He did not point to himself or benefit economically from his gifts. He pointed to Jesus Christ. Like modern charismatics, Kimbangu and his followers practiced faith healing and "speaking in tongues," but the prophet's preaching stressed basic Christian themes such as personal morality, prayer, repentance, forgiveness, and redemption through Christ. His theology was not antiwhite. Few of Kimbangu's sermons have survived. Some of his prayers are found in Kimbanguist documents, and one of those prayers shows the breadth of his message:

I thank Thee, Almighty God, Maker of heaven and earth. The heaven is Thy throne and the earth is Thy footstool. Thy will be done on earth as it is in heaven. Bless all peoples of the earth, great and small, men and women, whites and blacks. May the blessing of heaven fall on the whole world so that we all might enter heaven. We pray to Thee trusting that Thou dost receive us, in the Name of Jesus Christ our Saviour. Amen.[25]

Kimbangu is said to have prayed this prayer every day.

The Belgian authorities were less concerned with the new prophet's orthodoxy than with the fact of an emotional movement. They liked African prophets behind bars. Kimbangu and four assistants escaped arrest in early June, 1921. For three months they were fugitives. Then Kimbangu insisted on returning to N'Kamba, where he was taken without struggle. His family was transported to the district capital for questioning.

Simon Kimbangu was tried and found guilty of sedition and rebellion against the established order. His sentence was death, preceded by 120 lashes by a whip. The beating was administered. Partly because of appeal from Protestant missionary organizations, King Albert of the Belgians commuted the death sentence to life imprisonment. The Protestant groups did not approve of Kimbangu's religion but did not want him killed.

The prophet from N'Kamba was taken south, far south to a jail in Elisabethville (now Lubumbashi) and there held, often in solitary confinement, until his death on October 12, 1951. A very few people were allowed to see him during the incarceration of thirty years and nine days.

Its leader silenced, the Kimbanguist movement was outlawed and suppressed in the Congo. But it refused to fade. As it grew, so did the oppression. Followers by the thousands were exiled to remote parts of the country. N'Kamba was totally destroyed. Still the church flourished.

Limited toleration was extended to the Kimbanguists in 1957. Two years later the Belgian government officially recognized the movement. After the civil war wracking independent Zaire from 1960 to 1965, the church took its place along with Catholicism and Protestantism as one of the three major expressions of Christianity in the country. The Kimbanguist legitimacy in the Christian family was recognized in 1969 when it was admitted as a member of the World Council of Churches.

Devoted to Christ and proudly African, the Kimbanguists maintain a vast network of schools and social institutions in health, agriculture, youth work, and economic self-help for the poor. The church rejects all violence, polygamy, magic, and the use of tobacco and alcohol. Kimbanguists produce and sing moving hymns.

The wife of an army officer visiting Elisabethville managed to see Kimbangu briefly shortly before his death. She discussed with him the controversy surrounding him. "I was, and am," he said, "simply a servant of Jesus Christ and nothing more."[26]

Conclusion: Strong in the Way

"WHERE HAVE ALL THE HEROES GONE?" a newsmagazine asked in a 1979 cover story.

Where *gone?*

The Christian heroes and heroines of faith's history have gone nowhere—they come; they come from the memory and experience of the church along the way of holiness, bringing virtues and values, exemplifying the transcending love of God in ordinary life.

These saints of all the ages come in a diverse company whose members dared to be great hobblers for God, when hobble they did, and strong walkers with Christ's help over the best and worst terrains.

They come with lives transformed by holy love: Paul of Tarsus learned, in Frederick Buechner's words, "it is only when a person discovers that God loves him in all his unloveliness that he himself starts to be godlike"[1];

—with sin and pride laid low: Catherine of Siena knew God's fire of love "must burn up self-love and self-will and let the soul appear, beautiful and full of grace";

—with agony and tears for a troubled world: Simone Weil prayed to be stripped of everything and be "transformed into Christ's substance, and given for food to afflicted men whose body and soul lack for every kind of nourishment"[2];

—with gentle touch and mind: Clarence Jordan realized, "The Good News of the resurrection is not that we shall die and go home with him [Jesus], but he is risen and comes homes with us, bringing all his hungry, naked, thirsty, sick, prisoner brothers with him"[3];

—with encounter with the truth: Jonathan Edwards found that those of true religious affections, they have a "solid, full, thorough and effectual conviction of the truth of the great things of the gospel";

—with hearts and minds aflame for God: Pascal, said T. S. Eliot, had intellectual passion "reinforced by passionate dissatisfaction with human life unless a spiritual explanation could be found"[4];

—with mercy overflowing: Elizabeth of Hungary gave all the food to the poor; "As for her charities," said her husband, "they will bring upon us divine blessing";

—with the beauty of peacemaking: Dag Hammarskjöld saw the need: "In our era, the road to holiness necessarily passes through the world of action"[5];

—with lives poised ready to die for Christ on the way of holiness: Justin the Martyr told the Roman emperor, "You can kill us but cannot do us any real harm";

—And with the experience of the cross: Søren Kierkegaard said of himself, "That Jesus Christ died for my sins shows certainly how great his grace is, but also how great my sins are, and how infinitely far I am from God; so that God will deal with me only upon condition that Christ should die for me. . . . Only God himself knows how infinitely exalted he is. And here the remarkable thing is, that precisely by his condescension, God indirectly reveals his exaltation also."[6]

The saints, heroes, and heroines come in their Holy Company, each from their own experience knowing that great truth Pascal discovered:

Happiness is neither inside nor outside us; it is in God, both beyond and within us.

Notes

Introduction

1 *Letters of James Agee to Father Flye* (New York: George Braziller, 1962), p. 164.

2 Thomas à Kempis, *The Imitation of Christ*, trans. Richard Whitford (Garden City: Doubleday & Company, 1962), p. 81.

3 Karl Rahner, *Ignatius of Loyola*, trans. Rosaleen Ockenden (London: Collins, 1978), p. 36.

4 William Barclay, *The Gospel of Matthew*, Rev. Ed. Vol. I (Philadelphia: The Westminster Press, 1975), p. 88.

5 Walter Clemons, *Newsweek*, June 4, 1979, p. 79.

Chapter I

1 Dorothy Sayers, "The Zeal of Thy House," *Religious Drama 1* (Cleveland: World Publishing Company, 1964), p. 309; copyright 1937, originally published in U.S.A. by Harcourt, Brace and Co.

2 Dietrich Bonhoeffer, *The Cost of Discipleship*, trans. R. H. Fuller (New York: The Macmillan Company, 1963), p. 119.

3 Sayers, *op. cit.*, pp. 331–35.

4 Walter Rauschenbusch, *A Theology for the Social Gospel* (Nashville: Abingdon Press; originally published by The Macmillan Company, 1917), p. 155.

5 Evelyn Underhill, *Practical Mysticism* (New York: E. P. Dutton & Co., 1914).

6 Evelyn Underhill, Preface to Nicholas Arseniev, *Mysticism and the Eastern Church*, trans. by Arthur Chambers (Crestwood, N.Y.: St. Vladimir's Press, 1979), p. 15; originally published by SCM Press, 1926.

7 Arseniev, *op. cit.*, p. 87.

8 Translation from *The Orthodox Liturgy*, ed. by Nicon D. Patrinacos (Garwood, N.J.: The Graphics Arts Press, 1974), p. 77.

9 Paraphrased from William A. Clebsch, *American Religious Thought: A History* (Chicago: The University of Chicago Press, 1973), p. 44.

10 *Ibid.*, p. 56.

11 *Ibid.*, p. 55.

12 Each quoted phrase is the English title of a book by Kierkegaard.

13 Flannery O'Connor, "The Fiction Writer and His Country," originally published in *The Living Novel: A Symposium*, ed. by Granville Hicks (New York: The Macmillan Company, 1957), reprinted in *Mystery and Manners*, ed. by Sally and Robert Fitzgerald (New York: Farrar, Straus & Giroux, 1969), p. 32.

14 Flannery O'Connor, *The Habit of Being;* letters selected and edited by Sally Fitzgerald (New York: Farrar, Straus, Giroux, 1979), p. 104.

15 *Ibid.*, p. 125.

16 *Ibid.*, p. 90.

17 *Ibid.*, p. 92.

18 *Ibid.*, p. 90.

CHAPTER II

1 Clare Boothe Luce, ed., *Saints for Now* (New York: Sheed & Ward, 1952), p. 10.

2 *Ibid.*, p. 11.

3 *Butler's Lives of the Saints*, Vol. III, Herbert Thurston and Donald Attwater, eds. (Westminster, Md.: Christian Classics, 1956), p. 288.

4 Quoted by Simone Pétrement, *Simone Weil: A Life*, Raymond Rosenthal, trans. (New York: Pantheon Books, 1976), p. 483.

5 *Ibid.*, p. 470.

CHAPTER III

1 Antoine de St.-Exupéry, *The Little Prince*, trans. Katherine Woods (New York: Harcourt, Brace & World, 1943), pp. 66–73.

2 William Barclay, *The Gospel of Matthew* Vol. 1. (Philadelphia: The Westminster Press, 1975), p. 98.

3 A recent joint Roman Catholic-Lutheran study concludes that Matthew probably mentioned the four Old Testament women to show God's use of irregular unions in the messianic plan. See Raymond E. Brown, Karl P. Donfried, Joseph A. Fitzmyer, and John Reumann, eds. *Mary in the New Testament* (Philadelphia: Fortress Press, 1978), pp. 79–82.

4 "The Letter of Polycarp, Bishop of Smyrna, to the Philippians," trans. by Massey Hamilton Shepherd, Jr. in *Early Christian Fathers* Vol. I, *Library of Christian Classics*, Cyril Richardson, ed. (Philadelphia: The Westminster Press, 1953), pp. 133–34.

5 Letter to Simon Gabriel Bruté, later bishop of Vincennes.

6 Letter to Eliza Sadler.

7 W. P. Livingstone, *Mary Slessor of Calabar: Pioneer Missionary* (London: Hodder and Stoughton, 1916), p. 339.

8 From Mary McLeod Bethune, "My Last Will and Testament," printed in Rackham Holt, *Mary McLeod Bethune: A Biography* (Garden City, N.Y.: Doubleday & Co., Inc., 1964), p. 288.

9 Quoted from "The Apostle of Love: Toyohiko Kagawa," a multi-media presentation by Haruichi Yokoyama, translated by Masuo Kaneko, December, 1958 (unpublished), p. 29.

10 Quoted by Dallas Lee, *The Cotton Patch Evidence: The Story of Clarence Jordan and the Koinonia Farm Experiment* (New York: Harper & Row, 1971), p. 186.

11 Clarence Jordan, *The Cotton Patch Version of Matthew and John* (New York: Association Press, 1971), p. 16.

12 *Ibid.*, p. 22.

CHAPTER IV

1 *The Confessions of St. Augustine*, trans. E. B. Pusey (London: J. M. Dent & Sons Ltd., 1907), pp. 170–71.

2 From a condensation by Roland H. Bainton, *Erasmus of Christendom* (New York: Charles Scribner's Sons, 1969), p. 107.

3 Erasmus, *De Amabili Ecclesiae Concordia*, trans. Bainton, *op. cit.*, p. 266.

4 Edith Deen, *Great Women of the Christian Faith* (New York: Harper & Brothers Publishers, 1959), pp. 165–66.

5 G. K. Chesterton, *Autobiography* (Darby, Pa: Arden, reprint, 1978) p. 152.

6 G. K. Chesterton, *Orthodoxy* (Garden City, N.Y.: Doubleday, Image Books, 1959), p. 157.

7 Dietrich Bonhoeffer, *The Cost of Discipleship*, trans. R. H. Fuller (New York: The Macmillan Company, 1963; copyright, SCM Press Ltd., 1959), pp. 123–24.

8 Dietrich Bonhoeffer, *Letters and Papers from Prison*, edited by Eberhard Bethge; translated by R. H. Fuller (New York: The Macmillan Company, 1953), p. 26.

9 Martin Luther King, Jr., "Letter from Birmingham Jail," issued April 16, 1963; reprinted in *Why We Can't Wait* (New York: Harper & Row, 1964), pp. 93–94.

10 Eric Lincoln, ed., *Martin Luther King, Jr.: A Profile* (New York: Hill and Wang, 1970), p. xi.

11 "Letter from Birmingham Jail," p. 81.

12 *Ibid.*, p. 85.

13 Quoted by William Robert Miller in *Martin Luther King, Jr.: His Life, Martyrdom and Meaning for the World* (New York: Weybright and Talley, 1968), p. 290.

CHAPTER V

1 Mother Teresa of Calcutta, "Jesus My Patient," quoted by Malcolm Muggeridge in *Something Beautiful for God: Mother Teresa of Calcutta* (New York: Harper & Row, 1971), pp. 74–75.

2 See Barbara W. Tuchman, *A Distant Mirror: The Calamitous 14th Century* (New York: Alfred A. Knopf, 1978), p. 123.

3 See G.R.R. Treasure, *Seventeenth Century France* (Garden City: Doubleday & Company, Anchor Books, 1967), p. 113.

4 Walter Rauschenbusch, "Beneath the Glitter," first published in the *Christian Inquirer*, 1887; reprinted, Dores Robinson Sharpe, Walter Rauschenbusch (New York: The Macmillan Co., 1942), p. 81.

5 Robert T. Handy, ed., *The Social Gospel in America, 1870–1920* (New York: Oxford University Press, 1966), p. 10.

6 Quoted by Vernon Parker Bodein in *The Social Gospel of Walter Rauschenbusch and Its Relation to Religious Education* (New Haven: Yale University Press, 1944), p. 9.

CHAPTER VI

1 R. C. Dentan, "Heart," *The Interpreter's Dictionary of the Bible* Vol. II, ed. George Arthur Buttrick (Nashville: Abingdon Press, 1962), p. 550.

2 *Ibid.*

3 Aurelius Prudentius Clemens, "The Second Hymn: A Morning Hymn," trans. from the Latin by Harold Isbell in *The Harper Book of Christian Poetry*, ed. Anthony S. Mercatante (New York: Harper & Row, 1972), p. 10.

4 J. A. T. Robinson, *Honest to God* (Philadelphia: The Westminster Press, 1963).

5 Translated by James R. Woodford, 1820–1885.

6 Clyde Leonard Manschreck, *Melanchthon: The Quiet Reformer* (Nashville: Abingdon Press, 1958), p. 311.

7 Excerpts from Pascal's parchment from the translation by Emile Cailliet in *Pascal: Genius in the Light of Scripture* (Philadelphia: The Westminster Press, 1945), pp. 131–32.

8 T. S. Eliot, Introduction to *Pascal's Pensées*, trans. W. F. Trotter (New York: E. P. Dutton & Co., Inc., 1958), p. xviii.

9 Geoffret Treasure, *Seventeenth Century France* (Garden City, N.Y.: Doubleday & Co., Inc., 1967), p. 108.

10 Eliot, *op. cit.*, p. xix.

11 Gerald R. Cragg, *The Church and the Age of Reason: 1648–1789* (New York: Atheneum, 1961), p. 141.

12 Quoted by Margaret Cropper, *Life of Evelyn Underhill* (New York: Harper & Brothers, 1958), pp. 5–6.

Chapter VII

1 Quoted in Tony Gray, *Champions of Peace* (New York: Paddington Press Ltd., 1976), p. 50.

2 Charter of the United Nations.

3 Recorded in Moses Hadas, *A History of Rome from Its Origins to 529 A.D. as Told by the Roman Historians* (Garden City, N.Y.: Doubleday Anchor Books, 1956), p. 241.

4 Peter Meyer, ed., *The Pacifist Conscience* (New York: Holt, Rinehart and Winston, 1966), p. 65.

5 From an excerpt of *The New Cyneas*, translated by Meyer, *op. cit.*, pp. 68–69.

6 David L. Dodge, *Memorial. An Autobiography Prepared at the Request and for the Use of His Children* (Boston: S. K. Whipple & Co., 1854).

7 Quoted by Edwin D. Mean, *World Unity Magazine* XII, April, 1933, p. 33.

8 Jane Addams, *Twenty Years at Hull-House* (New York: Macmillan Publishing Co. Inc., 1938), p. 56.

9 *Ibid.*, pp. 77–79.

10 *Ibid.*, p. 109.

11 *Ibid.*, pp. 111–112, Miss Addams paraphrasing a clergyman.

12 Nathan Soderblöm, *Christian Fellowship, or The United Life and Work of Christendom* (New York: Fleming H. Revell Company, 1923), pp. 13–14.

13 Albert Luthuli, *Let My People Go* (New York: McGraw-Hill Book Company, Inc., 1962), p. 42.

14 *Ibid.*, p. 146.

15 Dag Hammarskjöld, *Markings*, translated by Leif Sjöberg and W. H. Auden (New York: Alfred A. Knopf, 1964), p. 205.

16 *Ibid.*, p. 85.

17 *Ibid.*, p. 115.

18 *Ibid.*, p. 213.

19 Gustaf Aulen, *Dag Hammarskjöld's White Book: An Analysis of Markings* (Philadelphia: Fortress Press, 1969), p. 107.

20 Charles Malik, *The Critic*, April–May, 1965, p. 74.

CHAPTER VIII

1 Gordon Zahn, *War, Conscience and Dissent* (New York: Hawthorn Books, 1967), p. 192.

2 Herbert Musurillo, *The Acts of the Christian Martyrs* (Oxford: Clarendon Press, 1972), pp. 43,45. (Excerpt has been reorganized into dialogue.)

3 "The First Apology of Justin, the Martyr," *Early Christian Fathers*, ed. Cyril C. Richardson (Philadelphia: The Westminster Press, 1953), p. 243.

4 W. H. C. Frend, *Martyrdom and Persecution in the Early Church* (Garden City: Doubleday & Co., 1967), p. 240.

5 "The Martyrdom of Saints Perpetua and Felicitas," Musurillo, *op. cit.*, pp. 109, 111.

6 *Ibid.*, p. 123.

7 *Ibid.*, pp. 125,127.

8 *Ibid.*, p. 131.

9 *Ibid.*, p. 129.

10 Norman F. Cantor, *Medieval History: The Life and Death of A Civilization*, 2nd ed. (New York: The Macmillan Co., 1969), p. 189.

11 *Celebrating the Saints* (New York: Pueblo Publishing Co., 1978), p. 141.

12 Barbara W. Tuchman, *A Distant Mirror: The Calamitous 14th Century* (New York: Alfred A. Knopf, 1978), p. 123.

13 Heiko A. Oberman, *Forerunners of the Reformation* (New York: Holt, Rinehart and Winston, 1966), p. 212.

14 F. E. Hutchison, *Cranmer and the English Reformation* (New York: Collier Books, 1962), p. 69.

15 Philip Hughes, *The Reformation in England, III: True Religion Now Established* (New York: the Macmillan Co., 1954), p. 282.

16 William Allen, quoted in Hughes, *op. cit.*, p. 285.

17 Biographical data in this section is drawn entirely from the research of Gordon Zahn, who has written extensively on Jägerstätter, including *In Solitary Witness: The Life and Death of Franz Jägerstätter* (New York: Holt, Rinehart and Winston, 1965), and *War, Conscience and Dissent, loc. cit.* Zahn acknowledges his debt to two priests, Heinrich Kreuzberg and Jakob Fried, who took note on Jägerstätter in written works following World War II.

18 Zahn, *War, Conscience and Dissent*, (New York: Hawthorn Books, Inc., 1967), pp. 179–180.

19 *Ibid.*, p. 181.

20 *Ibid.*

21 *Ibid.*

22 Marie-Louise Martin, *Kimbangu: An African Prophet and His Church*. Trans. D. M. Moore (Grand Rapids: William B. Eerdmans Publishing Co., 1976), p. 111.

23 *Ibid.*, p. 44.

24 *Ibid.*, p. 45.

25 *Ibid.*, p. 49.

26 *Ibid.*, p. 75.

Conclusion

1 Frederick Buechner, *Wishful Thinking: A Theological ABC* (New York: Harper & Row, 1973), p. 85.

2 Quoted by Simone Pétrement in *Simone Weil: A Life*, trans. by Raymond Rosenthal (New York: Pantheon Books, 1976), p. 486.

3 Quoted by Dallas Lee in *The Cotton Patch Evidence: The Story of Clarence Jordan and the Koinonia Farm Experiment* (New York: Harper & Row, 1971), p. 186.

4 T. S. Eliot, Introduction to *Pascal's Pensées* (New York; E. P. Dutton & Co., Inc., 1958), p. xi.

5 Dag Hammarskjöld, *Markings*, trans. by Leif Sjöberg and W. H. Auden (New York: Alfred A. Knopf, 1965), p. 122.

6 From Kierkegaard's *Papers*, in *T. H. Croxall*, ed. *Meditations from Kierkegaard* (Philadelphia: The Westminster Press, 1955), p. 68.

Bibliography

REFERENCE WORKS

Ahlstrom, Sydney E. *A Religious History of the American People.* New Haven: Yale University Press, 1972.

Aland, Kurt, *et al.*, eds. *The New Testament in Greek and English.* New York: American Bible Society, 1966.

Attwater, Donald, ed. *A Dictionary of Saints.* New York: P. J. Kenedy & Sons, 1958.

Barclay, William. *The Daily Study Bible Series.* 17 vols. rev. ed. Philadelphia: The Westminster Press, 1975.

Bettenson, Henry, ed. *Documents of the Christian Church.* New York: Oxford University Press, 1957.

Bruce, Alexander B. "The Synoptic Gospels," *The Expositor's Greek Testament.* Vol. I. Grand Rapids: William B. Eerdmans, 1951.

Butler, Alban. *Butler's Lives of the Saints.* Edited by Thurston, Herbert, and Attwater, Donald. Westminster, Md.: Christian Classics (copyright, P. J. Kenedy & Sons), 1956.

Buttrick, George A., ed. *The Interpreter's Dictionary of the Bible.* 4 vols and supplement. Nashville: Abingdon Press, 1962, 1976.

Delaney, John J., and Tobin, James Edward, ed. *Dictionary of Catholic Biography.* Garden City: Doubleday & Co., 1961.

Encyclopaedia Britannica. 30 vols. Chicago: Encyclopaedia Britannica, 1977.

Johnson, Paul. *A History of Christianity.* New York: Atheneum, 1976.

Kepler, Thomas S., ed. *The Fellowship of the Saints: An Anthology of Christian Devotional Literature.* Nashville: Abingdon-Cokesbury Press, 1953.

Latourette, Kenneth Scott. *A History of the Expansion of Christianity.* 7 vols. New York: Harper & Brothers, 1937–1945.

Laymon, Charles M., ed. *The Interpreter's One-Volume Commentary on the Bible*. Nashville: Abingdon Press, 1971.

The Library of Christian Classics, edited by John Baillie, 26 vols. John T. McNeill, and Henry P. Van Dusen. Philadelphia: The Westminster Press, 1953–1956.

McDonald, William, ed. *New Catholic Encyclopaedia*. 15 vols. New York: McGraw-Hill Book Co., 1967.

Neill, Stephen; Anderson, Gerald, and Goodwin, John. *Concise Dictionary of the Christian World Mission*. Nashville: Abingdon Press, 1971.

Richardson, Alan, ed. *A Theological Word Book of the Bible*. New York: The Macmillan Co., 1955.

Smith, H. Shelton; Handy, Robert; and Loetscher, Lefferts A. *American Christianity, An Historical Interpretation with Representative Documents, 1607–1820*. New York: Charles Scribner's Sons, 1960.

Walker, Williston. *A History of the Christian Church*. Rev. ed. New York: Charles Scribner's Sons, 1959.

GENERAL WORKS

Arseniev, Nicholas. *Mysticism and the Eastern Church*. Crestwood, N.Y.: St. Vladimir's Press, 1979.

Attwater, Donald. *Martyrs*. New York: Sheed & Ward, 1957.

Bacon, Margaret. *The Quiet Rebels: The Story of the Quakers in America*. New York: Basic Books, 1969.

Bainton, Roland. *Women of the Reformation in Germany and Italy*. Minneapolis: Augsburg Publishing House, 1971.

Batley, D.S. *Devotees of Christ: Some Women Pioneers of the Indian Church*. London: Church of England Zenanna Missionary Society, n.d.

Beardsley, Frank G. *Heralds of Salvation*. New York: American Tract Society, 1939.

Bonhoeffer, Dietrich. *The Cost of Discipleship*. New York: The Macmillan Co., 1963.

Buechner, Frederick. *Wishful Thinking: A Theological ABC*. New York: Harper & Row, 1973.

Cameli, Louis John. *Stories of Paradise*. New York: Paulist Press, 1978.

Cannon, William R. *History of Christianity in the Middle Ages*. Nashville: Abingdon Press, 1960.

Cantor, Norman. *Medieval History: The Life and Death of A Civilization*. 2nd ed. New York: The Macmillan Co., 1969.

Celebrating the Saints. New York: Pueblo Publishing Co., 1973.

Chesterton, G.K. *Orthodoxy*. Garden City: Doubleday & Co., 1959.

Clebsch, William. *American Religious Thought: A History*. Chicago: The University of Chicago Press, 1973.

Cogley, John. *Catholic America*. New York: The Dial Press, 1973.

Conway, J.S. *The Nazi Persecution of the Churches, 1933–45.* New York: Basic Books, 1968.

Coray, Henry W., ed. *Valiants for Truth.* New York: McGraw-Hill Book Co., 1961.

Cragg, Gerald R. *The Church in the Age of Reason.* New York: Atheneum, 1961.

Cross, F.L. *The Early Christian Fathers.* London: Gerald Duckworth & Co. Ltd., 1960.

Culver, Elsie Thomas. *Women in the World of Religion.* Garden City: Doubleday & Co., 1967.

Davies, J.G. *The Early Christian Church: A History of Its First Five Centuries.* Garden City: Doubleday & Co., 1967.

Dayton, Donald W. *Discovering an Evangelical Heritage.* New York: Harper & Row, 1976.

Deen, Edith. *Great Women of the Christian Faith.* New York: Harper & Brothers, 1959.

Delaney, John J., ed. *Saints for All Seasons.* Garden City: Doubleday & Co., 1978.

Dillenberger, John, and Welch, Claude. *Protestant Christianity.* New York: Charles Scribner's Sons, 1954.

Dunne, John S. *A Search for God in Time and Memory.* New York: The Macmillan Co., 1969.

Ellis, John Tracy. *American Catholicism.* Chicago: University of Chicago Press, 1956.

Eusebius. *Ecclesiastical History.* Grand Rapids: Baker Book House, 1962.

Finkelstein, Louis, ed. *American Spiritual Autobiographies.* New York: Harper & Brothers, 1948.

Fox's Book of Martyrs, ed. William Forbush. Philadelphia: John C. Winston Co., 1926.

Freemantle, Anne. *Saints Alive! The Lives of Thirteen Heroic Saints.* Garden City: Doubleday & Co., 1978.

————,ed. *The Age of Belief: The Medieval Philosophers.* New York: The New American Library, 1955.

————,ed. *Protestant Mystics.* London: Weidenfeld and Nicolson, 1964.

Frend, W. H. C. *Martyrdom and Persecution in the Early Church.* Garden City: Doubleday & Co., 1967.

Gray, Tony. *Champions of Peace.* New York: Paddington Press Ltd., 1976.

Hadas, Moses. *A History of Rome from Its Origins to 529 A.D. as Told by Roman Historians.* Garden City: Doubleday & Co., 1956.

Handy, Robert T., ed. *The Social Gospel in America, 1870–1920.* New York: Oxford University Press, 1966.

Hillerbrand, Hans J. *The Reformation.* New York: Harper & Row, 1964.

Hoffman, Peter. *The History of the German Resistance, 1933–1945.* Cambridge: The MIT Press, 1977.

Hudson, Winthrop. *Religion in America.* 2nd ed. New York: Charles Scribner's Sons, 1973.

Hughes, Philip. *The Reformation in England.* New York: The Macmillan Co., 1954.

Hutchinson, F.E. *Cranmer and the English Reformation.* New York: Collier Books, 1962.

Indian Christians. Madras: G.A. Natesan & Co., 1928.

John of the Cross. *Ascent of Mount Carmel.* Garden City: Doubleday & Co., 1958.

Jones, Rufus M. *The Luminous Trail.* New York: The Macmillan Co., 1949.

Kelly, Henry Ansgar. *The Devil, Demonology, and Witchcraft.* Garden City: Doubleday & Co., 1968.

Loud, Grover C. *Evangelized America.* New York: The Dial Press, 1928.

Lucas, Henry S. *The Renaissance and the Reformation.* New York: Harper & Brothers, 1934.

Luce, Clare Boothe, ed. *Saints for Now.* New York: Sheed and Ward, 1952.

Magalis, Elaine. *Conduct Becoming to A Woman.* New York: United Methodist Board of Global Ministries/Women's Division, 1973.

Maynard, Theodore. *The Story of American Catholicism.* New York: The Macmillan Co., 1942.

Merton, Thomas. *The Wisdom of the Desert: Sayings from the Desert Fathers of the Fourth Century.* New York: New Directions, 1970.

Meyer, Peter, ed. *The Pacifist Conscience.* New York: Holt, Rinehart and Winston, 1966.

Morrison, J.H. *The Missionary Heroes of Africa.* New York: George H. Doran Co., 1922.

Muggeridge, Malcolm. *Something Beautiful for God: Mother Teresa of Calcutta.* New York: Harper & Row, 1971.

Musurillo, Herbert. *The Acts of the Christian Martyrs.* Oxford: Clarendon Press, 1972.

Norris, Richard A. *God and World in Early Christian Theology: A Study in Justin Martyr, Irenaeus, Tertullian, and Origen.* New York: The Seabury Press, 1965.

Norwood, Frederick A. *Strangers and Exiles: A History of Religious Refugees.* 2 vols. Nashville: Abingdon Press, 1969.

Oberman, Heiko. *Forerunners of the Reformation.* New York: Holt, Rinehart and Winston, 1966.

O'Brien, John. *The Inquisition.* New York: The Macmillan Co., 1973.

Otto, Rudolf. *The Idea of the Holy.* London: Oxford University Press, 1952.

Oxnam, G. Bromley. *Personalities in Social Reform.* Nashville: Abingdon-Cokesbury Press, 1950.

Patrinacos, Nicon. *The Orthodox Liturgy.* Garwood, N.J.: The Graphic Arts Press, 1974.

Pauck, Wilhelm. *The Heritage of the Reformation*. Rev. ed. New York: Oxford University Press, 1961.

Peers, E. Allison. *Behind That Wall. An Introduction to Some Classics of the Interior Life*. New York: Morehouse-Gorham Co., 1948.

Prestige, G.L. *God in Patristic Thought*. London: S.P.C.K., 1959.

Rauschenbusch, Walter. *A Theology for the Social Gospel*. New York: The Macmillan Co., 1917.

Sayers, Dorothy L. *Christian Letters to A Post-Christian World*. Grand Rapids: William B. Eerdmans, 1969.

Schmemann, Alexander. *The Historical Road of Eastern Orthodoxy*. New York: Holt, Rinehart and Winston, 1963.

Söderblom, Nathan. *Christian Fellowship, or the United Life and Work of Christendom*. New York: Fleming Revell Co., 1923.

Steuart, R.H.J. *Diversity in Holiness*. Freeport, N.Y.: Books for Libraries Press, 1937.

Teresa of Avila. *Interior Castle*. Garden City: Doubleday & Co., 1961.

Thomas à Kempis. *The Imitation of Christ*. Garden City: Doubleday & Co., 1962.

Treasure, G.R.P. *Seventeenth Century France*. Garden City: Doubleday & Co., 1967.

Tuchman, Barbara W. *A Distant Mirror: The Calamitous 14th Century*. New York: Alfred A. Knopf, 1978.

Vedder, Henry C. *Christian Epoch-Makers: Story of the Great Missionary Eras in the History of Christianity*. Philadelphia: American Baptist Publication Society, 1908.

Walker, Williston. *Great Men of the Christian Church*. Chicago: University of Chicago Press, 1908.

Ward, Benedicta. *The Desert Christian*. New York: The Macmillan Co., 1980.

Washburn, Henry Bradford. *The Religious Motive in Philanthropy*. Philadelphia: University of Pennsylvania Press, 1931.

Westcott, Glenway. *A Calendar of Saints for Unbelievers*. New Haven: Leete's Island Books, 1976. Reprint, originally published 1932.

Zahn, Gordon. *War, Conscience and Dissent*. New York: Hawthorn Books, 1967.

AUTOBIOGRAPHIES AND BIOGRAPHIES

Addams, Jane. *Twenty Years at Hull House*. New York: Macmillan Publishing Co., 1938.

Augustine, Aurelius. *The Confessions*. London: J.M. Dent & Sons Ltd., 1907.

Aulèn, Gustaf. *Dag Hammarskjöld's White Book: An Analysis of Markings*. Philadelphia: Fortress Press, 1969.

Bailey, J. Martin, and Gilbert, Douglas. *The Steps of Bonhoeffer*. New York: The Macmillan Co., 1969.

Bainton, Roland. *Erasmus of Christendom*. New York: Charles Scribner's Sons, 1969.

Barker, Dudley. *G.K. Chesterton*. New York: Stein & Day, 1973.

Battenhouse, Roy W., ed. *A Companion to the Study of St. Augustine*. New York: Oxford University Press, 1956.

Bethge, Eberhard. *Dietrich Bonhoeffer: Man of Vision, Man of Courage*. New York: Harper & Row, 1970.

Bodein, Vernon Parker. *The Social Gospel of Walter Rauschenbusch and Its Relation to Religious Education*. New Haven: Yale University Press, 1944.

Bonhoeffer, Dietrich. *Letters and Papers from Prison*. New York: The Macmillan Co., 1953.

Bosanquet, Mary. *The Life and Death of Dietrich Bonhoeffer*. New York: Harper & Row, 1968.

Bretall, Robert, ed. *A Kierkegaard Anthology*. Princeton: Princeton University Press, 1951.

Brown, Raymond, et al., eds. *Mary in the New Testament*. Philadelphia: Fortress Press, 1978.

Cailliet, Emile. *Pascal: Genius in the Light of Scripture*. Philadelphia: The Westminster Press, 1945.

Cherry, Conrad. *The Theology of Jonathan Edwards: A Reappraisal*. Garden City: Doubleday & Co., 1966.

Chesterton, G.K. *Autobiography*. Darby, Pa.: Arden, 1978. Reprint, originally published 1936.

———. *St. Francis of Assisi*. Garden City: Doubleday & Co., 1957.

Colette, Jacques, ed. *Kierkegaard: The Difficulty of Being Christian*. Notre Dame: University of Notre Dame Press, 1968.

Cropper, Margaret. *Life of Evelyn Underhill*. New York: Harper & Brothers, 1958.

Croxall, T.H., ed. *Meditations from Kierkegaard*. Philadelphia: The Westminster Press, 1955.

Curtis, C. J. *Söderblom, Ecumenical Pioneer*. Minneapolis: Augsburg Publishing Co., 1967.

Deissman, Adolf. *Paul: A Study in Social and Religious History*. New York: Harper & Brothers, 1927.

Dibelius, Martin, and Kümmel, Werner G. *Paul*. Philadelphia: The Westminster Press, 1953.

Dodge, David L. *Memorial. An Autobiography Prepared at the Request and For the Use of His Children*. Boston: S.K. Whipple & Co., 1854.

Drake, Robert. *Flannery O'Connor: A Critical Essay*. Grand Rapids: William B. Eerdmans, 1966.

Dumas, Andre. *Dietrich Bonhoeffer: Theologian of Reality*. New York: The Macmillan Co., 1971.

Hammarskjöld, Dag. *Markings*. New York: Alfred A. Knopf, 1964.

Harmon, Rebecca. *Susanna: Mother of the Wesleys.* Nashville: Abingdon Press, 1968.

Holt, Rackman. *Mary McLeod Bethune: A Biography.* Garden City: Doubleday & Co., 1964.

Joy, James Richard. *John Wesley's Awakening.* New York: The Methodist Book Concern, 1937.

Kepler, Thomas, ed. *The Evelyn Underhill Reader.* Nashville: Abingdon Press, 1962.

Kierkegaard, Søren. *The Point of View for My work as An Artist: A Report to History.* New York: Harper & Brothers, 1962.

King, Coretta Scott. *My Life with Martin Luther King, Jr.* New York: Holt, Rinehart and Winston, 1969.

King, Martin Luther, Jr. *Why We Can't Wait.* New York: Harper & Row, 1964.

Knox, John. *Chapters in A Life of Paul.* Nashville: Abingdon Press, 1950.

Lee, Dallas. *The Cotton Patch Evidence: The Story of Clarence Jordan and the Koinonia Farm Experiment.* New York: Harper & Row, 1971.

"The Legacy of Clarence Jordan." *Sojourners,* special section. December, 1979.

Lewis, A.J. *Zinzendorf the Ecumenical Pioneer.* London: SCM Press, Ltd., 1962.

Lincoln, C. Eric, ed. *Martin Luther King, Jr.: A Profile.* New York: Hill and Wang, 1970.

Livingstone, W.P. *Mary Slessor of Calabar: Pioneer Missionary.* London: Hodder and Stoughton, 1916.

Lowie, Walter. *A Short Life of Kierkegaard.* Princeton: Princeton University Press, 1942.

Luthuli, Albert. *Let My People Go.* New York: McGraw-Hill Book Co., 1962.

McConnell, Francis J. *John Wesley.* New York: Abingdon-Cokesbury Press, 1939.

Manschreck, Clyde M. *Melanchthon: The Quiet Reformer.* Nashville: Abingdon Press, 1958.

Martin, Marie-Louise. *Kimbangu: An African Prophet and His Church.* Grand Rapids: William B. Eerdmans, 1976.

Melville, Annabelle M. *Elizabeth Bayley Seton.* New York: Charles Scribner's Sons, 1951.

Merton, Thomas. *The Last of the Fathers.* Westminster, Md.: The Newman Press, 1960.

Miller, Perry. *Jonathan Edwards.* New York: Meridian Books, 1959.

Miller, William Robert. *Martin Luther King, Jr.: His Life, Martyrdom and Meaning for the World.* New York: Weybright and Talley, 1968.

O'Connor, Flannery. *The Habit of Being.* Edited by Sally Fitzgerald. New York: Farrar, Straus & Giroux, 1979.

————. *Mystery and Manners*. Edited by Sally and Robert Fitzgerald. New York: Farrar, Straus & Giroux, 1969.

Pascal, Blaise. *Pensées*. New York: E.P. Dutton & Co., 1958.

Payne, John B. *Erasmus: His Theology of the Sacraments*. Richmond: John Knox Press, 1970.

Pétrement, Simone. *Simone Weil: A Life*. New York: Pantheon Books, 1976.

Rogness, Michael. *Melanchthon, Reformer Without Honor*. Minneapolis: Augsburg Publishing House, 1969.

Rohde, Peter. *Søren Kierkegaard*. London: George Allen & Unwin Ltd., 1963.

Sharpe, Dores Robinson. *Walter Rauschenbusch*. New York: The Macmillan Co., 1942.

Smith, Amanda. *Amanda Smith's Own Story*. Chicago: Meyer & Brothers, 1893.

Smith, John Holland. *Francis of Assisi*. New York: Charles Scribner's Sons, 1972.

Smith, Kenneth L., and Zepp, Ira G. *Search for the Beloved Community: The Thinking of Martin Luther King, Jr.* Valley Forge: Judson Press, 1974.

Sterne, Emma G. *Mary McLeod Bethune*. New York: Alfred A. Knopf, 1957.

Topping, Helen. *Introducing Kagawa*. Chicago: Willett, Clark & Co., 1935.

————, ed. *Kagawa in Australia, New Zealand and Hawaii*. Tokyo: Friends of Jesus, 1936.

————, ed. *Kagawa Comes Home*. Tokyo: Friends of Jesus, 1939.

Undset, Sigrid. *Catherine of Siena*. New York: Sheed & Ward, 1954.

Van Dusen, Henry P. *Dag Hammarskjöld: The Statesman and His Faith*. New York: Harper & Row, 1964.

Walsh, William Thomas. *St. Teresa of Avila*. Milwaukee: Bruce Publishing Co., 1943.

Ward, Masie. *Gilbert Keith Chesterton*. New York: Sheed & Ward, 1943.

Weinlick, John R. *Count Zinzendorf*. Nashville: Abingdon Press, 1956.

Wesley, John. *Journals*. 2 vols. New York: Methodist Book Concern, n.d.

Zahn, Gordon. *In Solitary Witness: The Life and Death of Franz Jäggerstätter*. New York: Holt, Rinehart and Winston, 1965.